STORYTELLING FOR USER EXPERIENCE

CRAFTING STORIES FOR BETTER DESIGN

Whitney Quesenbery

Kevin Brooks

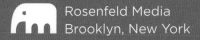
Rosenfeld Media
Brooklyn, New York

Storytelling for User Experience: Crafting Stories for Better Design
By Whitney Quesenbery and Kevin Brooks

Rosenfeld Media, LLC
457 Third Street, #4R
Brooklyn, New York
11215 USA

On the Web: www.rosenfeldmedia.com
Please send errors to: errata@rosenfeldmedia.com

Publisher: Louis Rosenfeld
Editor: Marta Justak
Development Editor: David Moldawer
Interior Layout Tech: Danielle Foster
Cover Design: The Heads of State
Indexer: Nancy Guenther
Proofreader: Kezia Endsley

DEDICATION

This book is dedicated to

Brother Blue—Dr. Hugh Morgan Hill

who taught us that our stories have the power to change the world.

HOW TO USE THIS BOOK

Who Should Read This Book?

This book is for any user experience practitioner or, really, anyone who designs, whether you are taking your first steps in the field or looking for ways to improve a long practice. If you are curious about storytelling as part of user experience design, we hope this book will give you a nudge to try it out. We've tried to cover the big points, but also to include practical ideas for using stories to enrich your practice and improve your work.

The stories in this book are *real* stories from *real* projects, as well as some examples created just for the book. Some are more polished; some are more ad-hoc and raw. There is not one style for the stories. We hope the range in this book will help you find your own storytelling voice.

If you are already a storyteller, this book can show you some new ways to use your storytelling skills.

As we worked on this project, we heard from many people in user experience who were thinking about stories. You will find many of their stories throughout the book as well.

If you...

- need to share research and design insights in a compelling and effective way

- struggle to communicate the meaning of a large body of data in a way that everyone just "gets"

- want to explore a new, innovative idea, and imagine its future

...then this book can help you, by showing you how and when to choose, create, and use stories.

What's in This Book?

The book is organized into three sections:

Section One: The first five chapters are a look at why stories can be useful in user experience and how they work. The section includes a chapter on some of the ethical issues you should consider when you are using stories based on real people.

Section Two. The middle section is an overview of the user experience process, looking at how stories can be a part of all stages of work, from user research to evaluation, including plenty of practical tips and examples.

Section Three. The last six chapters dive into the craft of creating and using stories, looking at how to address the right audience with the right story, the "ingredients" of a story (perspective, character, context, imagery, and language), the framework of structure and plot, and the different mediums you can use in the process of crafting effective stories.

What Comes with This Book?

This book's companion Web site (ꙮ rosenfeldmedia.com/books/storytelling) contains more stories and short articles about stories. You can also find a calendar of our workshops, talks about storytelling and storytelling performances, and a place to engage others in conversation. We've also made the book's Story Triangle diagrams and other illustrations available under a Creative Commons license for you to download and include in your own presentations. You can find these on Flickr at ꙮ www.flickr.com/photos/rosenfeldmedia/sets/.

FREQUENTLY
ASKED QUESTIONS

Why stories in user experience design?

Stories have always been part of user experience design as scenarios, storyboard, flow charts, personas, and every other technique that we use to communicate how (and why) a new design will work. As a part of user experience design, stories serve to ground the work in a real context by connecting design ideas to the people who will use the product. This book starts with a look at how and why stories are so effective. See Chapters 1 and 2.

Is storytelling a new UX methodology?

No. We are not here to promote a new methodology based on using stories. Whether you believe in user-centered design, goals-based design, or even a more technical approach like domain-driven design, stories have a place in your work. Stories can be a part of almost any user experience activity. The middle section of the book is arranged in a loose lifecycle, so you can dive in at whatever point you are in your current projects. See Chapters 5–10.

Can I start using stories in the middle of a project?

Yes. Although user experience is improved by having good user research (and the stories you will collect), there are many reasons why you might find yourself working on a design or running a usability evaluation without a good collection of stories to draw on. The chapter on using stories in the design process includes several techniques for working with, or creating, stories. See Chapter 8.

I don't think I tell stories well. What do I do?

You may not think you tell stories, but you probably already do. Most of us tell stories as a way to explain a perspective on a problem or describe an event. The goal of this book is to help you learn to use stories in a new way. We hope the varied stories in this book will be an inspiration. Your storytelling will improve with each telling opportunity. See Chapter 2.

How do I create a good story?

Creating a story isn't hard. Your first ones may feel awkward, but storytelling gets easier—and your stories get better—with practice. Storytelling is a craft as much as an art. If you start by knowing your audience, add character, perspective, context, and imagery, and put it all together within a structure, it will all come together. See Chapters 11–15.

How much does the audience matter?

Knowing your audience is critical. Whether you can plan in advance, or have to adjust on the fly, you can't tell a good story unless you can get the audience involved. After all, the goal of the story isn't to tell it, but for the audience to hear it and take away something new. See Chapters 3, 10, and 12.

Is it OK to use other people's stories?

When we do user research, one of our goals is to bring back a useful picture of the people we design for. Telling their stories is one way to share what you have learned. But you have to remember that they are human beings who must be treated ethically. See Chapters 4 and 6.

Is this a book about performing stories?

Not really. For performance storytelling, the crafting and telling of stories is a goal in itself. Nor is the book about scriptwriting or writing short fiction. While some of the story structures and ingredients covered in the last section can help add drama to stories, that is not our focus. When we use stories in user experience practice, we borrow from these worlds, but put them to use in new ways. See Chapter 15.

Do you cover storytelling in games?

This is also not a book about narrative hypertext, games, interactive fiction, virtual reality, or immersive interfaces where stories and storytelling are a central feature of the user interface. Although we believe that every interaction tells a story (even if only a mundane one), this book is not primarily about how to weave stories into a digital interactive experience.

If you are interested in how stories are woven into user experience and hypermedia narrative, we can recommend two excellent books:

- *Hamlet on the Holodeck: The Future of Narrative in Cyberspace* by Janet H. Murray, which looks at how hypermedia and other new technology can make new forms of story possible.

- *Computers and Theatre* by Brenda Laurel. A seminal book on Aristotelian storytelling as the basis for user experience design.

What's next for storytelling in user experience design?

While working on this book, we have been excited to watch storytelling take off as a useful concept in many more aspects of user experience design. People have started talking about how to make the product tell a story or use story structures to help structure the user experience. Others have borrowed ideas from filmmaking to add emotional resonance to applications and make the concept of designing a better experience more concrete. And there's a swarm of people writing on the topic of storytelling and business management, which touches on some of the same issues as user experience.

There's always another story waiting to be written.

TABLE OF CONTENTS

CHAPTER 4
The Ethics of Stories   **45**

CHAPTER 5
Stories as Part of a UX Process   **55**

CHAPTER 9
Evaluating with Stories   129

CHAPTER 10
Sharing Stories
(Managing Up and Across)   139

LIST OF STORIES

FOREWORD

Janice (Ginny) Redish *has been actively doing user experience design since long before it took on that name. Ginny's books on usability testing (with Joe Dumas) and on user and task analysis (with JoAnn Hackos) have helped many practitioners hone their skills in user research. Her most recent book is* Letting Go of the Words—Writing Web Content that Works, *published by Morgan Kaufmann.*

I've been talking about stories and scenarios—and how useful and powerful they are—for a long time. And I've been wishing for a book that would both make the case for stories in user experience and help us all become better at collecting, crafting, telling, and using stories in our work

Well, here it is. You are holding a book that combines the stories and skills of a professional storyteller who designs user experiences and a user experience designer who tells stories.

Just as personas make users come alive for user experience designers, stories make users' lives real. User experience design is about experience. Stories are those experiences.

As Kevin and Whitney say in this book: We all hear stories. We all tell stories—every day in all parts of our lives. What happened in school today? What happened at work today? How did you manage that? What would you do if...?

As Kevin and Whitney also say, you are probably already hearing stories in the user research that you do. If you write scenarios for design or for usability testing, you are already telling stories. This book will help you do what you are doing—even better.

Stories are immensely powerful, as I realized many years ago on a project to help an airline company understand what happens in travel agencies. For four months, a colleague and I crisscrossed the U.S., spending several hours in each of many types of travel agencies around the country. We watched and listened as travel agents took calls, helped walk-in customers, and told us about their other clients.

When we sifted through our notes back at our hotel at the end of each day, we found ourselves reminding each other of the stories we had heard and seen. Part of the drama in those stories was in the life of the traveler: The father who had promised his daughter that their trip to Disneyland would include renting a red Mustang convertible... The gal who wanted to visit her boyfriend for a weekend but needed a cheap fare... The reporter who had to get to the scene of a disaster in another state immediately... The family planning a once-in-a-lifetime trip to France...

The other part of the drama in those stories was in the work of the travel agents, especially in how difficult it was for them to meet these customers' needs with their current software.

When we reported our findings to the client, we had facts. We had numbers. We had flowcharts. And we had stories—lots of stories. It was the stories that people remembered. It was the stories that became the focal points for innovation in the software.

I wish I'd had this book when doing the project with the travel agents—and for many projects after that. This book will help you become a better story collector, story crafter, story teller, story user—all in the context of your work in user experience design.

The examples (yes, lots of stories, as you'd expect) and the direct, clear advice will help you become

- a better listener, so you have users' words to tell their stories

- a better observer, so you can include the real context of use in your stories

- an ethical storyteller, knowing how to craft stories (like personas) that are archetypically true even if they are composites

- an innovative designer, using stories to help teams see problems and solutions in new ways

- a person who people enjoy listening to because your stories are both interesting and meaningful for your projects

Have fun!

—Ginny Redish

www.redish.net

CHAPTER 1

Why Stories?

W̲e all tell stories. It's one of the most natural ways to share information, and it's as old as the human race. This book is about how to use a skill you already possess in a new way: in the field of user experience (UX) design.

As a part of user experience design, stories serve to ground your work in a real context. They let you show a design concept or a new product in action, or connect a new idea to the initial spark. But most importantly, they help you keep people at the center of your work. However you start a project, in the end it will be used by people. Stories are a way of connecting what you know about those people (your users) to the design process, even if they can't always be part of your team.

Stories can be used in many ways throughout any user experience process:

- They help us gather (and share) information about users, tasks, and goals.

- They put a human face on analytic data.

- They can spark new design concepts and encourage collaboration and innovation.

- They are a way to share ideas and create a sense of shared history and purpose.

- They help us understand the world by giving us insight into people who are *not* just like us.

- They can even persuade others of the value of our contribution.

Here's one way that stories can be part of user experience design.

STORIES HELP US SEE THE USER EXPERIENCE MORE CLEARLY
The Open University (OU) is the largest university in the UK. Its programs are offered through distance learning, so its Web site is critical to connecting students to the university and helping potential students find out about it.

One of our ongoing projects is the online prospectus, the catalog of academic programs offered by OU. Originally, this prospectus was presented like a typical catalog or database, starting with a list of departments and drilling down to specific courses. This design assumed that most people would be looking for the details of a particular course.

But we were wrong. We found out instead that students wanted to talk about their dreams. For example, one was bored in his job and wanted to make a change into something more challenging. Another loved being a party planner, but wanted to build his career from a part-time endeavor into a full-scale business that would make his fiancée proud. They told us how the OU had helped them succeed beyond their teachers' expectations. Or how they had found that they really loved studying, or had discovered an aptitude for science through the short courses. A few people had a simple, straightforward goal like "Get a degree in psychology," but most were deciding not only what they wanted to study, but where they wanted their studies to take them.

In one usability test, an older Pakistani woman, Priti, had put off her own education to raise her family. Now, she wanted to get the university degree she'd missed when she was younger. Her first course, she thought, should be the one that would help her with her English reading skills and get her back into good study habits.

She and a friend worked diligently, reading each page carefully. They talked through each decision, and had good reasons for each link they chose. But in the end, they selected an upper level linguistics course, which would have been completely wrong for her. The cues about the level and content of the course that seemed so obvious to us were just invisible to them. How could a course called *English Language and Learning* not be perfect?

It happens that the OU has a program specifically for people like Priti. Opening courses are a gentle introduction to university study skills like re-learning how to write essays, and they would have been a perfect match. So it wasn't just that she had picked a bad starting point; she had missed a really good one.

This wasn't a case of a single usability problem that could be fixed in a simple way. The site just wasn't speaking *her* language.

This story, and many more that we collected, convinced the team that we needed to engage people in the *idea* of the subject before pushing them to choose their first course. We started talking about needing to *tell the story* of the subjects that you could study at the OU.

More importantly, we had to find ways to help them think about how to plan their education. The site offered good guidance about planning a student's time, but we'd seen that the best reactions occurred when we presented small personal stories like this one on the Web site:

David Beckenham got his Bachelor of Laws (Honours) through the Open University. Here is how he managed his time:

It was six years' hard work, 16+ hours a week for me, and I missed watching television, but it was definitely worth it in the end. I kept Sundays free so that I could relax and spend time with the family, but I always made sure that I set aside the right amount of time each evening and on Saturdays to keep up with the timetable. That meant sometimes I had to work to 1 a.m., but I always did it. ■

It makes sense. Stories like this one, or a video welcome from a course lecturer, help students make a connection, translating dry information into personal terms.

What's the next step? More ways for the community to share its own stories.

What is a story?

Story and *storytelling* are such big concepts that we'd better start by defining what kinds of stories are helpful in user experience design.

In this book, we will be focused on stories whose goal is to describe or communicate some aspect of user experience. We will include scenarios, user stories, stories for personas, storyboards, (some) narrative use cases, and many other story forms that are part of different user experience methodologies.

As far as the mechanics go, we'll include all forms of storytelling:

- A story can be written or spoken.

- A story can be told through pictures, moving images, or words.

- A story can be told live or through recorded audio or video.

A story can have a beginning, middle, and an end—usually, though not necessarily, in that order—or it can simply suggest a time and place.

Types of stories we are **not** talking about include: bedtime stories, stories about that really cute thing you did as a child, news stories, stories about cats rescued from trees, shaggy dog stories, ghost stories, novels, love stories, confessions, how I met your father (unless we're designing a dating service), the end of the world, the beginning of the world, and dreams (not to be confused with conceptual visions). We love these stories, but they are for another book, and a context outside user experience design.

There are many types of stories in UX design

Stories can be a natural and flexible way of communicating. Some of the values often attributed to stories include their effectiveness as a way to help people remember, as a way to persuade, and as a way to entertain. This is as true in UX as anywhere else.

User experience includes a wide variety of disciplines, each with its own perspective. Stories bridge the many different languages you bring to your work. By providing tangible examples, stories can provide a common vocabulary for everyone.

- Stories can describe a context or situation.

- Stories can illustrate problems.

- Stories can be a launching point for a design discussion.

- Stories can explore a design concept.

- Stories can describe the impact of a new design.

Stories that describe a context or situation

Stories that describe the world as it is today help us understand that world better. They not only describe a sequence of events, but they also provide insight into the reasons and motivations for those events.

Stories that accompany personas often describe something about their activities or experiences. This story, from a persona for a cancer information Web site, describes how someone with good Web and search skills helped a cancer patient find pertinent information. It describes how and why someone might look for information about cancer, using sources that are beyond the norm for most people.

A STORY FROM A PERSONA:
BARBARA—THE "DESIGNATED SEARCHER"

Barbara has always liked looking things up. Her job as a writer and editor for a technical magazine lets her explore new topics for articles. In addition to the Web, she has access to news sources, legal and medical databases, and online publication archives. Recently, a friend was diagnosed with colon cancer. She helped him identify the best hospitals for this cancer and read up on the latest treatments. She looked for clinical trials that might help him, and even read up on some alternative treatments being offered in Mexico and Switzerland. She was glad to be able to find articles in journals she trusted to give her the depth that more popular medical sites lacked. ■

Stories that illustrate problems

Stories can also be used to illustrate a *point of pain*—a problem that a new product, or a change in a design, can fix. They are used to help a design or product team see a problem from the perspective of the users.

A POINT-OF-PAIN STORY

Sister Sarah sighed. She and Sister Clare ran the youth group in their church, and today they had taken the kids to a Phillies baseball game. They had gotten everyone from the parking lot, through the gates, and into their seats, losing no one in the milling crowd. Sister Sarah was about to go buy some drinks when she realized she'd left the cash in the car.

She stood at the stadium entrance, trying to remember where they had parked. Usually, their small bus was easy to spot, but today it seemed as though every church group in the area had shown up. She saw dozens of vehicles that might be hers.

She closed her eyes and tried to remember the walk to the entrance. Had they turned to the right or the left? Left, she thought, and she headed out toward one of the rows. But that wasn't her bus.

After 30 minutes of walking in one direction and another, she would have to go back and tell Sister Clare that, once again, she'd failed to pay any attention to where she was going or where they had left the bus. The children would know, she thought. She could take one of them. Again. She couldn't even phone. Their one mobile phone was back at her seat. She sighed. ■

This story describes a current problem. In this case, it's a lost bus in a vast parking lot, and someone without a good way to solve the problem.

Did the story make you start thinking of innovative ways to solve Sister Sarah's problem? There are many different possible solutions, and you probably thought of several. That's the point of this kind of story: to describe the problem in a way that opens the door to brainstorming new ideas.

Stories that help launch a design discussion

You can also end a story in the middle with an explicit call for a new idea, finishing it with a better ending, or identifying a situation that might open the door to new products. Stories that you will use as a starting point for design brainstorming must have enough detail to make sense, but also leave room for the imagination. Their goal is to open up thinking about a design problem, suggest the general area for work, or start a discussion.

A STORY TO LAUNCH A DESIGN DISCUSSION

Joan was filling in on payroll while Kathy, the office manager, was away. Kathy left her a message to remind her about some special bonus checks for that week.

Joan had not used the payroll program for a while and only remembered that special checks could be difficult. Reading the Post-it notes on the wall next to the computer, she scanned for instructions and was relieved to find one for bonuses.

Following these brief notes, she found the right screen. Her first try to print the checks came out wrong, and she had to reverse all of the transactions. She puzzled over it some more and finally matched the instructions on the Post-it notes to the messages on the screen. In the end, she managed to get the checks to print, but she also left a note on Kathy's desk to have her check everything when she returned. ■

How could you make creating special checks and filling in on bookkeeping tasks easier? Did the story spark your mind for solutions? Have you encountered a similar situation?

Stories that explore a design concept

Stories can help you explain and explore a new idea or concept and its implications for the experience. They help shape a new design by showing it in action, even before all the details are complete.

One way to create an expressive story is with video, although this can be more difficult than a comic, storyboard, or verbal narrative. Bruce Tognazzini, now a member of the Nielsen Norman Group, led a project at Sun Microsystems to envision the future of computing. The result was *Starfire: The Movie*, a video that imagined a day in the life of a knowledge worker 12 years in the future. *Starfire* was created in 1992 and set in 2004. It featured a workspace made up of several displays controlled with gestures, well before the movie *Minority Report* or recent innovations like Microsoft Surface.

Instead of spending time describing problems to solve, the story explored a completely new way of interacting. The events of the story were pretty simple, showing a designer going about her work. It said, "What if all these technologies were in current use?" and told the story as if they were. *Starfire's* goal was to provoke new thinking, rather than to prescribe a design in the kind of precise detail needed to build a new product.

The next story also explores unknown territory, in this case an interactive entertainment system that flips the usual shopping and reality TV formulas on their heads.

REALLY INTERACTIVE TELEVISION

Bob, Carol, and their 17-year-old son Robert Jr. replaced their old cable system with a new Acme IPTV system. Not only did they have access to all the media they had with their old system, but now they also got special channels with interactive content.

Carol loves soap operas. With the interactive remote, her favorite show, *All My Restless Children*, becomes a shopping catalogue. If she likes the earrings of the lead actress, she can order them. If she likes her blouse, she can order that, too—right from the TV. And the best part is, no commercials.

Even Bob is getting into it. During the show, he chooses to enter the soap opera's car contest using the remote and onscreen interface. First place is the lead actress's 1970 Corvette convertible.

Robert Jr. entered a different contest, where first place is dinner for two with the female lead. Not dinner with the actress who plays the lead, but dinner with her as the character she plays!

But Carol topped them all. Because the interactive options are available even when watching on-demand, late one night, Carol ordered the latest episode and entered the show's babysitter contest. First place is one night of free babysitting by the lead actor. Does Carol have a baby? No. What a shame if she wins. She'll have to figure out some other way to occupy the actor's time. ◼

Stories that prescribe the result of a new design

Prescriptive stories describe the world as it will be in more detail. They are similar to descriptive stories, except they describe a user experience that doesn't exist yet.

Software specifications often contain prescriptive stories in the form of scenarios that accompany use cases or other narrative ways of describing the user experience. These stories can be quite detailed, especially if they are used to illustrate the requirements documents.

A PRESCRIPTIVE STORY

John is a 32-year-old who had been working for a mid-size company. He recently decided to start his own consulting company and is currently working as a sole proprietor.

John wants to take the money out of his former employer's pension plan and open a new account at YourMutuals, where he can roll over the pension money without tax consequences and then start adding to it himself every year.

He begins by signing on to the YourMutuals Web site with his username and security password. He finds the link to open an account and fills in several forms with information about the type of account he wants to create. When he is done, he sees that the new account is now listed on his home page along with his IRA accounts.

He picks up the letter with the information about the pension plan. It says there is an option to transfer his money into a new account directly. Clicking on the account, he sees that "Transfer funds from another account" is one of the options. He enters the plan name, bank name, and his old member account number. When he is done, he gets a message that says that his money will be available as soon as the transfer is confirmed. He prints out the message and signs off.

The next day, he gets an email from the pension plan confirming the transfer and giving him a phone number to call, in case the information is incorrect. When he goes online to YourMutuals, he can now see that the new retirement account shows the correct amount deposited to it.

Now, he can decide which mutual funds he wants to invest in. ◼

This story could continue to describe more steps in the process or other functions that John could use. This is not a programming specification, but a narrative description of an interaction.

More work? Not really!

Perhaps you think, "There's quite enough to do without adding anything else to my process."

Don't worry. If you already have a good user experience process, you are probably already collecting and using stories. This book can help you do it more *consciously* and more *effectively.*

If your process doesn't include much contact with users, this might be a good time to start. You'll find that it improves your work, and gives you more confidence that you are creating something people will really find useful and usable.

Either way, collecting stories and telling them as you work on a design will make your work richer and more innovative.

The radio show *This American Life*, from U.S. National Public Radio, tells stories of everyday experiences. Each show takes a theme and looks at it from different perspectives, each based on a real person's story. Ira Glass, the producer, blends journalism and storytelling to create oddly compelling portraits.

> "Until you hear a story and you can understand that experience, you don't know what you are talking about. There has to be a person's story that you hear, where finally you get a picture in your head of what it would be like to be that person. Until that moment, you know nothing, and you deal with the information you are given in a flawed way."
>
> —Ira Glass, *This American Life*, speaking at GEL 2007 (gelconference.com/videos/2007/ira_glass/)

More reading

If you are interested in how stories are woven into user experience and hypermedia narrative, we can recommend two excellent books:

Hamlet on the Holodeck: The Future of Narrative in Cyberspace, Janet H. Murray. How hypermedia and other new technology can make new forms of story possible.

Computers and Theatre, Brenda Laurel. A seminal book on Aristotelian storytelling as the basis for user experience design.

Summary

Stories are a powerful tool in user experience design. They can help you understand users—and their experiences—better, communicate what you've learned, and use that understanding to create better products. Whether you are a researcher, designer, analyst, or manager, you will find ideas and techniques you can put to use in your practice.

Stories have many uses in user experience design and can be integrated into your own process.

- They can describe a context or situation, like stories that are part of personas.

- They can illustrate problems and "points of pain," explaining why a new experience is needed.

- They can be the starting point for a design discussion, explore a new design concept, or describe a new design.

CHAPTER 2

How UX Stories
Work

Some people think of telling a story as a form of broadcasting. Claude Shannon, sometimes called the "father of information theory," looked at communication as a sort of transmission of a message from one place to another. From this perspective, a story would be something simply transferred from one person to another, like an exchange of goods or a signal on a wire, as shown in Figure 2.1.

This seems simple enough. You write a story, and then you tell it. You might consider your audience as you write the story, but telling the story is just broadcasting it. A lot of bad speakers seem to see it this way as well.

But it's not that simple.

Good storytelling is interactive. It's more like a conversation than a broadcast, even when the stories are carefully crafted and rehearsed. Actors and directors talk about how the audience is different at every performance, even if the script or the stage action is the same from night to night.

Stories work the same way. They are as much a part of the audience as of the storyteller. They come to life in the imaginations of the audience members, whether it is one person or hundreds of people.

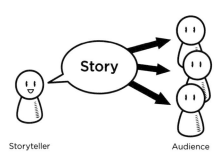

Storyteller   Audience

FIGURE 2.1
Some people think of stories as a broadcast, a one-way communication from storyteller to audience.

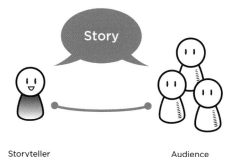

Storyteller   Audience

FIGURE 2.2
The Story Triangle shows the connection between storyteller and the audience: the audience hears the story, but also shares their reactions with the storyteller.

This is especially true when you are telling a story in person, as part of a presentation or in a discussion. The story becomes part of a dialogue between the storyteller and the audience, even if the audience is silent. This set of relationships between the storyteller, the story, and the audience is called the Story Triangle (shown in Figure 2.2). It defines the interdependency of these three elements in any story experience. You can see how it works in Figure 2.3

1. First, the storyteller shapes the story.

2. As they listen, the audience members form an image of the story in their own minds.

3. As the story is told, the storyteller and the audience continuously interact, with energy flowing back and forth. Each affects the others and shapes the story they create.

4. In the end, the most important relationship is between the audience and the story. They are part of the story each time it is told.

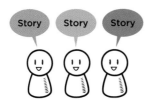

FIGURE 2.3
How stories work.

Something similar happens with written stories, except that the dynamic exchange between storyteller and audience is missing. The audience still makes the story their own, understanding it in their own terms. They might be engaged or uninterested, believe the story entirely, or doubt it. But they are still part of the full story experience.

What this means is that it is not enough to have a good story. You must have a good story *for your audience*. It has to suit the purpose for which you created it and fit the context in which you will share it. The stories you tell to entertain are very different from the stories you tell for business purposes. Stories in user experience are usually created for a specific audience and for a specific reason.

Stories are more than just narrative

The core of a story is usually a sequence of events. Without that sequence, nothing "happens." You might have a description of a scene or a character, but it's not really a *story* until you have events, decisions, and actions, or at least a reaction to a situation or environment (see Figure 2.4).

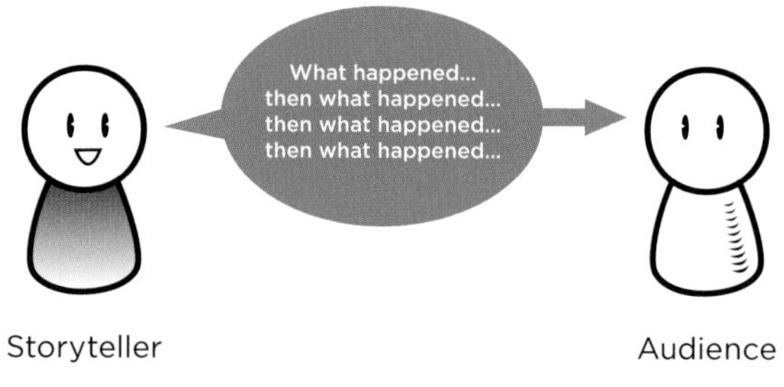

FIGURE 2.4
Stories are more than just a description of a series of events.

Storyteller

Audience

What happened… then what happened… then what happened… then what happened…

Sometimes, events can be implied through context, but you'll learn more about that in Chapter 13, "Combining the Ingredients of a Story." Stories that are just narrative events—a series of statements of "what happened"—aren't very interesting. They can be useful as a way to describe the details of an interaction. Use cases and flow charts are like that. They strip away everything except the specific actions that are at the core of a user experience.

Stories play a more complex role. They not only describe actions, but also explain them and set them into a context that helps you understand why they happened.

The first step in building a story is to add motivation. The goals and motivations of the characters can be clearly described, or they can be implicit, but it's the notion that people do things for a reason that makes stories so interesting. We want to know *why* something happened, not just what happened (see Figure 2.5). If we aren't told why, we are likely to invent a reason for ourselves.

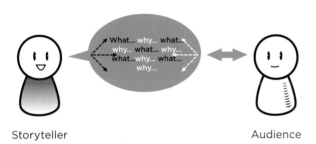

Storyteller   Audience

FIGURE 2.5
Why things happen can be as interesting as *what* happened.

Adding the reasons why the events occurred is the first step in creating a good user experience story, that is, a story that communicates enough information to be useful as a way of explaining a user context or triggering design ideas.

Motivation and goals are often deeply embedded in a cultural context. Many stories rely on some level of shared cultural context as a kind of shorthand. When folk stories are told and retold in different cultures, they are adapted. Details are changed to make the context for the story more familiar—or stranger—to the audience.

THE ANT AND THE GRASSHOPPER:
TWO VERSIONS OF THE SAME STORY
Laura Packer retells one of Aesop's fables to show how one basic story can be cast in different settings and told in different ways. The first version is loosely based on the Harvard Classics.

1: The Classic

Once upon a summer's day, a Grasshopper was dancing and singing in a field. She saw an Ant walk by, sweating and struggling to carry a kernel of corn twice as big as she was. The Grasshopper kept dancing and singing, then later saw the same Ant struggling by with another kernel of corn, on her way to the nest.

"Why not stop and talk with me? We could sing and dance instead of you working so hard."

"I am putting food away for the winter, and I suggest you do the same."

"Why should I worry about winter?" replied the Grasshopper. "I have plenty to eat right now." The Ant shook her head and continued her hard work. Summer passed and soon enough winter came. The Grasshopper had no food and found herself starving, while she saw the Ants feasting on the corn and grains they had collected all summer. It was only then that the Grasshopper understood that it is best to think about tomorrow, today.

(Æsop. Fables, retold by Joseph Jacobs. Vol. XVII, Part 1. The Harvard Classics. New York: P.F. Collier & Son, 1909–14; Bartleby.com, 2001, www.bartleby.com/17/1/)

2: Laura's modern retelling

Ann knew life as an administrative assistant wasn't glamorous, but she liked her job, worked hard, and saved her salary. Her apartment was modest but pleasant. Ann always thought of herself as having enough, except when she had lunch with Suzen, an old friend from college. Suzen was a derivatives trader and loved living the high life. She went out every night to the swankiest restaurants, her house was huge, her car was fast and sexy, and her clothes were the best. Everything Suzen did was designed to impress.

Whenever these two met for lunch, Suzen would say to Ann, "Live a little! Come on, you're always telling me you need to be careful. What fun is that?" Ann would smile and sip her drink while Suzen slugged back her second or third. "I just want to make sure I have enough, just in case," Ann would say. Suzen would shrug and tell Ann about her latest exotic vacation or the designer shoes she was wearing. Usually, this didn't bother Ann; she just listened to her old friend and thought that, while Suzen had a very exciting life, she liked her security and her home and knowing that she was safe, just in case.

Things stayed that way for years. Ann was promoted to office manager, but didn't change the way she lived. Suzen stayed in derivatives, making more money and spending it as fast as she earned it.

Then the housing bubble burst, taking with it the stock markets and derivatives trading. No one trusted derivatives anymore.

At first, Suzen pretended nothing was wrong. She kept buying Manolo Blahnik shoes and Gucci handbags. But she drank more at lunch and talked more about the vacations she wanted to take and less about the vacations she had taken. Then the lunches became less frequent. One day, Ann realized it had been many months since she had heard from Suzen, so she left her a voicemail, then later a second voicemail, and much later a third.

Finally, Suzen called back and left a message on Ann's home voicemail during the day when Ann was at work. "Yeah, I'm looking for work now. I have a part-time job at Starbucks, and I'm thinking about moving back in with my parents. I just don't have anything, I don't know where all that money went. I'd love to go out to lunch sometime, but I can't really afford it. Would you mind buying? I'd love to know how you're doing and hear about anything you've been up to. Gimme a call. See ya."

When Ann listened to the message, she thought about all those times when Suzen hadn't picked up the tab for lunch, about how she had laughed at Ann's frugality so she could retire someday, and how Ann had hidden her discount shoes so Suzen wouldn't see them. She deleted the message. ■

Remember that the story really lives in the minds of the listeners. As the storyteller, you can't include every single detail or motivation, even if you wanted to. This means that you must rely on the audience to interpret some of the elements in the story for themselves and therefore you must craft the story to help them do just that (see Figure 2.6).

The positive side of this is that the more the audience draws on their own lives and experiences, the more the story becomes their own. In the process, it elicits other shared stories, building connections.

On the other hand, when you and the audience bring different cultural assumptions to a story, it opens up opportunities for misunderstanding. Or opportunities for distraction, as the audience veers away from the point you want to make.

So, a story is more than just a transfer of information. It's an active mechanism for communicating events, communicating contextual information, and for developing connections between people.

FIGURE 2.6
We fill in details
about a story from
our own culture and
experiences.

This active role is what makes stories so useful in user experience design. One of the hardest parts of your work is understanding other people—people who may have different motivations and goals than your own. All of the user research and analytics techniques are a way to bridge that gap. Stories are not only a good way to learn about users, but also a good way to share what you have learned with your colleagues (and anyone else who has a stake in your work).

Stories have many roles in user experience design

Some of the most important roles that stories can play in a user experience design process are the following:

- They explain.
- They engage the imagination.

- They spark new ideas.

- They create a shared understanding.

- They persuade.

Stories explain

Most stories offer a description of events—a narrative. They place a set of actions into a time and place, arranging them into a sequence.

> When she was on her way to the store, she...

User experience stories often focus on explaining those events. They can describe behavior and emotional attitudes, showing how the people in the stories react to the events.

> Every time he tried to enter the 26-digit code, he got a message that the two fields did not match. Every time it happened, he got a little angrier, and hit the keyboard a little harder...and typed the code a little less accurately. Finally....

They can also add context to actions, providing an explanation for motivation or the goals driving the behavior.

> She wanted to get to Charleston for her cousin's wedding, but was on a tight budget. As she looked for the cheapest way to travel, she visited site after site: big travel sites, airlines, budget travel sites, auctions, trains, even car rentals. It was hard to compare her options because none of them gave her the full cost with all the expenses added up.

Placing a *character* in a *context* and communicating not just the *events*, but also using the *imagery* of the sensory experience is what differentiates a story from other techniques for modeling interaction, like flow charts and use cases. Some of the best storytellers are people who can present a collection of rules or facts as a story that you can easily remember. For example, they can illustrate the importance of guidelines for good design and usability by revealing what can happen when you ignore them.

This is not just about being entertaining. A good story weaves together causes and effects in a narrative so you can best remember them. It captures context and tacit knowledge and does so more efficiently than any other form of communication.

Stories engage the imagination

Stories engage the imagination of the listener, help the listener make intuitive leaps that surpass linear logic, and evoke new ideas. They rely on the way listeners create mental images, because they fill in the gaps and complete the images to fully create the story.

KEVIN'S STORY ABOUT TOKYO

I'm walking around a particularly busy and noisy part of Tokyo, with dense crowds and music playing, and I see a sign pointing around a corner that seems to indicate that there's a shrine down there.

So I turn right and walk down the cross street. As I walk, the air seems to change, because it gets quieter and quieter the farther I walk. The shrine is only a short block away from the main street with all its noise and crowds, but by the time I get to the shrine, it's quiet. It's peaceful. It's like there's a force field of peace surrounding this shrine.

I walk into this shrine, start walking through it on wide wooden floorboards, and it's so quiet. There are other people there walking by me, with me, and around me, but everyone is quiet. These people walked through the same frenetic noise that I walked through to get there, but everyone is quiet and respectful as we walk through this beautiful building.

I make my way to the center of the building where there is this Zen garden. I'm compelled to sit down on the edge and be with the huge rock in the middle of beautifully combed pebbles. I sit and let my eyes follow the path of the pebbles. I can hear my breathing. I can hear my heartbeat. I can hear my thoughts. All I can do in the middle of this patch of tranquility, in the middle of this gigantic busy, noisy metropolis, is sit and listen to the silence.

There was no place I knew—in the busy metropolis where I live—that is so easy to reach in the middle of the noise, where I could find such peace. ▨

Now, let's think about what you've learned from this story. Kevin told this story to a group of UX folks at a UsabilityNJ meeting and asked them what they saw in the story. Here's how they replied:

What was the street like?

Answer: You said the street was very noisy. It was turning the corner, I think, that I could just visualize, just from the way you described it, just gradually walking to the silence, to the peace from that noisy, chaotic area. From the noise into this peaceful area Zen garden.

What color was the sign for the shrine that you saw?

Answer: It was white and the arrow was black.

Anyone else see the sign?

Answer: It had some kind of picture on it of a building, something that somehow indicated the shrine. I knew you couldn't read the words so I was picturing that there must be some kind of design on it.

What color was the shrine; did anyone see the shrine?

Answer: Bamboo.

Answer: I'm seeing a green shrine.

Answer: Stone shrine.

Answer: And small.

What color were the rocks in the Zen garden?

Answer: Gray.

Answer: Beige and brown.

Answer: Different shades of gray.

We don't know what that shrine really looked like: bamboo, stone, or green. Kevin's story omitted that detail. But each person imagined a specific place, filled in the details so they were seeing a place almost as real to them as Kevin's memory is to him.

Stories spark new ideas

Because we instinctively fill in the gaps, stories can hint at details, rather than having to spell them out. Our ability to fill in gaps makes stories a good way to spark innovation. You start by imagining a new product or a change in the environment. Then you tell a story about it, showing how people behave differently in that new situation. Here's an example:

> I live in a lovely old two-floor apartment and when I have parties, they take up both floors. What I wanted was a way for my party music to be heard all over the house, not just in the living room, and not blaring so loudly that people couldn't hear themselves think. And I didn't want to string wires all over the place. After some research, I bought an Acme Receiver. I have nice speakers next to it in the living room, of course, but all I had to do was plug in a set of satellite speakers in the kitchen, the office, and the upstairs hallway. There are no wires strung all over and no blaring music in any one place. So now when I create that perfect playlist for the evening, all my guests can enjoy it.

This story describes a solution to a problem without going into any technical detail about that solution. But when you read the story, did you imagine any parts of that solution?

- What are the possible ways for the audio signal to get from the receiver to the satellite speakers?

- How would the receiver know about the existence of the satellite speakers and is there any user setup for that?

- How would the user control the volume in the various parts of the apartment?

Steve Denning, author of several books on storytelling as effective business communication, talks about a special kind of evocative story he calls a *springboard story*. These are short stories, almost fragments, which illustrate a typical predicament. They capture the listener's attention by illustrating a familiar situation while suggesting how things might be different in the future. They are evocative because their goal is not to suggest a specific solution, but rather to spark the imagination and get people thinking about the problem in new ways.

> "A springboard story has an impact not so much through transferring large amounts of information, but through catalyzing understanding. It can enable listeners to visualize from a story in one context what is involved in a large-scale transformation in an analogous context. It can enable them to grasp the idea as a whole not only very simply and quickly, but also in a non-threatening way. In effect, it invites them to see analogies from their own backgrounds, their own contexts, their own fields of expertise"
>
> —Stephen Denning, *The Springboard*

Springboard stories highlight one powerful aspect of the Story Triangle. When an audience is inspired to think about a solution in new ways through a story they have heard, they can take ownership of the story. Once they own the story, they can sculpt and develop it in their minds. More importantly, because they own the story, they are much more likely to take that action if the story suggests it. For instance, if the solution to their story suggests reorganizing a corporate department, they might be more likely to actually do that reorganization. And they would be doing so because it was their idea, suggested by *their own story*, which was inspired by *your springboard story*.

Stories create a shared understanding

In UX work, stories about users can bring a team together with a shared understanding of their goal. These stories can be examples of the problems a product will solve, or a vision of what life might be like with the new product.

Stories can also reveal different perspectives on an experience. The stories people choose to tell and retell say a lot about their concerns and interests.

WHAT KINDS OF STORIES DO YOU TELL?
I used to work in theatre. Like some user experience projects, a theatrical production brings together a group of specialists. When I worked on a version of *The Nutcracker Suite*, each group had its own stories.

The design and technical staff told success stories. They focused on how they had made things go right, even in the face of real problems. These stories portrayed the staff as heroes for saving the production with their knowledge and skill.

The parents and other adults who traveled with the show to supervise the young dancers told stories about times when things went wrong, lingering over the "disasters" and chaos of a live performance. These stories emphasized the excitement of being part of a live event.

The dancers were responsible for teaching the choreography to the local children for two sections of the ballet. Their stories expressed their pride in their young students, as well as emphasizing their own skill as teachers.

The stories each group told helped them create a sense of their work on the production, but their stories also revealed differences in what this shared event meant to them. ■

Stories persuade

Because they are so compelling, stories can change people's minds.

Stories can be a way to persuade others to follow your ideas. (If you are a manager or a design leader, you might want to read Steve Denning's book, *The Secret Language of Leadership*. In it he looks at stories as a management tool, just as we are looking at them here as a UX design tool.) Instead of giving orders, leaders can persuade by using stories to create a vision that others want to be part of.

Good lawyers are often good storytellers. Part of a lawyer's job is to joust using stories. Lawyers use the power of words to change the images that a story evokes in people's minds and the emotions that go along with those images.

 USING ANALOGIES TO CHANGE PEOPLE'S MINDS
Michael Anderson is a First Amendment lawyer and a performing storyteller. He tells this story about how he uses story imagery and story logic to make his point.

Telling the law is about analogies. Lawyers have to retell the stories of past cases so that they sound eerily familiar, like the characters in the legend have been reincarnated here and now. With your opponents as the losers, of course.

I'm a union lawyer. I was recently arguing against a conference full of management lawyers. The issue was whether bosses have a right to force workers to attend anti-union indoctrination sessions. For 80 years, this has been an unquestioned privilege of management. Any sign of union organizing, and bam! Every worker in the plant gets marched into a mandatory anti-union "education program." When unions complain, the employers weep about their First Amendment rights. Boo-hoo, how could anyone try to silence their free speech?

I have to explain why this is wrong. So I dig up an old religion case. An evangelical Christian construction firm tells its workers they have to attend mandatory prayer sessions. It doesn't discriminate: it hires Jews and atheists just like anyone else. And the boss doesn't bribe or threaten anyone. Non-Christians are free to hold to their beliefs, but they are required at the beginning of every shift to listen to a sermon or watch a film about Jesus. In the ensuing civil rights suit, the court laughs the employer out of the courtroom. Yeah, Mr. Christian construction guy, you have a sacred right to preach the Gospel. But on your own time—you have no First Amendment right to force your workers to listen as part of their jobs.

So I ask the audience of management lawyers: "Give me a show of hands, how many people think this case was wrongly decided? Who thinks an employer has a right to force its workers to listen to sermons about Jesus?" No one raised a hand.

Then I asked, "OK, so why do union-avoidance programs have more privileges than God?" ■

Maybe you're not convinced

Before we get too far, let's take a moment to address any little voices still nagging at you. You may think that stories are an unscientific way of communicating data. Or that the people you work with won't take them seriously. Or that you don't have the talent or skill to create and tell stories.

In a field where you sometimes feel the need to sound authoritative, stories can seem, well, not *serious*. Whitney once had a proposal for a presentation on stories and personas rejected with the explanation that "We're *engineers*!" We're not talking about "Once upon a time" here. User experience stories aren't made up. They are based on data from listening and observing in formal and informal settings. They are just as valid as scientific research papers or business reports.

Nothing says that talking about user research can't be engaging, or that brainstorming has to be so formal that you can't relax and let the ideas flow. Stories are a form of communication built deeply into the human psyche. Because of this, you can use them to pack a lot of information into a small space. This makes stories an easy way to learn and an effective way to teach. In a presentation, you may take notes on the bullet points, but it's the illustrations, examples, and anecdotes that help you remember the key points or grasp a new concept on an emotional level. A few well-chosen stories might be just the thing to get everyone to put down their Blackberries and join the conversation.

Because stories are such a natural way to communicate, anyone can create and use them well. You don't have to be a great presenter, actor, or stand-up comic. Sure, storytelling can be awkward at first. Conducting a user interview or running a card sorting exercise can be difficult the first time, too. But once you start thinking about stories as a way of describing a user experience, with characters, motivation, context, and emotions driving their actions, you may find it easier than you think.

All it takes is a little practice. Just dive in and try it.

Summary

Stories are more than just a way of broadcasting information. They are interactive, and come to life in the imaginations of the audience members.

Stories are as much a part of the audience as of the storyteller. The Story Triangle describes the relationships between storyteller, story, and audience.

Stories have many roles in user experience design:

- They explain research and ideas.

- They engage the imagination and spark new ideas.

- They create a shared understanding.

- They can persuade.

CHAPTER 3

Stories Start with Listening (and Observing)

Our world is full of things to listen to: theatre, books, movies, radio, recordings, and television. The World Wide Web has brought new ways to listen to radio, watch movies and TV, read books, and read blogs all over the Internet. YouTube and podcasts let you talk to people all over the world using video and audio. With all this media, all this expression, all this need for people to read, watch, and listen, you might think that listening to one another would be second nature, and that we would all be very good listeners. Instead, all of these possibilities have sometimes encouraged us to express more and listen a little bit less.

Don't get us wrong. Expression is important. But in user experience design, a great idea can often start from a quiet moment of listening or observing how people act and interact.

Think about the last time you had free rein to say whatever you wanted to say, taking as long or as short a time as you needed to say it, absolutely sure that you were not going to be interrupted, redirected, or distracted. It may have been a long time ago, perhaps never. That sort of listening not only allows people to say what they need to say, but it also gives you an opportunity to listen deeply—what we call *really listening*.

This careful attentive listening has valuable benefits: it holds space open to allow other people to form their thoughts and express their minds. When you *really listen*, you may hear or see things that surprise you, like emotions or ideas that you haven't considered in your design process yet.

LISTENING CAN TAP INTO EMOTIONS

In 2005 I taught a workshop on Listening for Creativity at a design conference. It was the first time I had focused on the listening section of my Beginning Storytelling workshop. I really wasn't sure if it was going to work. I knew the 18 people in the room were all designers and design students, and I knew that a large part of design is story listening and storytelling. But I wasn't sure if a session on listening would touch people in a way that made a difference. Would they think that listening was just an idle task?

After an hour, I could tell that many of them weren't convinced of the importance of listening. But to my delight, all but a couple of people came back from the break! As we continued, each exercise was designed to be a little more intense and challenging. One challenge was that simply being listened to can bring up unexpected emotions. In our culture, we are chronically un-listened-to, both at work and home.

After the fifth exercise, a woman raised her hand to make a comment and started crying. She said the exercises helped her see how little she had been listened to in her life, and remarked how strange it was that she was crying in the middle of a conference. As she was speaking and crying, I glanced around the room at the other people. The few remaining cynics sat stunned. I could almost hear them thinking, "Wow! You mean this listening stuff is for real?" ■

UX design requires good listening skills

As user experience designers, we have a lot of people to listen to. One of our jobs is connecting different groups of people: users, business stakeholders, and our colleagues.

The users

A lot of our work involves listening to the people who will use what we create. Maybe your company calls this "The Voice of the Customer." The users of your product are experts in *what they do* and *how they do it*. Perhaps you spend time with them understanding their complex tasks. Or observing their activities and interactions to discover gaps that you can turn into new product ideas. Learning to *really listen* to users is important if you want to discover what they need, not just what they say they want.

Listening is a critical part of user research and usability testing. Almost all user research activities involve paying attention to other people: listening to what they say and watching what they do. Whether you are working in the field or in a lab, your goal is to understand someone else's perspective. You may be in the first phase of learning about their world, or seeing how people you know well react to a new product or concept. Either way, you are gathering their stories. You can't hear the stories the participants are telling you, or see stories playing out in front of you, unless you are paying attention, not just checking off answers to questions.

If you have listened carefully to users' stories, you can weave that understanding into your design presentations, showing that you not only heard their words, but also understood their perspectives.

Business stakeholders

For a user experience designer, the business organization provides many listening opportunities, especially in larger organizations with many different people and roles involved, from your clients to your boss. Each of these groups tells different kinds of stories:

- The **money stakeholders** who directly approve budgets and tell stories of cost versus benefit.

- **Management stakeholders** may have a story of their vision for the company or product, and have credibility and career riding on the project.

- **Political stakeholders** in other departments or divisions have stories about their relationship with the project, whether they are declared friends or undeclared foes.

- **Sales and marketing stakeholders** also tell customer stories, reflecting the give and take of the sales relationship.

A user experience designer translates "business speak" into "design" and vice versa. If you have listened to business stakeholders, you can incorporate their perspectives into your stories, showing how they are in harmony or conflict with user stories.

Our colleagues

As the field of user experience grows, we have an increasingly important group of people to listen to—our colleagues. More and more often, we see teams that include an information architect, interaction designer, user researcher, authors, visual designers, and many other roles. Whatever role you fill, being able to listen actively to others makes the collaboration deeper and easier.

Listening and observing leads to better understanding

Really listening lets you understand someone, or a situation, on several different levels. This leads to better understanding, and gives you deeper, more detailed information to use in your work.

Really listening lets you hear subtext and overtones. You can hear not just what people are saying, but also the *way* they say it. This second layer can give you a deeper sense of who they are, what's important to them, and how they view the world. With attentive eyes and body language, someone really listening communicates that what the speaker is saying is important to them. The speaker then pays more attention to themselves, too.

When you don't listen to these deeper layers of meaning, you can miss important information.

MISUNDERSTANDINGS ABOUT THE AGENDA

Françoise Brun-Cottan is an ethnographer who works in business settings. In a recent book, Ethnography and the Corporate Encounter *(edited by Melissa Cefkin), she described an experience of "losing the personal" in her relationship with one of the people at the site. In doing so, she missed an important part of their experience.*

I was studying how a large manufacturing company manages its records. I was part of an interdisciplinary team of five. The fieldwork included shadowing employees, videotaping them as they went about their daily work. Like many of the records staff, one informant, Dee, did not start out particularly thrilled at the prospect of being followed, observed, and recorded on tape while working. She tolerated us with forbearance verging on amusement. At the end of the project, I had an opportunity to talk to Dee one last time. We were all feeling pretty good about the project, even Dee. She felt that maybe she'd gotten some new respect for the work she did, although she didn't expect that it would translate into a better salary. Then she said, "You're trying to get rid of people, aren't you, heh heh heh?"

Whoa! Stop the train.

Dee had been working with us all along with this notion of her easy "replaceability" in her mind, this image of herself as expendable. And I, who had been so self-assured in representing her as she was manifest in her work, had been oblivious to all the other parts of her that made her who she was (Dee) and to the high degree of grace involved in her cooperation in the face of her belief.

And how does this little anecdote end? Dee noticed my consternation and said, "Would you care to go out and have a cup of coffee?" She was consoling me. ■

Really listening allows people to share their deeper thoughts. When you listen and observe carefully, you can hear and see the way people shape their thoughts, how they think about what they are about to say, and how they respond to hearing themselves say it. In this way, listening empowers speakers to speak with more awareness of what they are saying and to take the time to consider what they mean carefully. In other words, you allow them to expose and improve their thought process. That's a real benefit when you are trying to understand more about them.

SECOND THOUGHTS CAN BE DEEPER

Some users of the National Cancer Institute's (NCI) Web site are grassroots cancer advocates. These folks talk to patients, educate the community, and help raise money for cancer research. Most of them got started when they or someone in their family was diagnosed with cancer, so this work is deeply personal. The NCI is very important in the fight against cancer, and they are often hesitant to criticize it.

At the end of every session with these advocates, I ask if they have any thoughts about the site that they would like to share. Their first comments are usually what they think NCI wants to hear—that it's a great site with wonderful resources. But if I just give them my full attention and wait, they often start to share stories about problems they've had: information that is hard to find or too complex for the people they work with, or their ideas about how it can be improved.

I always hope that if they see their suggestions implemented, they will think, "NCI is a big place, but they *listened to me.*" ▪

Really listening means observing, too. Sometimes, you will find a story in the details that you observe. People may not mention things that they consider to be just another part of the natural environment—things like exactly *how* or exactly *when* something gets done. In other words, watching what people do and how they interact with their environment is part of listening.

WE FORGET TO MENTION EVERYDAY FACTS

Ginny Redish tells a very simple story about usability problems with a hand-held device for an inventory system. What no one thought to mention to the designers was that the device was used by people working in a refrigerated environment. The keys were too small for their gloved hands. ▪

Combining listening and observing can lead to greater insights as well. As important as it is to pay attention to exactly what people say, listening for deeper meaning may allow you to find contradictions between what they say and what they do that are key to understanding them better.

Discussions about usability testing are full of examples of people who say one thing and do another. Or who insist that something is easy, even as they go to greater effort to complete a task.

 WHEN ACTIONS CONTRADICT WORDS
Steve Portigal is a strategist who studies how people interact with technology. For one project, he investigated how people managed their digital music. In some cases, what he observed contradicted what they said.

We talked to some people who used iTunes and some who used Windows. Those who were using Windows to manage their music kept it in multiple drives in a variety of music folders. Each person might have a number of different ad-hoc naming schemes—in folders by album, artist, or both, or neither. We asked people to show us how they would find and play music. While everyone said they were comfortable with this task, the non-iTunes users spent minutes opening folder after folder, hunting for the right one. We'd see "click-open-click-click-browse-close-open-browse-click-click" and then they'd launch the file and play it for us.

What they said: They have their music in control.

What we saw: No coherent organizational structure.

How they behaved: Music definitely was not at their fingertips; a lot of hunting and clicking.

This wasn't just our opinion. By comparing the Windows and iTunes users, we could see the gulf between how easy, fast, and effortless this task could be, and thus the gulf between what they told us and what we saw. ■

Really listening lets people know they are being heard. The listener empowers the speaker to share thoughts and observations they might otherwise keep to themselves. This can be especially important in situations where people have not been heard in the past—for example, in the relationship between a company and its customers.

StoryCorps' (storycorps.net) goal is to inspire people to tell their stories. Some are broadcast on National Public Radio, but their goal is to make the act of recording the story, having the conversation, available to everyone. They set up "story booths" that people can visit to record a story with a friend or relative. The thing that is amazing about these stories is how extraordinary they are. These are not the stories of famous people; it is the connection between the storyteller and the listener that gives them depth and resonance.

> "Whenever people listen to these stories, they hear the courage, the humor, the trials and triumphs of an incredible range of voices. By listening closely to one another, we can help illuminate the true character of this nation, reminding us all just how precious each day can be and how truly great it is to be alive."
>
> —Dave Isay, StoryCorps

Being listened to is addictive

We would be remiss if we did not caution you that good listening can be addictive. If you have ever been *really listened to*, then you know its power. We then want it, even crave it, and seek it constantly.

You know that feeling when you're talking and you were afraid to stop for even a moment because you knew that those listening to you were biding their time until they could jump in? That's a form of "not-really-listening." They aren't actually hearing what you are saying, just waiting for words or phrases to trigger what *they* will say.

> **Speaker:** I had some trouble coming up with exactly the right... (speaker pauses searching for the right word).
>
> **Non-Listener:** Oh, I've had that trouble too, but that's no problem. What I've done is... (and they launch into telling their own story, rather than listening).

The listener may never know exactly what the speaker was trying to say. The original thought may be lost, or simply plastered over by the listener's suggestion.

Many of us are so accustomed to being interrupted that we have developed highly effective interruption defense mechanisms. For example, with the threat of interruption, we might raise our voice so we can continue. We might pause only for a moment and then interrupt the interrupter with words like, "I know! I know! And..." and try to finish the thought.

Perhaps you know someone who never seems to stop talking. You might ask yourself: "Where's the *off* button?! Why are they going on and on and on about the same thing? It's not like I even asked them a question." Perhaps at one point, perhaps even recently, they've had someone who listened hard enough and long enough that they could express and work out what was on their mind. And the only way they can find a really good listener is to talk to everybody a lot. They know they'll recognize a good listener again once another one comes along. They may not even be aware of it, but they remember how good they felt when they were well listened to.

At the risk of sounding overly simplistic, often all people need is to be given the freedom to find intelligence and creativity on their own. We need time to "think out loud" without the threat of interruption, without a listener's apparent allergy to what is often the most precious thing in our culture— moments of silence. Listening to others that deeply is a gift the listener gives the speaker.

Learn to be a good listener

Being a good listener takes practice. It can be especially hard for consultants, who often join a project as an expert and can feel pressure to talk more than they listen.

One of the ways to be good at listening is called *active listening*. Mind Tools, a career skills development site, lists five elements of good listening.

1. **Pay attention.** Give the speaker your undivided attention and acknowledge the message.

2. **Show that you are listening.** Use your own body language and gestures to convey your attention.

3. **Reflect back.** Show that you understand what is being said by paraphrasing and summarizing periodically.

4. **Defer judgment.** Allow the speaker to finish. Don't interrupt.

5. **Respond appropriately.** Be candid and open in your response.

At MathWorks, Donna Cooper and Michelle Erickson created a workshop on active listening. This skill helps them work together better as a team and also do their work with other groups more effectively. They compiled a list of 10 skills based on research by Marisue Pickering and the University of Vermont (see Table 3.1). These skills are all good listening behaviors that you can practice in your work, as well as during any kind of user research.

TABLE 3.1

10 SKILLS FOR ACTIVE LISTENING			
Skill	Behavior	Do	Avoid
Attending, acknowledging	Provide verbal or nonverbal awareness of the other person.	Face the speaker and maintain eye contact, nod, etc.	Looking around the room or fidgeting.
Restating	Respond to the person's basic verbal message.	Repeat the phrase you would like clarified.	Changing the subject.
Reflecting	Reflect perceptions of content that are heard or perceived through cues.	Listen for what is not said. Respond with phrases such as, "So you feel that..."	Discounting or downplaying the speaker's feelings.
Interpreting	Offer a tentative interpretation about the person's feelings, desires, or meaning.	Keep an open mind about what you are hearing; try to picture what the speaker is saying.	Assuming you know what the speaker is trying to communicate without listening.
Summarizing, synthesizing	Bring together feelings and experiences to provide a focus.	Repeat back what you heard briefly but accurately; paraphrase.	Elaborating on what the speaker is saying.

TABLE 3.1

10 SKILLS FOR ACTIVE LISTENING (CONTINUED)			
Skill	**Behavior**	**Do**	**Avoid**
Probing	Question the speaker in a supportive way to request more information or clear up any confusion.	Wait for the speaker to pause to ask clarifying questions; try "dangling" or open-ended questions.	Interrogating or challenging the speaker.
Giving feedback	Share perceptions of the person's ideas or feelings, disclosing relevant personal information.	Wait three seconds, and then respond with phrases such as: "So you feel that...", or "I felt that way when...".	Interrupting or offering solutions; preaching or teaching.
Supporting	Show warmth and caring in one's own individual way.	Pay attention to what isn't said—to feelings, facial expressions, gestures, posture, and other nonverbal cues.	Judging the speaker or rehearsing your response in your head while they are speaking.
Checking perceptions	Find out if interpretations and perceptions are valid and accurate.	Check the accuracy of your perceptions with phrases such as, "I think that you are saying..."	Making assumptions or jumping to conclusions.
Being quiet	Give the person time to think as well as to talk.	Try to understand what the speaker is feeling and have empathy for the speaker.	Filling pauses; instead, let the speaker set the pace.

The next time you are in a situation where you need to listen to other people, try observing yourself. See what happens when you consciously turn on good listening behaviors. You might be surprised.

Teach your team to listen

One of the first steps toward a good user experience is to start *really listening* to your customers and users. This does not mean starting a fancy program with a nice corporate title, but teaching and practicing good listening skills.

For a company or team, *really listening* means not only hearing the words, but also understanding what's behind those words and being ready to act on what they hear. This clearly applies to listening to users, and we often *have* to listen to business stakeholders, but we can easily forget to listen to our colleagues.

For example, it's easy to let design sessions become little more than a series of monologues as each person waits for an opening to jump in with his or her own ideas. This can be especially true when the group includes people who are not used to being part of a design team. Your goal is to create an environment where everyone is free to just say what he or she has to say with the knowledge that the others are listening—and listening intently. They are not reading emails, paying attention to their inner monologues, running through task lists, or deciding what they would like to say next. Your job as a facilitator is to make sure that everyone is listened to.

LISTENING IS THE KEY TO SELLING

When I worked for a small consulting company, I went on many sales calls. I'd helped create some of the company's marketing materials, so I thought that *selling* meant talking to potential customers about *us:* our great services and how clever we were.

Doug Crisman, our president, put me straight. "You make more sales by listening. If you are talking for most of the meeting, you're not taking the time to hear what problem they want you to solve." When I started to listen more carefully, I quickly learned that the specifics of the project were just the tip of the iceberg. There was often an underlying issue that they didn't mention. Maybe this product was the start of a new direction for the company. Or they were facing defections from long-time customers. Or...or...

If we listened carefully first, when we finally spoke about how we could work with them, we could weave our awareness of their issues into the pitch for our services. Years later, I realized the irony: our design process always started by understanding the *client's* users, but we forgot that our clients were *our* users, and we needed to understand them, too. ■

You may not work with a sales team, but anyone in user experience design has to "sell" their deliverables, whether that deliverable is an information architecture, a visual design, a usability report, or a new product concept. If you've not only done your work well, but also listened carefully for the problem that needs to be solved, you will find that you can weave business needs and your user experience work together. You may find a better reaction to your work.

The point here is that good listening gets you ready to talk effectively. The things you say will speak directly to your listeners, and the stories you tell will include them more effectively.

We'll cover more about using stories (and listening) in Chapter 10, "Sharing Stories," when we talk about sharing stories as part of managing.

More reading

MathWorks distributes these links about active listening to the UX team. They are drawn from a variety of contexts—business, agricultural labor management, family counseling, and corporate training—but all have a similar emphasis.

Eight Barriers to Effective Listening: www.sklatch.net/thoughtlets/listen.html

Mind Tools's Active Listening: www.mindtools.com/CommSkll/ActiveListening.htm

Empathic Approach—Listening First Aid: www.cnr.berkeley.edu/ucce50/ag-labor/7article/listening_skills.htm

Empathic Listening: www.beyondintractability.org/essay/empathic_listening/

7 Tips for Effective Listening: findarticles.com/p/articles/mi_m4153/is_4_60/ai_106863366/?tag=content;col1

10 Tips to Effective & Active Listening Skills: http://powertochange.com/students/people/listen/

Summary

Good listening can be contagious. We started this chapter by saying that stories start with listening. When you get in the habit of *really listening*, you may be surprised to discover how many stories you will hear. You are listening more, so you will have more opportunities. Because you are listening more deeply, the stories you find will be more useful, meaningful, and interesting.

- Listening carefully allows you to hear subtext and overtones in what people say, especially when you combine it with observing them.

- When you allow people time to speak, they can think more carefully about what they are saying and share deeper thoughts.

- You can learn to be a good listening, using *active listening* techniques.

CHAPTER 4

The Ethics of Stories

W e have already talked about the triangular relationship between story, storyteller, and audience. But there's a second triangle.

This triangle is critical for user experience, where you use stories collected from real people. This triangle switches the relationships around. At the beginning of the process, *you* are the listeners, and your ethnographic informants, usability participants, or research interlocutors are the storytellers (see Figure 4.1).

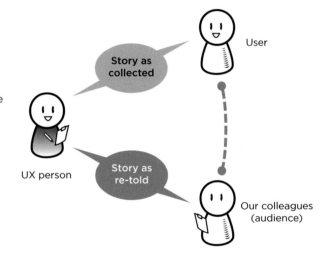

FIGURE 4.1
When you create and tell a user experience story, it is one you have originally collected from another person. Your retelling of the story creates a connection between the user from whom you originally heard the story and your audience.

Because you are using material from other people in your user experience stories, you have an ethical responsibility not only to the story, but to your sources as well.

Good research ethics—good storytelling

There is no conflict between research ethics and storytelling. A story is not just a collection of facts, but of information structured to appeal to an audience's logic and emotion. To be a good storyteller in user experience, you need honesty and authenticity, along with a simplicity or clarity of expression. These are tools the storyteller uses in any application of storytelling to craft the material and the presentation so that the audience sees something new.

- An honest story portrays user research accurately, not distorting the evidence through the selection of the story or the details that are included.

- An authentic story is true to the feeling of the original events, and it is told in a way that reflects how the participants themselves might tell it.

When you tell a story with simplicity, you use just enough details to be clear and to help your audience recognize the honesty and authenticity of the story and no more.

Stories and storytelling are very powerful parts of the human experience. It's not simply that people happen to enjoy stories; they need them and want to believe them. Where pure logic and reason are not effective, stories provide a form of reason that is often so effective that it moves people to thought and action.

This means that storytellers have an important ethical responsibility to their audience and possibly to the world. History is full of examples of people who have told good stories, in the right way, at the right time, to the right audience, and moved them to radical change—sometimes for good, but often enough not. Every revolution or coup starts with a good story. And after a revolution, it is often the storytellers—the artists, the journalists—of the former regime who are silenced.

At this point one might think, "But I'm just redesigning the Web site for my startup. I'm not interested in regime change." Fine. Understand, though, that the tools for both are the same. Stories and storytelling are important for design in part because stories can shape and change minds. Use that power well and use it wisely.

Professional societies give us relevant ethics for stories

The Code of Ethics of the American Anthropological Association addresses many of the issues that you must consider when creating stories from user research material. This includes your responsibility to the people with whom you work and those you study. Their guidelines begin with the overarching requirement to "avoid harm to the individuals or groups you work with" (including both your colleagues and people you meet during user research), and they continue with four specific requirements that are just as relevant to stories as to any other user research.

- Actively establish a working relationship that is beneficial to everyone involved.

- Do everything in your power to ensure that your work does not harm the safety, dignity, or privacy of the people with whom you work.

- Determine in advance whether the people you work with want to remain anonymous.

- Ensure that the people you work with are informed of the goals of your work and what you will do with the information, and that you have obtained their informed consent, with a clear understanding of the impact of their participation in your work.

The Code of Professional Conduct of the Usability Professionals' Association (UPA) includes similar guidelines, as do those of many other user experience professional organizations. The Code of Ethics of the Human Factors and Engineering Society (HFES) includes another principle relevant to storytelling: "Avoid sensationalism, exaggeration, and superficiality that constitutes deception." The American Psychological Association (APA) has a detailed code of ethics covering similar aspects of working with people as part of your research.

All of these ethical considerations come into play when you are collecting, creating, or telling user experience stories.

Acknowledge your own influence

Think carefully about your own ability to influence user research. This influence, or "reflexivity," works in both directions: Our presence, attitudes, and behavior can affect the people we work with, and they can affect us.

For example, there is a narrow line between providing people with an opportunity to tell their story and leading them to perspectives, opinions, or ideas that they might not express without your urging. This sort of influence might include the following:

- Suggesting terminology, especially emotional terminology

- Asking leading questions that hint at a "right" answer

- Going beyond eliciting stories to suggesting issues before the participant brings them up

- Translating concepts from the participant's frame of reference to your own

These are, of course, pitfalls of any user research. It's just good practice to think carefully about how much the situation in which you collected your observations is an accurate reflection of "real life." It's especially important in stories because their emotional impact can magnify any distortions or simply convince you (or someone else) of something that may not be exactly true.

Tell the story accurately

Stories can be a good way to communicate uncomfortable truths or even to shock. For example, when you have learned something in a user research or evaluation session that contradicts the team's current beliefs, a story can provide the explanation and context to help make the news believable.

 A STORY CAN DELIVER GOOD NEWS...AND BAD NEWS
Ginny Redish, an early advocate of the value of observing users, tells this story about using information collected in the field to share bad news about a product idea.

This is a story from the days when many companies were first moving from dumb terminals with green screens to graphical user interfaces (GUIs), and object-oriented programming was just becoming popular. One of my clients was very excited about the new possibilities, and the developers decided to redo one of their major applications as a test case.

They sent business analysts out to the field to gather requirements from the field staff who were the users of this application (and many others that the company had). The business analysts went out all fired up to tell field staff about the new computers they would be getting—after all, GUIs couldn't run on the old dumb terminals.

But their enthusiasm was dampened by the users' realities and the users' stories. The business analysts brought back photos of the users' workspaces (incredibly cramped, with not an inch of space for a second monitor), and they told the story of meeting with Jack, a 50-year-old who had been doing the job in one town for more than 20 years. They played their tape of Jack asking, 'Are you changing all of our applications? No? Then we'll still need our old terminals for all our other work. Where are we going to put the computer we'll need to use your new program?'

Jack's story was bad—but very important—news for the developers. No one had thought beyond the excitement of picking one application to change." ■

The more difficult the message your story has to communicate, the more careful you must be to ensure that the story reflects reality.

When stories are presented as part of research, you have an obligation to be sure that they reflect the full picture of the people and context. You need to make sure that the stories are "true," meaning that they are an accurate representation of the situations involved, whether you are telling the story of a single event from a single participant or creating a composite with material from several different people.

All of this does *not* mean that the story should be a verbatim account. For instance, you might change details to protect the anonymity or privacy of the participant. But the story must reflect the real details, not be overstated or idealized beyond what you would present in any other analysis report.

This is just good practice. If you are using stories to help guide user experience design, you want them to accurately express what you know about users and their context. Another way to think about accuracy is to look at whether the stories you have chosen to tell reflect the big picture. It's easy to be seduced by an interesting story that is an outlier, an interesting or amusing anecdote that does little to illuminate the user experience (or worse, seems to poke fun at the person). It's also easy to avoid stories that carry a message you don't like. Maybe it suggests a design direction you don't agree with. Or it reinforces an idea that your audience doesn't want to hear.

The need to keep stories true is especially important if you work in a domain where there are experts. If you distort details, you risk creating a story that distracts the expert audience from the point of the story with its inaccuracies. And by sticking close to the original story, you can shift easily into a more detailed account when necessary by going back to the original research.

The common saying, "Never let the facts get in the way of a good story," presents a fine line that storytellers walk all the time. Performing storytellers have a greater latitude here, as the story *is* their product, and the audience's perceived value of their story is something close to instantaneous. The audience doesn't have to hold it, handle it, click on it, operate its menus, plug it in, or interface it to their PC. They simply have to experience the story.

Experience designers have a much finer line to walk, but walk it they must. To only relate facts is not storytelling, it's regurgitation. On the other hand, to play fast and loose with the facts risks distorting the truth, which diminishes the value of the story.

Keep the story authentic

An audience may not actually comment on your story's authenticity. But if it isn't authentic, they will absolutely notice. One of the challenges in using research data as the basis for a story is deciding how much to "clean up" the language or details from the way you originally heard them.

There are many issues here. For example, if there is a large difference in socioeconomic class or authority between the participant and your audience, you have to decide whether a verbatim transcript will keep a story "true" or whether it might inadvertently make the person you heard it from seem less educated or competent than they are. There is a careful balance between preserving the original form of expression and harming the dignity of your source.

**CLEANING UP SPOKEN LANGUAGE
FOR WRITTEN PRESENTATION**

*Caroline Jarrett works with government agencies on their
communication with citizens and businesses. In these projects,
she is aware of her role as an intermediary between ordinary people
and their government.*

I conducted a series of informal visits with small business owners, where
they chatted happily to me as we looked at a group of Web pages, letters,
and forms from a government agency.

They were intelligent and articulate people, but most of them hadn't had
much education. My audience was a government agency, which tended to
discount less educated citizens.

In retelling their stories for my report, I decided to clean up incorrect
grammar or dialect that might be interpreted as a lack of education or
sophistication. My solution was to use the same terminology and basic
sentence construction as I'd heard, but to correct the sort of grammatical
errors that most people make when speaking. ■

You may decide to create slightly different versions of a story for different
audiences or for when you place the story in different contexts. Think
carefully about how to preserve the authenticity of the story as you
transform it.

Accepting the responsibility for changing the details of a story to amplify
the truth is part of building an experience. You may create a composite
story based on several incomplete stories from your research or a composite
character, like a persona. In any case, you, the storyteller, must be a careful
judge of whether you have slipped too far from an ethical story that reflects
the *truth* you want to communicate.

End the story well

We offer one final word on the ethics of stories. When you tell a story, you
make a connection with the audience, who in turn makes a connection
to your story. Your job as the storyteller is to facilitate those relationships.
When the story ends, the audience has been through something of a journey,
whether it is one of narrative events, challenging ideas, or emotional states.
The final resolution of the story—the last images or emotions the audience

experiences—affect their impressions of the story as a whole, no matter what came before. You need to end the story in a safe place for the audience, one from which they can complete that journey in their minds. This does not mean that every story needs to have a happy ending, but that the ending affects the audience's receptivity to the entire experience.

This is an ethical issue because as a storyteller, you lead the audience to ideas, experiences, and emotional terrain they would not have traveled on their own.

The storyteller has a responsibility to choose an ending that not only suits the purpose of the story, but also allows the audience to incorporate that story safely into their lives and work.

More reading

Professional ethics codes

American Psychological Association Ethical Principles of Psychologists and Code of Conduct: www.apa.org/ethics/code2002.html

Code of Ethics of the American Anthropological Association: www.aaanet.org/committees/ethics/ethcode.htm

Usability Professionals' Association Code of Professional Conduct: www.usabilityprofessionals.org/about_upa/leadership/code_of_conduct.html

ICC/ESOMAR International Code on Market and Social Research: www.esomar.org/index.php/codes-guidelines.html

Market Research Society: www.mrs.org/uk/standards/codeconduct.htm

Human Factors and Ergonomics Society Code of Ethics: www.hfes.org/web/AboutHFES/ethics.html

Summary

When you use material from other people in your user experience stories, you have an ethical responsibility not only to the story, but to your sources as well.

- When you collect stories from other people, you have to consider how you can treat them—and their stories—responsibly.

- Research ethics from professional associations offer useful guidance.

- You must think carefully about your own ability to influence user research and how you will "translate" users' stories (if at all).

CHAPTER 5

Stories as Part of a UX Process

55

N ow that we've explored what a story is, the ethics of telling them, and how stories empower people through listening, it's time to think about how all of this fits into user experience design.

If you are looking for inspiration at a specific point in a project, the chapters in this section each focus on one aspect of user experience design, in a roughly chronological order.

We are not going to promote one approach to user experience design over another, nor are we going to promote a new methodology based on using stories. Whether you believe in user-centered design, goals-based design, or even a more technical approach like domain-driven design, stories have a place in your work.

Despite the number of approaches to user experience design, the core is usually quite simple, so we will stick to this generic process: start by understanding the context, put that understanding to work in creating the design, and then test the design as it is fleshed out to be sure that the product will be a good fit.

There's even an international standard that describes this generic process—the "human-centered design process for interactive systems." Its official name is ISO 13407, but it's being updated as ISO 9241-210 to broaden its scope from usability to user experience. Figure 5.1 shows a simplified diagram of the stages of the process.

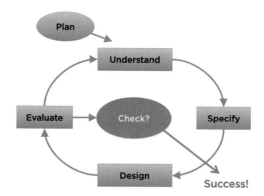

FIGURE 5.1
A model of a human-centered design process.

It starts with planning, working within a process—any process—that provides a structure for your work. It doesn't have to be a rigid plan (although some of you may work within a highly structured product lifecycle). But if you don't plan time for user experience work, or make room for understanding users within your methodology, it just won't happen.

The rest of this process is a cycle of activities through which you will build and test your design:

- **Understand** (conduct user research and investigate the context of use)

- **Specify** (analyze the business and user research to define what the product will do)

- **Design** (create the actual product design, from early sketches to final designs)

- **Evaluate** (check the designs to be sure they meet the goals for the product)

There are three important features of this process.

First, it's iterative. Ideas can be tested and either accepted or discarded. Designs can be created and tested until a good solution is found. This also allows a user experience design team to start with rough sketches or wireframes and build them into a finished design, testing at each stage.

Stories can iterate with the rest of the design. For example, they might start with a small anecdote and then get shaped into a complete scenario that illustrates a function. New stories can be found during evaluation that will help shape the next iteration of the design.

Second, it's scalable. Different parts of a product can be moved through this process at different times. An early version of a design might include only the most basic sketch of a feature, which will be designed in detail in a mini-process. Stories can also scale from short fragments to a more complete story as your understanding of the product grows.

Finally, it applies to any type of project. Whether you are building an informational Web site, defining a taxonomy, creating a new electronic device, developing an online application, writing documentation, or designing a piece of furniture, this general cycle is useful for building, from understanding to evaluation.

As you go through this process, stories help you keep people at the center of your work. This can be hard, especially when you do not have easy access to users. A good story can remind you of the real-world contexts in which your products will be used.

UX is a cross-disciplinary practice

Although we're not the first to say it, the vision for user experience design is for a cross-disciplinary practice, with everyone working on one team, bringing together all of the skills needed to create an excellent product. This vision is not universally achieved.

We've seen everything from one-person UX teams to companies where the entire team (including designers and project managers and development staff and marketing and all of the UX disciplines) participated in the user research, analysis, and design. As William Gibson has famously said, "The future is already here. It's just not very evenly distributed."

In whichever way your team is structured, when we talk about working with stories, we are not suggesting that this is a new specialty, requiring adding a "storyteller" or "story thinker" to the team. In fact, we hope that "story thinking" can help everyone be more creative, no matter what their roles are.

When we talk about how "you" can collect stories, or how "you" can select stories to use as design inspiration, anyone on the team might be that person at any point in the process. Or it might be a group of "you" collaborating on one piece of a larger project.

Using stories in user experience design is not a new idea

We are not the first people to notice that stories can be incorporated into user experience design. Many different approaches and methodologies use story forms as a way of communicating information about the user experience.

Ethnography, one of the disciplines that is the basis for field methods in user research (that is, observing people and their behavior in context), also focuses on the human story and the ability of that story to communicate. AIGA's *An Ethnography Primer* says that one role of the ethnographer is to "tell the story in a way that helps people embrace recommendations and create a shared vision."

Tom Erickson, an interaction designer and researcher for IBM (and before that, for Apple), uses stories throughout the design process. In his view, story gathering begins the design process, and stories are then used to communicate design requirements and user information to the development team. Prototypes based on stories allow the team to explore a new vision, especially one that is innovative, rather than a small improvement on a previous design. His essays on storytelling in design emphasize the value of stories as a way to stimulate design thinking and enhance communication among a design team.

John Carroll and Mary Beth Rosson's scenario-based design uses stories to ensure that user experience is included in software development. They recognize that scenarios are a way to communicate important information about the human-computer interface without writing technical specifications. Their scenarios describe the goals, behaviors, and experience of the people using the system.

Sometimes, scenarios sound a lot like use cases, but use cases typically focus on describing all of the events in an interaction, including actions performed by the system (or "actors" within the computer system). They are intended to document the interaction that will be part of a program, rather than describe the environment and the broader user experience, too. In their "usage-centered design," Larry Constantine and Lucy Lockwood use the basic format of use cases and other software models to define user goals and the features or activities that let people meet those goals.

These stories are collected and then later filled out in conversations with users and other stakeholders. They are usually simple requirements in a format that describes the user role, the goal, and the reason for the goal. These stories are collected and then later filled out in conversations with users. However, agile development methods emphasize that the role of user stories is to capture testable requirements in a rapid, simple way. They are often no more than a single sentence. One of many good agile Web sites "Agile Software Development Made Easy!" (www.agile-software-development.com/2008/04/writing-good-user-stories.html) relates, "User Stories are a simple way of capturing user requirements throughout a project—an alternative to writing lengthy requirements specifications all up-front. The basic construct of an agile user story is, "As a [user role], I want to [goal], so I can [reason]," for example:

> As a job seeker, I want to search for a job, so I can advance my career.

> As a recruiter, I want to post a job vacancy, so I can find a new team member.

JoAnne Hackos and Ginny Redish focused on scenarios and stories in their seminal book, *User and Task Analysis for Interface Design*. They traced scenarios through the process as a way of communicating analysis. Their understanding of scenarios was as broad as our view of stories and storytelling.

> "Scenarios can be about users, their work, their environments, how they do tasks, the tasks they need to do, and all combinations of these elements. Storytelling has the advantages of bringing people, places, and actions alive. It can also give you insights into the attributes of tasks you need to accommodate in your design, what users value, and what they see as aids and obstacles to accomplishing their goal."
>
> —*User and Task Analysis for Interface Design*

They identified several types of stories (or, as they call them, *scenarios*) from *brief scenarios* and *vignettes*, which provide a concise view of a situation, environment, or how a user currently does something, to *elaborated task scenarios* and *use scenarios*, narratives that describe an interaction from beginning to end. They suggested using these scenarios in several different ways. First, the brief scenarios are a way to collect insights. Task scenarios help document user, information, and interaction needs, while setting them in a context. Finally, use scenarios tell a story about the new design and how people will interact with it.

Stories can be part of many UX activities

We'll focus on five parts of the UX process where storytelling can be most useful, thinking about the audience for the stories in each:

- When you are collecting input

- When you are exploring user research and other information

- When you stimulate or experiment with design ideas

- When you want to test your designs

- When you need to share (or sell) your ideas

When you are collecting input

Anytime you work with users, you have a chance to listen for the stories they tell about their home or work lives, how they can work better, and what they want (see Figure 5.2). During this phase of the work, you (and your fellow user experience colleagues) are the primary audience for the stories because you are listening to stories from users and other stakeholders.

FIGURE 5.2
You collect input from
many sources.

You are probably already hearing these stories. All you have to do is make a conscious effort to recognize them as stories and collect them. You can also make a note of what pieces of the stories might be missing that you can fill in later with additional research.

In the human-centered design process, this is part of the *understanding* stage. Your story focus in this stage is to listen for stories that provide an interesting experience, viewpoint, or way of describing an experience.

When you are exploring user research and other information

The stories you collect complement other data, from site logs to functional analysis. They can provide explanations for what surveys, usage analysis, or other data are telling you, or point to places where you need more information. During your analysis, you can select the stories that illuminate the data, as shown in Figure 5.3.

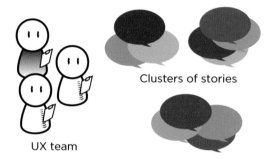

Clusters of stories

UX team

FIGURE 5.3
Stories illuminate data
during analysis.

Although the user research team is still the primary audience for these stories, you are already thinking about which stories and which story images will resonate with designers, developers, managers, or anyone else who may rely on your work.

In the human-centered design process, this is part of both *understanding* and *specifying*, as you transform your first understanding into a view of the needs that the project must meet. Your story focus in this stage is to select the stories that are compelling examples, those which illustrate patterns and personas.

When you experiment with design ideas

Stories are raw material for design innovation. Story fragments can stimulate new ideas. Stories from the field can describe problems to solve or scenarios of how things might be improved. They can help you explore new ideas or test an early draft of a design (see Figure 5.4). Because stories focus on people and their motivations, they can help realign a drifting or divergent design process back toward the people who will use the product.

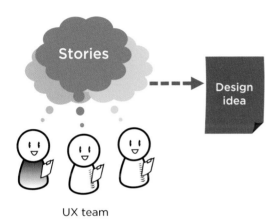

UX team

FIGURE 5.4
Stories can lead to design ideas.

In this stage, your audience begins to grow. The stories you create are valuable to the user experience team, but also must be credible to the full product team.

As you and your colleagues become accustomed to using stories, you will find that you have a wider choice of story formats and more ways to use them.

In the human-centered design process, this is part of the *design* stage, as you start to envision a new design and user experience. Your story focus in this stage is about using stories to help generate ideas and keep the emerging design grounded in real user needs. You can also create new stories that show the design in context and action.

When you want to test your designs

Stories even have a function in evaluation (see Figure 5.5). They can give you a scenario to kick off a task or define what you want participants to do during the test.

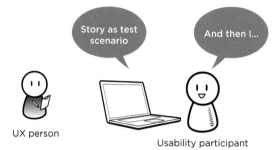

FIGURE 5.5
Stories make good
scenarios for testing
tasks.

Going back to these original stories will ensure that the new product has stayed true to your user needs and initial inspiration.

In the human-centered design process, this is part of the *evaluation* stage, as a check that the design works as intended for real people. Your story focus in this stage is on reusing and adapting your stories to be suitable as test scenarios.

When you need to share (or sell) your ideas

We may like to think that a great design or a great idea will sell itself, but if a picture is worth a thousand words, a story can be just the right number of words needed to explain what that picture (or design prototype) is all about. Stories become part of the connections between the user research and design (see Figure 5.6). They can explain why a design will work because they connect the design with the inspiration for the designer's idea.

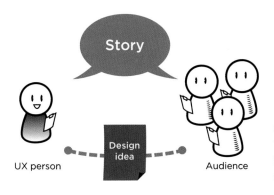

FIGURE 5.6
The team can share ideas by sharing stories.

More reading

"Notes on Design Practice: Stories and Prototypes as Catalysts for Communication," Tom Erickson, in *Scenario-Based Design: Envisioning Work and Technology in System Development*, edited by John Carroll

Usability Engineering: Scenario-Based Development of Human Computer Interaction, John Carroll and Mary Beth Rosson

Software for Use by Larry Constantine & Lucy Lockwood: www.foruse.com

User and Task Analysis for Interface Design, JoAnn Hackos and Janice (Ginny) Redish

AIGA, An Ethnography Primer: www.aiga.org/resources/content/3/7/4/5/documents/ethnography_primer.pdf

Summary

Storytelling is not a new methodology, but can be part of any approach to user experience design.

- Including storytelling in user experience design is not a new idea. Many approaches and methodologies include some form of stories as a way to communicate how users will interact with a product.

- Stories can be helpful at many points in a process: collecting input, analyzing data, creating new designs, evaluating a design, and sharing insights with colleagues.

Each of the next five chapters focuses on one of these topics, with examples and details about how to put storytelling to work in user experience design.

CHAPTER 6

Collecting Stories (as Part of Research)

S tories in user experience design are not "made up"—they are based on real user data and then distilled to effectively illuminate the design process. It all starts with collecting stories during user research. Whether you are building a picture of audience demographics, doing an in-depth task analysis, or seeking a broader understanding of user motivations and desires, you, too, can collect valuable stories.

The stories you hear from users give you a first-person view of the world from many unique perspectives. They help you understand the goals, motivations, and preferences of the people you design for. They help you understand their personalities and their quirks, which you can use to create a rich, textured experience.

MEETING REAL CUSTOMERS LEADS TO A WHOLE NEW WAY OF TALKING

Rahel Bailie is a content strategist who helps organizations create and manage their communication products better. She told us this story about how listening to customers can change the way a company markets its products.

Recently, I was asked to "do the writing" for a new company's Web site. Naturally, I started by asking about the audience. Their idea was to spin off a new company to provide a platform as a service (PAAS) for small businesses. The company owner's vision was "software so easy to use, even my grandmother could figure it out." The idea was to have "drag-and-drop" code that could be used by small businesses to develop customized software modules to meet their business needs.

I quickly realized that they hadn't really thought about their audience. While they'd certainly done market research on similar services in the market, they didn't actually know how small business owners worked or searched for such a service, so I had to back up and do the entire UCD (user-centered design) process in order to be able to write the copy.

I started by interviewing some potential customers. What I found surprised everyone. They told me that their new product would be for small businesses, generally defined as having under 100 employees and under $5 million in annual revenue. By the second interview, I'd discovered that the target market wasn't small businesses, but microbusinesses— owner-operated businesses with fewer employees (under 10) and generally doing under $1 million of annual sales.

Not only did these customers not know what "platform as a service" was or how it could benefit them, but they also didn't know how to look for such a beast. When they did search for information, it was for specific business-focused features, such as online invoicing.

When they found a solution they thought was feasible, they sent the information to "my guy"—generally, it turned out, a developer who built or maintained their site—to figure out how to use it. While the technical aspect, the service, remained an important part of their offering, that aspect was now explained only in the section for developers, the people who actually cared about the technical side of how it worked.

After listening to these potential customers, we decided that the product had to be described in a completely new way. The marketing now talks about providing "business applications and services" with "more than on-demand CRM."

The funny thing was that in the end there wasn't really much copy on the home page. Instead of the long explanation of why PAAS was good for microbusiness owners, we chose to name the high-performance modules, point to a real success story (which the audience said was an important feature for them to understand the offering), and combine that with a brief instructional home page video.

Oh, yes, and the cost, which also turned out to be a key factor in whether they would explore the offering further. ■

The best stories come from being there

The most obvious place to collect stories is in qualitative research: ethnography, contextual inquiry, focus groups, and interviews all center on observing (and listening to) people. As we listen, we hear not just what they choose to say, but also how they say it and what they leave out. Some stories are explicit, offered as a straightforward explanation and ready to be collected. Others must be teased out, deduced from what is not said, or discovered by also collecting details about the context.

When you are *there,* you can hear and see all of the small details that make up an experience. This is especially true of emotional reactions, or those happy accidents that only occur when you don't plan them.

WHICH REMOTE CONTROLLER IS MORE FUN?

Back in the early 90s when I was in grad school, Philips was in the process of developing a short-lived technology called *CD-I* or Compact Disc Interactive. As part of their sponsorship of my graduate program, they loaned us one of their CD-I players, along with some games designed for the system and two different controllers. When Christmas time rolled around and all the other grad students were going back home for the holidays, I asked if I could borrow the CD-I player and its accessories to try out in our home, something I knew my three small children were going to love. I loved it too because it was *free*, that magic price for grad students.

We had a big Christmas dinner with friends and other families with small children, so there were plenty of people to try it out. As I watched them, I came away with two important observations to share with Philips.

First, apparently no product testing had been done in an actual home with children, because when little feet ran through the house or even just walked heavily, the vibrations from the wooden floor would cause the CD-I player to skip or even cause a program to hang. The system probably worked great in a lab building with a concrete floor, but not in an actual home, the very place Philips intended for its use.

The second observation had to do with the two wired remotes. One was simple, small, black, and completely unremarkable. It had directional buttons and action buttons. You eventually learned how to use this utilitarian piece of equipment.

The second controller was a "children's controller," but in reality it was a better fit for the adults, too. The six-inch trackball was bright yellow, the base was white, and the various large side buttons were red and blue. The plastic it was made from was comfortable and felt substantial.

It was fun to use, worked well, and required no learning—you just used it! It was the best piece of design and engineering we had seen from Philips. We all loved it. I'm not sure if it ever hit the market. If it did, it probably did much better than the CD-I player itself. ■

Other sources of stories are all around you

If you can't be there, you can find stories all around you. For example, user research that primarily aims at learning answers to a specific set of closed questions can also be a source of stories. Surveys and usability testing usually include opportunities for people to answer open-ended questions or to comment. These comments may be very short stories, or might hint at a story that can be collected later.

Even if you can't do direct user research, you can glean stories from many indirect sources.

- **Search logs and server logs.** Web server logs, path analysis, search logs, and other ways of measuring user behavior give you a quantitative look at what people are doing as they interact with your site or product. This data is one side of a conversation between users and the site. By seeking the story behind the data, you can get a better view into how and why people use your products. The story in Chapter 7 on "Golden Pages" is a good example of how data from server and search logs can lead to a more detailed story.

- **Customer service records.** If you have access to records from customer service or support queries, you will find many stories hidden there. Emails or Web contact forms will have questions in users' own words, often with a rich description of the context. Customer support logs provide an overview of the types of questions being asked. You can treat these entries as a form of observation.

- **Training and sales demos.** People who teach training classes or do sales demonstrations have direct contact with users as they learn a new product. This information is rarely collected, so you can tap into a new source of information by taking the training department to lunch. They often will have a great collection of anecdotes about questions they are asked in their classes, stories they have heard about how the product is used, or the way users explain a problem. All of these can be the beginning of a story.

- **Market research.** General industry research with a specific audience or market segment often contains raw material for stories like images, emotional responses, or even small snippets of interviews.

- **Attitudinal data.** Satisfaction surveys of customer opinions and attitudes are useful sources of stories, especially if they include open-ended questions or if they ask for examples.

You can use material from these sources along with stories gleaned from the user research you are currently doing. Each source will provide you with slightly different types of stories, all useful in creating a rich and well-rounded view of the user experience.

Another source of stories are the many social media networks. Official and informal support sites and user forums can be an easy way to find stories about using specific types of products or solving problems. More general social networks can provide insights into many different kinds of activities and interactions.

It can take work to dig through these sites, but they can be rich repositories of information. Not only do people tell stories, but others in the group react to them and often expand on a first comment or question with stories of their own. This gives you ready-made clusters of stories on a related topic.

Listen for stories

You don't usually set out to capture stories directly. But with a little effort, you can watch for story opportunities and structure your user research to allow time to listen to them.

When you plan a user research session, you usually have a series of questions in mind, and you set up the session so you can get those answers. You probably include time for follow-up questions or to probe more deeply into motivations and attitudes. Listening for stories is no different. When you allow time for a bit of wandering, or give the people you work with space to think carefully, you can get beyond the top layer of information to explore not only the background but also the deeper layers of experience behind their answers. That's where you will often find the best stories.

For example, you might be testing a new concept for a television remote control. You ask each person you work with to complete a series of tasks to see how easily they can use the new design and how well the features fit into the way they might use the remote. After each task, you might ask them to assess their experience. That conversation might go something like this:

>   **Researcher:** How was that? Was that easy for you? Did you have any problems?

Participant: Oh, no, no, no. I had no problems. It was very easy. My husband would never be able do this. But I had no problems with it.

As the researcher, you now have two choices. After you write "no problems" or "successful in task" on your notes, you can continue to the next task. Or you can back up to that throwaway comment about the participant's husband. There is a story there, and you have a chance to find out what it is. What is the difference between these two people? How do they use technology in their household to work around (or make use of) this difference? This sort of story is not just a source of material to spice up a final report. These stories encourage new understanding and point to previously unnoticed usage areas. In other words, these stories can lead to new product ideas!

The simplest way to elicit stories is to ask for them. Give the people you are working with permission to give you more than the shortest possible answer. Instead of asking several short questions, you can just ask one open-ended question. Or you can follow up with a broad invitation to talk. It might go something like this:

You: How often do you buy things online?

User: At least once a week. Sometimes more. Or do you mean for work? I do that all the time.

You: Let's stick with things you buy for home, for right now. What was the last thing you bought online for yourself?

User: Oh, it was a sweater I saw in a catalog.

You: Tell me about that.

User: I still get all this junk mail, but some are from stores I like. I flip through them and mark things I might want. Most of the time that's all I do, but sometimes I'll go to the Web to see if it's still on sale. Waiting...that's a good way to keep from spending too much money. All the good things are gone, so it takes the decision away. But if I really like something ...

Now you know that this person not only buys things online, but also still browses catalogs to find things to purchase. You also know that they play a little game with themselves to make sure they only buy things they really want. This is a detail that you can weave into a larger story about how people mix different sources of information as they shop.

Once you get into the habit of asking "Why?" or "Tell me about that," you will find that just asking people to tell you about themselves is often enough to get them started. Remember: Stories start with listening. Your job as an interviewer is to give the participants your attention and make it comfortable for them to talk.

Get groups to tell stories to each other

Another way to collect stories is to get a group of people to tell stories to each other. There's a natural tendency for one story to lead to another and for each person to want to tell their own story. You can make use of this bad listening habit to create more story-collecting opportunities.

One of the classic problems in focus groups is that the more confident participants can overwhelm those who are less confident about speaking up. This often includes people from lower social backgrounds or those who are not as well educated. According to Jon Cohen, who helped develop the BBC's Read and Write literacy strategy in 2005, storytelling is a powerful means to allow people with low literacy to express themselves.

> "It lays the foundation for personal stories which bring to life how respondents feel about any commercial and social issue, brand, or product in their lives."

> —Matthew Secker, *Research Magazine*

For example, you can weave storytelling into a focus group session. In a typical focus group, you might start with a prototype of some kind, perhaps just an image or a story that the moderator tells. Then the moderator asks a series of questions. Some people will leap forward to answer the questions. Some of them will tell a quick story as an example. As the moderator, you can use this moment to encourage others to tell their own stories, with each one building on the last. As with any group, you have to make sure that everyone gets their turn. These quiet participants may be more comfortable telling a story, or adding a little bit to another story, than expressing an opinion or answering a direct question.

SOMETIMES YOU LEARN MORE THAN YOU EXPECT

I did a small research project exploring a new concept for a physical therapy device for people recovering from a stroke. This was a hard context for me to understand. I knew little about the routines of physical therapy and rehabilitation centers. Stroke patients have their entire world turned upside-down in ways I could only begin to imagine.

We didn't have a product to work with, just a few drawings to illustrate the concept. Instead of running one-on-one interviews, we put together groups of three people and encouraged them to talk to each other. They quickly began asking each other about their experiences in rehab, almost ignoring me. All I had to do was listen to this conversation.

One of the more interesting things we learned was how much they hated rehab. The concept included a way for patients to monitor their own progress. It turned out that this feature tapped into the deep frustration they felt about how helpless they were after their stroke. We learned a lot more than simply whether they liked a new product concept. ■

One of the side benefits of small groups like this is that it gives people a chance to be listened to and to have their experiences acknowledged by others. When you can create a safe place for this to happen, you will gain much deeper insights into the user experience.

Explore memorable incidents

The technique of collecting narratives is at the heart of the Critical Incident Technique developed by John Flanagan. Instead of asking for an opinion about a product or experience, you ask the person to tell you about a specific recent experience. This formal methodology is often used for evaluating the performance of mission-critical systems, but you can use the general approach to get people to tell you the story of a single event. It can be an interesting way to get people to tell you about routine experiences.

LIFE AND DEATH—AN INCIDENT THAT CHANGED MY PERSPECTIVE

Chauncey Wilson, who has an encyclopedic knowledge of research methods, describes this as a practical use of the Critical Incident method.

When I'm visiting a customer site, I try to ask the people I interview to tell me a story about how an application or system helped or hurt their work or reputation. One of the most memorable stories that I've heard when I asked this question occurred during interviews at a prestigious medical center.

I was discussing the usability of backup and recovery software with an information technology (IT) manager and asked him if there were any critical incidents with this software in the last few months. He thought for a second and recounted a story about how the system had worked well for many months with no problems.

During this time, the person who set it up left for a better job and a new, much less experienced technician was the replacement. A few months before my visit, the medical center had a major power failure and the new technician, unfamiliar with how to start the recovery (which required some manual intervention), took several hours to get the system back. My interviewee said, "That was really bad because we have come to depend on computerized data in patient rooms and even in some surgery rooms. Not having data for even a few minutes earlier could be a life or death situation."

I knew that time lost for getting a system back after a power failure or other catastrophe could cost a company a great deal of money—millions of dollars in the case of major financial institutions—but this short story from the IT manager changed my perspective about the consequences of unusable backup and recovery software. Since then, I've thought that poor usability for some systems can have harsh, even dangerous repercussions for those who depend on timely, accurate data.

A second more practical lesson was that, when you automate processes and they run fine for a long time without intervention, you need to make memorability a key focus for the user interface used to fix or restore a system that breaks. ∎

These stories not only give you examples of events or user behavior, but also information about the context in which those events occurred. You'll use these contextual details later when you construct your own stories.

You can observe stories, too

If you are watching as someone does something, watch *how* they do it in addition to listening to what they say about it. Their behavior may offer a story as rich as their words.

Sometimes the simplest activities may offer unexpected insights into the user experience. While we were collecting stories for this book, we heard a lot of anecdotes about seemingly small observations that led to large improvements to the user experience:

- One group watched people unpacking a large, heavy piece of equipment and had the insight that they could design the box as a lift-off lid: instead of lifting the equipment out of the box, the packaging could slide off the top.

- A documentation manager didn't discover until visiting customer sites that many of the users had never even unpacked the product manuals.

- At a call center that covered three states, the best customer representatives kept a window open for each state, giving each of them a different background color.

You probably have your own stories like that. Details so small that no one would think to mention them that became the basis for an innovation.

When you go into a new situation, everything is unfamiliar and strange to you. Those early moments, before you become an "insider," are your opportunity to observe stories about how people interact with objects in their environment and with other people. In their chapter on conducting site visits in *User and Task Analysis for Interface Design*, Ginny Redish and JoAnne Hackos talked about the importance of taking specific notes on the environment, including the way the furniture is arranged, the decorations and notes around someone's workspace, the lighting, or any special clothing or safety equipment. Similarly, if you are in someone's home or personal environment, you want to take notes on how they have arranged that environment to make it their own.

Anthropologists talk about contextual observation as a way of making the familiar strange or the strange familiar. Genevieve Bell and her colleagues at Intel study the home and familiar settings like kitchens. They talk about *defamiliarization* as a way of looking critically at a context or object to see it in a new way. In an article, "Making by Making Strange: Defamiliarization and the Design of Domestic Technologies," they describe how they use detailed descriptions to force themselves to observe well-known settings closely and see a familiar environment and its objects in a new light.

Seeing the familiar in a new way can be difficult if you work in a specialist field like technology or medicine. You may have absorbed basic concepts to the point that you can't imagine not knowing them. Stories from people encountering a situation that incorporates these concepts for the first time can help you and your colleagues remember what that experience is like.

Careful observation of the physical environment is also important if you are working in a situation that is new to you. We don't usually tell stories about routine things. As Steve Denning puts it, "fish don't tell stories about water." So it's up to you to notice these details and how they affect the people in the environment.

When you question basic assumptions, you'll find new opportunities.

TRAIN DOORS OPEN FROM THE INSIDE, RIGHT?

You'd think there's nothing easier than opening a door. On my first trip to England, I attended a conference that was in two parts, the first part in Brighton and the second in Southampton. The two cities are located only 60 miles apart on the southern coast of Britain, but at that time, to travel between them by train, I had to travel north most of the way to London, then get a connecting train back down south to the other city.

Over dinner in London, my colleagues gave me detailed instructions. Even after two or three large glasses of wine, I figured I'd be able to get on and off the proper trains.

The time came when we had to leave our quaint British pub, and they took me to the station. I got on the train, sat down, and got out my train timetable, keeping close track of the passing stations. As the train approached my stop, I got up, walked to the nearest door, and prepared to get off.

That's when I noticed there was no door handle. I couldn't open the door. Must be an entrance-only door, I thought, and walked to the next door in the train car. Again, no door handle, as the train slowed at my stop. I quickly walked to the next train car, three doors—no handles. Next car—same thing.

By this time, the train had stopped. I was about to miss my stop and end up lost. The next door I came to had a window that was partially open, so I reached through the window to the handle on the outside, opened the door, and jumped from the accelerating train.

When James Bond jumps from a moving vehicle, he deftly rolls and gets up without a spot on his white tuxedo. Landing there in a crumpled heap, I was so not 007. That's when it hit me: I JUST JUMPED FROM A MOVING TRAIN! I COULD HAVE BEEN KILLED!

At the end of the conference, I was on the train again to get to Heathrow airport. Traveling with a small group this time, I asked a native Brit why there were no handles on the inside of train doors. "Oh, you're supposed to reach through the window and open the door from the outside. It's a safety feature." ■

You may want to bring back pictures as a way of reminding yourself of what you saw and to give you images to illustrate your stories. Your notes and photos can also shed new light on what you heard. Do the users' descriptions match what you observed? If not, you may have the beginning of an interesting story about different perceptions.

THEY MEANT WHAT THEY SAID

In one usability test, we worked with older women who used the Web but reported that they often had trouble finding information they wanted. During the session, the participants used several different sites to look for answers to their own questions. They were allowed to browse in their own way and to take as much time as they wanted. Several of them mentioned feeling "uncomfortable" on the Web, even people who seemed to navigate around sites with no problems.

It wasn't until a week or so after the sessions that we realized the significance of the word "uncomfortable." We had assumed they meant that they were unsure about what they were doing, but we were wrong.

We had videotaped the sessions, using a camera in the corner of the room, giving us a diagonal view of the people with a wide enough angle to see their whole upper body. Many of the women were straining their necks forward so they could see the screen without their reading glasses. Sitting in that position for almost an hour must have been physically difficult, especially for people who were not used to working at the computer for long periods of time.

They really were uncomfortable—physically uncomfortable. It wasn't a metaphor at all. ■

Tips for collecting stories

If you are used to conducting very structured research sessions, you may find that gently directing the conversation and flow of information is harder than just asking a series of prepared questions. Even when you are experienced at collecting stories, you need to be ready to deal with things that can derail your work.

Don't get distracted

Sometimes what people have to tell you is important to them but not that valuable to your research. Other times, it's the opening to a much richer understanding. As a researcher, you have to be in control and practice the art of listening without being distracted from your goal. You don't want to cut off someone who has a story they need to tell. (Remember, stories start with listening.) But you don't want to let a story take you off track, either. Most of the time, you need to keep the user research session on track while remaining open to valuable tangents.

If someone veers off into a story that isn't exactly what you are interested in, you need to decide how long to let them talk and find ways to redirect the conversation into the areas you want to hear about. You can do this by asking them to tell you more about an aspect of the experience they are describing that might be more relevant to your research. Or you can let them finish and then move on to *your* next topic.

> **You:** How often do you buy things online?
>
> **User:** All the time. The last thing I bought was a sweater. I used to knit my own sweaters. Actually, I was really into wool and did a lot of experimenting with dyes. Did you know that you can make dyes from natural products? They are a lot better for you than the

chemicals that most commercial sweaters are colored with. I even collect things from the woods. Like there are certain barks that you can boil to make really nice brown colors.

You: That's really interesting. Thanks for telling me about that. To come back to shopping, are you able to find knitted products that you like online?

If the person seems determined to avoid the topics you are interested in, that in itself might be an important piece of information, and you might want to take some time to find out why.

PEOPLE MAY HAVE REASONS THAT ARE NOT OBVIOUS
During a user research session looking at women's health information online, one participant decided to use our session as a chance to look up something that she wanted to know. She was so insistent that we decided to let her do it, but also asked her to tell us why this information was so important.

She told us that she had a question about a medical condition. She had not been able to find the answer and was worried. Her question had nothing to do with what we were testing, but it was hard to tell someone not to search for health information she really wanted. We were also interested in why she hadn't been able to find the answer.

In the end, she took almost 10 minutes searching on different sites. She kept entering the same search terms, but finding nothing relevant. Finally, on one of the sites, something in the search results page gave her a clue. She entered the term the site used—the medically correct word—and found the answer immediately.

In this case, it wasn't that the participant was trying to avoid our tasks...she just had something else on her mind, and thought our usability test would be an opportunity to get the answer.

We learned something important about the problems she'd had using the search feature and a lot about how persistent patients can be in looking for information about their own medical conditions. ■

As you learn to handle these situations, keep focused on your research goals. Most of the time, you don't want to go down a rabbit hole following a tangential story unless you are sure that there's something interesting to be learned.

Create a structure that supports story collection

If you want to collect stories, you have to create a structure for your research sessions that allows the time for that to happen. One way to do this is to mix closed and open questions. You can start with simple questions that establish the topic and then ask a question that invites the person to give you more detail. For example, look at Table 6.1.

TABLE 6.1

A STRUCTURE FOR AN INTERVIEW	
Do this...	**Like this...**
Start with a question that establishes the activity you want to talk about. This question can be simply answered with a yes or no.	"Have you ever [done something]?"
Then ask questions that build up a picture of how this activity fits into their work or life. You can even suggest answers from a standard list for these questions.	"How often do you [do that thing]?" "What makes you decide to [do that thing]?" "Would you say this is something you mostly do at work or at home?"
Now, ask a question to get them to think about a specific example.	"When was the last time you [did that thing]?"
Once they have a specific event in mind, you can repeat the situation, to be sure you have it right, and then ask for the whole story.	"Tell me about that."

Sometimes, there is not much more to say about the event, but if there is, you have accomplished two goals: found answers for your basic questions *and* given the person a chance to give you a rich example of the context and situation.

Something else to remember is that people respond to their environment. If you are sitting in a conference room with a camera looking over your shoulder, taking notes on a clipboard with a list of questions on it, don't be surprised if people respond by trying to answer each question as succinctly as possible.

If you want them to open up, they need things to react to. These can be your own products or prototypes, but they might also be all the things in their office or even a "stage set" of a home. Proctor & Gamble, for example, built a Future Home Lab, which was a house complete with a laundry room, kitchen, and living room (along with a focus group room), where they could talk to customers within a context similar to the one in which their products would be used. They felt that they could get more accurate information from research when people were reminded of "real life." Something about being in a kitchen, for example, reminds people that it can be messy and wet and hot. Or having their kids with them reminds people of how busy and sometimes chaotic their lives can be.

SEEING IT IN CONTEXT CHANGES THE ANSWER

Caroline Jarrett was asked to find out about an annual pack of materials that was sent to every employer in the UK—about 1.3 million packs, each of them an inch thick, containing a mixture of forms and guidance, including a set of 22 "help cards," nicely printed in color on good-quality card stock.

The annual customer satisfaction survey rated the cards as "easy to use," but I persuaded the agency to let me interview small business employers on their own premises. I took a pack with me, so we had realistic materials, and we were in a realistic setting—their actual offices.

The typical incident that became the story: one nice lady started leafing through the pack, setting aside the parts that weren't relevant to her business (almost all of them). She got to the help cards: "Oh yes, these are really useful." Myself: "That's interesting. Could you go through those cards then and show me which one you used most recently? And if it's not too much trouble, perhaps you could find your own copy from your filing system?" She rifled through the cards, looking thoughtful. A moment later, "Ah, I remember now. What I actually did was use the one from last year and changed this number here."

The government was sending her 22 rather expensive pieces of recycling.

P.S. As a result, the whole pack was redesigned. ■

Keep the conversation flowing naturally

You need to make people feel comfortable talking. If they haven't been listened to very much, they may need cues that it's OK to tell their story in their own way. Or they may not be sure just what kind of information you are after, so you should be ready to ask more questions to gently keep them talking.

In casual conversation, people usually try to reach a state of equilibrium in which everyone contributes equally. As an interviewer, you want the person you are working with to talk more, so you have to create an unequal conversation pattern. There are some simple techniques to help keep the conversation flowing with minimal intervention from you. Judy Ramey's "Methods for successful 'thinking-out-loud' procedures" describes techniques that are helpful. All of them allow you to take your turn in the conversation without interrupting the story.

- **Echoing.** Repeat their last words or phrases back to them as a question. Echoing sets up a social dialogue and reinforces social conversation expectations: They say something, you repeat it; they say the next thing, because that is what is expected in conversation. Sometimes, even a nonverbal signal can be enough. What's important is that you "take your turn" in the conversation and then give control back to them without distracting them from their train of thought.

  User: This is confusing.

  You: ...confusing...

  User: Yes, confusing. I wasn't sure whether I should use *this* link or *that* one.

- **Conversational disequilibrium.** Let your statements trail off and end in an upward pitch, as if you were asking a question. The other person will usually complete your statement. This is another way to "take your turn" in the conversation and toss it right back to them.

  User: I wanted to download that application, but the instructions were so confusing... (trails off and stops talking).

Here are five good ways for you to get them going again:

You (1): The instructions were confusing?

You (2): And you expected....

You (3): Confusing? ... Because....

You (4): So then you....

You (5): Mmmm hmmm.

In using any of these techniques, be careful not to put words in their mouth or offer interpretations. If you use their words, instead of trying to come up with a new way of saying the same thing, you are usually on safe ground.

When you build time for story collecting into your user research, you uncover completely new ideas. A rigidly structured interview only gives you the answers to the questions you ask. Giving people space to tell their own stories lets you learn about things you would never have thought to ask about.

When all else fails

Often, people insist on giving the shortest possible answers. When you absolutely need to pull something out of someone who is either shy or otherwise uncommunicative, you can tell stories to get stories. When people hear a story, they are often compelled to respond with their own. So have a collection of small personal stories in your back pocket that you can pull out and tell if a participant is not giving you enough. For example:

You: Have you ever used an ecommerce Web site?

Participant: Yes.

You: How recently?

Participant: Last week.

You: What did you do when you were there?

Participant: I bought something.

You: Tell me about it.

Participant: I bought a sweater.

You: (wait)

Participant: (silence)

You: I got a sweater recently, too. It was for my husband... a blue one. For his birthday. Who did you buy yours for? Was it a special occasion?

Participant: Myself. I'd been wanting something bright and cheery, and I saw this red sweater...

The goal is to open up the discussion by sharing a small piece of personal information, putting you and the participant on a more equal conversational footing. The trick is to do this without asking a leading question. It doesn't have to be more than a few words, but it does have to be true. Don't pretend to like something you don't or claim an experience you haven't had.

Once you get them telling stories, you can use all the techniques above to keep them going. If they go back to short, crisp unhelpful answers, pull out another story. Remember, both your probing questions and short crisp stories establish and feed your relationship with the users. You like telling stories to people you have a relationship with, even if that relationship is paper-thin and transient.

In Chapter 2, we described the relationship between the storyteller, the audience, and the story as the Story Triangle. That bottom connection of the triangle between the storyteller and audience, or in this case between the user and you, is very important. So make sure they have a warm body to tell their stories to and not a cold paper survey with arms and legs.

Write stories into your notes

You won't have any stories (or even story fragments, images, or great quotes) if you didn't take good notes. There's nothing more frustrating than to half-remember a story, but not be able to find it in all your observation notes. If you don't capture this information in a retrievable way, you will never go back and get it later. The way you write your notes can help.

There must be an ideal world in which there is enough time for everything we want to do, but the realities of most project schedules make it hard to fit in anything "extra." And the rich detail that you need for stories is often "extra."

The most important place to start is by turning on your "juicy story" filter so you are ready to take notes on any exceptional stories that come along. These field notes don't have to be elaborate—just enough to remind you of the story so you can go back and write down all the details later.

Anytime you take notes, you are making selections about what is worth writing down. It might seem possible to record a description without any interpretation at all, but even the decision about where to place a video camera eliminates some parts of the story and emphasizes others.

When you are taking notes, it's very helpful to write down the real words. The specifics of terminology or expression can be key to a story. With the specific words, patterns or other realizations may emerge during later review of your notes that you would never see if you didn't have those words. Look at these four notes about someone deleting something by accident.

> User deletes sentence.

> User deletes sentence, comments that it was a mistake, retypes.

> User deletes sentence. (Makes a face.) "Oh, I deleted what was already there." Retypes sentence.

> User deletes sentence. "Damn it. Why doesn't it know that I wanted to *add* this information, not *get rid of* what I typed before!" (Bangs on the keyboard as he retypes the sentence.)

The first situation describes the event, but includes no emotional or behavioral detail. The second adds a richer description of the entire event. The third and fourth provide a direct quote and an indication of the user's level of emotion, showing a different level of intensity in the reaction to the situation.

Since you are probably not just listening for stories, but collecting a lot of other information at the same time, you need to organize your notes so that there is time and a place for notes that might lead to stories. Ginny Redish, the author of one of the first books on usability, suggests using a multi-column format, as shown in Figure 6.1. The first column is for your observations, and the second for inferences you draw from those observations. In the final column, you can easily record both quotes and notes on potentially good stories.

Observations	Inferences	Stories They Tell
Uses a plastic protector to hold the cookbook page open.	Any computer used in the kitchen needs to be protected (and cleanable).	
Reads recipe.		
Gets all ingredients for the recipe out and lines them up on the counter.	Making sure that she has all of them? Would a shopping list be helpful?	
"I learned this from watching the chefs on the Food Channel. They all have everything in these little bowls."	Wants tips and tricks she can use.	Tells: How she first found the Food Channel and watched it with a friend. Her story about "competing" to master new techniques.
Crosses kitchen 5 or 6 times to find everything in different cabinets.		Image: Kids helping in the kitchen and everyone bumping into each other.
Measures some ingredients in advance.		

FIGURE 6.1

Organizing your notes in columns (or marking them as you write them) makes it easier to find those insights that occur to you as you listen and observe, as well as the stories that might otherwise get lost.

Of course, you may be taking your notes in an electronic recording tool like Techsmith's Morae or simply typing in a document or spreadsheet. If so, make two different markers for stories. You might use "Q" for a great verbatim quote and "S" for a possible story or word image. That way, it's easy to find your story material among all the other notes and data that gets recorded, so that you can go back and listen to that part of the recording later.

You may not have time to write as much as the last example when you are taking notes "live," but you will want to develop a note-taking style that lets you capture as much of the richness of the experience as possible.

One place to start is by capturing as much of the real words as you can. Capturing exact words can also be a fast way to provide cues about details, like the level of domain knowledge, for example:

"I just closed the window."

"I clicked on the little x thing."

All of these techniques also work if you are taking notes by reviewing audio or video recordings. Whether you are watching the tapes for the first time or just going back over sessions or events where you were present, you still need to listen for the users' own words and the way they tell their stories.

In this example, both users manage to close the window, but one uses technical language to describe her actions, while the other does not, suggesting very different relationships to the computer.

Another trick that helps make analysis easier is to write a summary of each person, pulling together all of your notes. A summary sheet might include the following information:

- Demographic details and a description of the person

- A log of their actions (where they went, what they did)

- Quotes or observation notes that describe their attitudes

- A brief note on any stories you heard

- Any other specific details you are collecting, such as task success, preference, or other questionnaire data

Put this into a structured format, and it will be easy to flip through your notes to find the stories. Figure 6.2 shows the basic template, and Figure 6.3 shows an example of a structured notes form.

This may seem like a lot of work, and you may not have time to do this for every participant on every research project. But when you can do this, it makes the analysis go much faster. It does something else, too. It gives you a chance to summarize the session while it is still fresh in your mind. You can get down on paper all the impressions that you took away from the session. In her writing on field studies, Judy Ramey calls this "collecting your head notes." If you are working on a research team, it's a good chance to pull everyone's observations into one place. And it's fodder for personas.

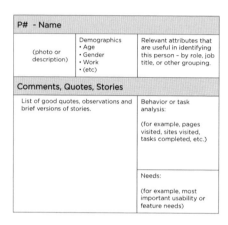

FIGURE 6.2
Template for structured notes.

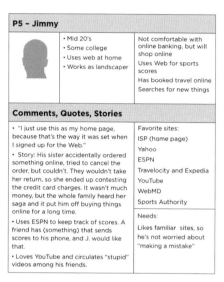

FIGURE 6.3
Example of structured notes.

More reading

"Making by making strange: Defamiliarization and the design of domestic technologies," G. Bell, M. Blythe, and P. Sengers, in ACM Transactions on Computer-Human Interaction (TOCHI) 2005, Volume 12, Issue 2

"Methods for successful 'Thinking-Out-Loud' procedures," Judy Ramey, in the STC Usability Toolkit: www.stcsig.org/usability/resources/toolkit/toolkit.html

Summary

Stories are all around us, if you just listen for them. The trick to getting good stories in your user research is to make the time for them.

- Look for juicy stories in any user research, as you observe or review your notes.

- Learn to ask questions that encourage people to tell you stories.

- Thinking out loud procedures can keep the conversation and stories flowing comfortably.

- You can find stories in many places, including search logs, customer service records, survey data, and even internal staff who work with users.

- Take notes in a way that lets you find possible stories easily.

CHAPTER 7

Selecting Stories (as Part of Analysis)

N ow that you've collected stories, you have to select those to develop for use in analysis. These stories serve a purpose and must be more than simply "great" anecdotes.

A performance storyteller may start from a story that "just feels right" and develop it over many years, letting it evolve in front of different audiences. In user experience, that process often happens as you (and your team members) go through all of the user research material to understand what you have learned.

As you select and develop your stories, you have to consider both your audience and your goal. These stories must help you understand the user experience in a new way or help support your user analysis as you communicate with the rest of the user experience team, the broader project team, and management.

Your first audience: yourself

You (and your colleagues) are your first audience. Your first use of stories is to help your team understand what you have learned about users and their context. If you don't find these stories useful and meaningful, no one else will either, because you won't be able to use them effectively.

The process of selecting stories is iterative, just like any other analysis. At the beginning, you may notice stories that illuminate the problems you are working on. But, as you dive deeper into the analysis, you will find stories that point out new, previously unnoticed aspects of the design space.

The more often you work with the information, the easier it is to connect individual data points to make a coherent picture. You may find some of the stories you collected popping into your mind as you work on other parts of the analysis. For example, a story might be a great illustration for a quantitative data point, or it might provide the background to explain users' attitudes about a product or task. For example, published research suggests that Latinos who are more acculturated—who have been in the U.S. longer, were educated in English, or speak English more fluently—

often act as intermediaries in helping their families navigate the healthcare system in the U.S. With that data point tucked away in your mind, when you hear a user research participant talk about finding information for her mother, your ears should prick up. Perhaps there is a concrete story here that can help make the research more vivid.

This isn't that different from any other analysis process. It can work both *top down* and *bottom up*. You may select stories to illustrate a concept. Or you may combine story fragments and other data points to draw a larger conclusion. (You have taken your notes in a way that makes it easy to find those stories, right? If not, go back to Chapter 6, "Collecting Stories," where we have some pointers for writing notes.)

Remember that you may not find complete stories popping out of your notes fully formed. Often, you will have a collection of anecdotes, notes on behaviors, and imagery. These can be equally valuable as the building blocks for rich stories. Here are a few examples:

> A user describes his system for storing information as "a junk heap—like my kids' closets, with everything tossed in wherever it will fit"—and suggests that he needs "one of those consultants who organizes your closets."

> Someone else talks about "the laundry basket of junk on my computer—I just pick the newest things off the top and never get all the way to the bottom."

> During a usability test, participants seem to get lost in part of the program. They talk about how much information there is on the screen, using words like "cluttered," "crowded," "junk heap of valuable things," and "overwhelming."

> A participant tells a story about losing information that she is *sure* she saved...somewhere.

> Another describes her "perfect toy" as a "Mary Poppins bag that never gets full, no matter how much you put into it."

These are all different viewpoints on managing the objects in our lives. Any one of them could be the starting point for a story, or you could combine snippets from different people into one story. If you have the data, you can go further and mix in the insights from metrics. For example, perhaps cluttered screens are making it harder for users to find information

What are you looking for?

What you are looking for are juicy stories: stories with plenty of texture, dripping with good detail.

Some of the signs of a juicy story are the following:

- **Stories that you have heard from more than one source.** They don't have to be identical, but when you hear similar anecdotes or ways of talking about an event, pay attention.

- **Stories with a lot of action detail.** Stories describing the way things happened thoroughly are valuable because they offer more than an opinion or a quote. They capture a narrative sequence and can be the basis for further development as a scenario for how a product might be used.

- **Stories with details that make your user data easy to understand.** Stories with a lot of contextual detail help anyone who hears them relate to the people they describe. These details might describe when, how, or why something happens. They might be a turn of phrase, a way of describing someone's goals or actions, or an anecdote that just seems to sum up a type of person or event.

- **Stories that illustrate an aspect of an experience that the UX team is particularly interested in.** They may not be your focus of attention, but you can always look for stories that have come up organically during any story collecting. If you know that your team is starting to work on a mobile interface, a story about how someone used your site through their cell phone will be particularly juicy at that moment.

- **Stories or story images that surprise or contradict common beliefs, yet are clear, simple, and compelling.** These can be the hardest, because (like Ginny Redish's story, "A Story Can Deliver

Good News...and Bad News," in Chapter 4), they may deliver bad news. However, stories can provide early anecdotal evidence that can suggest new design directions or new user needs.

Stories are most valuable when they help you explain something about the user experience in a way that gets beyond simple demographic facts or even complex data analysis. They should bring your data to life by grounding it in a specific context.

Finding the stories

When you find a juicy story fragment, you can work with it to see if it develops into a useful story. You might start from a user quote or an anecdote and see if it still holds your interest when you try retelling it a few times. Or you might find that part of a story from one person complements stories from other participants. Sometimes, these stories illustrate a single usability problem or a single user experience goal, giving you more specific data to work with. Sometimes, several pieces of stories start to collect into something richer than you would get simply by tying analysis points into a single narrative. The story can let you pull it together in a way that helps you focus on the bigger problem, even as you weave in some of the specific examples of how that problem affects users.

PULLING BITS OF INFORMATION TOGETHER

When a colleague and I were working on a user research project for the National Cancer Institute, we had a lot of notes on problems we'd seen with people getting lost in the site. We started to write these up as a set of individual usability issues. The problem was that there were so many of them, and they all seemed so specific to the individual participants and exactly what they were doing on the site.

We tried creating little narratives for each person to get each one down to the shortest description. When we put them together, the issues started to crystallize, and we could see the pattern. No one single observation was coherent enough to stand on its own, but when we put fragments from several different participants together, we could tell a compelling story about how the structure of the site encouraged people to browse in circles.

Once we had the story clear in our heads, we could see how it affected people in many different ways. In our report, we used a series of screenshots to illustrate the problem, similar to Figure 7.1. It looked a little bit like a storyboard, but we used it to describe what we saw instead of proposing a new design.

It wasn't fancy, but it helped everyone follow the path, and understand the frustrations of the experience better. ∎

FIGURE 7.1
Saving screenshots of the pages that the participants see during a research session makes it easier to put these stories together. It's especially important on dynamic sites where headlines, user-generated content, ads, or other elements of the site change frequently.

Telling stories is a natural activity, an easy way to sort through what you have learned. If you work with other people on user research or usability testing, you have probably done it without thinking, "I'm telling a story." You just share bits and pieces that seem particularly memorable and juicy to you.

Finding stories in data

So far, we have mostly talked about stories that come directly from participants in user research or from your own observations. As we mentioned in Chapter 6, there is another source of user research, though you may have to dig a little deeper to find the stories in it: user information from search logs, Web logs, or other collected data about user behavior. These sources can give you details to use in your stories, such as the most frequent (or infrequent) types of searches, how long someone reading intently might stay on a page in your site, paths through the site, or even nonobvious connections between parts of a site.

GOLDEN PAGES

Like most universities, the Open University's Web site is a huge collection of smaller sites maintained by the administration, individual departments, and faculty members. The OU Web services team pays a lot of attention to Web statistics as a way of understanding how people use the site to find courses and register for them. One of the things they were watching was how people moved from general academic information into the online course catalog. Caroline Jarrett did an analysis of which paths from within the site led from general information to the registration pages.

I noticed that there were a lot of people coming to the creative writing course pages in the prospectus from the Arts Faculty pages. When I traced those links, I found a great site about how to get started as a writer. It had good organic placement on Google, so people searching for "creative writing" found it even if they didn't know about the OU. I call pages like these "golden pages." Obviously, a lot of people were impressed enough by what they read to follow a link to learn more about the course...and some of them registered. ■

This analysis tells us a lot about how people connect one activity to another, and how important having good, useful content is for attracting people to your site. Analysis insights like these can be the start of a story that illustrates why some pages are so attractive. These stories could be incorporated into a persona or combined with other user research to make the analysis memorable.

You can also use sources of information like technical support logs or questions in an online knowledge base to find raw material for "points-of-pain" stories. Do the problems users report match up to the problems you see in usability tests or the needs you hear about in other user research?

When you can triangulate between different data sources—draw the same conclusions by looking at the user experience through several different lenses—you are almost always on the right track.

Building stories into personas

If you create personas, they are a natural place to use stories. The stories you write for your personas let you transform facts into situations that bring static personas to life, giving them context and motivation.

The stories you tell about personas are a natural way of understanding people and events. Let's look at three ways to describe a group of people:

Aged 30–45

Well educated: most have attended college or have a college degree

45% married with children

Over half use the Web 3–5 times a week

65% use search engines

This profile is not very specific. It looks very precise with its percentages and statistics. But it does little to bring these statistics to life. Add some specific details: pick an actual age, not just a range. Then add some of the story fragments you have collected. These are things participants told us during a pre-test usability interview when we asked for examples of reasons they had used the Web recently:

Elizabeth, 35 years old

Married to Joe, has a 5-year-old son, Mike

Attended State College and manages her class news on the alumni site

Uses Google as her home page and reads CNN online

Used the Web to find the name of a local official and how to contact that person

Now you have a person with some real activities. You can now develop those activities into stories (see Figure 7.2). The demographic details and other data are still there, but they provide a background for the richer description of the experience.

Elizabeth
"What did we do before the Web?"

For Elizabeth, the Web is a library, post office, and town hall. Between working part time and spending time with Justin, her 5-year-old son, she's always rushing. But once she has the house put to bed at night, she can go back to being a gadfly and local activist.

Her most recent campaign is an effort to get her whole town designated as a Wildlife Zone. She's done all the research on the Web, and she's ready. She's written an article in her town newsletter, posted on the town forum, and set up a Facebook page.

She's looked up all of the businesses in town on the Web, and is planning to email all of them to see if they will support her. She'll write to them this weekend, and then on Monday, she and Justin will pay a visit to all of them, and see if they will put up a sign.

After that, she's going after support from everyone on the Borough Council. She's already looked up their emails, so she's ready.

About Elizabeth:
• Age 32
• College graduate
• Married
• Works in an office

Goals:
Information I can use.
Communication on my schedule

Usability Needs:
Efficient: Give me a search box and I'll tell you exactly what I want.

Bookmarks:
• Town government site
• Wildlife World
• Son's school

FIGURE 7.2
A persona.

If you already have personas, you can connect your stories to them. This can have a number of advantages:

- Stories add more richness (and underlying data) to the personas, making them more useful and helping keep them fresh and updated.

- Using the personas as the cast of characters lets you explore internal conflicts, attitudes, or choices the personas make under pressure.

- If you are working with personas that are little more than named categories, stories can help you understand the concepts behind the categories better.

- Stories inspire more stories, so combining stories with personas inspires collaborators, stakeholders, and other team members to inject more life into the design project.

- Stories breathe life into implicit cultural context of personas—like "35-year-old married, college graduate office worker"—which helps the audience identify better with the characters.

Sometimes, stories can even expose gaps in your user analysis. If a story doesn't seem to "fit" well with any of the personas, and you are sure that the story illustrates an important analysis point, you need to stop and figure out what's happening. You may be missing a persona, or you may find that there are some things you don't know about your personas. Either way, the stories can help bring out those gaps before you design a product without considering them.

Including user research data in stories provides a powerful new way to communicate your work. Personas can combine stories from people with similar perspectives. Connecting different user experience techniques strengthens all of them, as each connection between them validates the conclusion, and adds to your ability to triangulate on user experience needs.

Summary

Your goal in analysis activities is to find juicy story fragments that you can develop into stories. When you start from a quote, anecdote, or image, add it to other fragments, and then distill it down into a narrative, you have a story that can explain "what's going on here" in a clear way.

Selecting stories puts your "story thinking" to work, identifying stories that support other analysis. A useful set of stories makes sense of scattered pieces of information by doing the following:

- Illustrating points you want to emphasize from the user analysis.

- Bringing out details that are hard to communicate in any other way.

- Connecting with other sources of information.

- Resonating, not just by ringing true, but also because they are so natural and convincing that they spark action, like a discussion or a design change.

CHAPTER 8

Using Stories for Design Ideas

The stories you have collected are not blueprints for design, but they can serve as unparalleled inspiration for the design process. They hint at the goals, attitudes, and needs of the people you are designing for. They can also lead to the story the design must tell.

When we say that the design must "tell a story," we are not just talking about games or interactive fiction, or even about turning a work application into an adventure ("Conquer the benefits allocation maze..."). Instead, we mean the kind of stories that help you create new designs. These stories are used to make you think of new possibilities, give you the tools to encourage a self-reflective kind of thinking—design thinking—or so you can imagine designs that will improve the lives of other people. Stories explore ideas from user research.

In Tom Erickson's view, design is as much about communication as it is about the end result. This includes communication with the eventual users, as well as communication among a collaborative team. The stories are a tool to help designers "grapple with the messy, ill-defined issues" that are part of the design process. They do this by not only creating small scenarios, but also by communicating the emotional overtones, the social and organizational dynamics that are just as much a part of the story as the factual narrative. Used in this way, stories activate the mind by providing rough sketches with openings for discussion.

Imagine that you have been researching attitudes toward new "green technologies" as you work on a product to help people use resources more wisely. You might have heard people talking about how difficult it was to tell how much electricity or water they were really using. And you probably heard attitudes ranging from the altruistic ("We should use fewer resources for the good of the earth.") to the selfish ("Why should I be the one to scrimp?"). You probably have a few story fragments. But you still need to turn this information into a design. That process might involve sketching ideas for screens as Jeremie Jean and Aaron Marcus did in "The Green Machine: Going Green at Home" (in UPA's UX Magazine 8.4) when they imagined a smart phone application that would help people visualize their energy use by showing a graph that compared their goal to average use by others. Or you might create a story showing how your design idea would work.

PURPLE BUILDINGS

Tom Erickson's story describes a design solution to the problem of how one might use monitoring of resources to encourage people to moderate their usage habits while at the same time not having a Big Brother scenario where every toilet flush is metered and reported to the utility.

Xiang-Wei left the transit station and turned onto her street with foreboding in her heart. She looked down the street, and her fears were confirmed: Her building's skin, normally a healthy green, was discolored with purple streaks. How embarrassing—their building was overdrawn on its water allotment.

It wasn't her fault. That morning, alerted by feedback in their apartment, she and her husband had skipped their showers and made certain that their children used no more than their 10-liter allotments.

But it was difficult to believe that their building-mates were to blame. She'd gotten to know the 24 other families that lived in the co-op over the last two years, and they were all generally responsible. Her husband thought that there was a leak somewhere in the building. That seemed unlikely to her because most appliances monitored their resource usage and sent out requests for assistance when out-of-band consumption events occurred. But her husband said not everything was instrumented—pipes for example—and that there could well be a leak, especially since they'd had a mild earth tremor last week. Old Dr. Lee, who lived just down the hall, spoke darkly of hackers, implying that vague enemies had broken into the resource monitoring system with the aim of embarrassing them. But Dr. Lee was well known to be a bit...odd and, besides, the penalties for hacking into resource control systems were severe.

Xiang-Wei reached her building, and hurried up the walk through the front garden, feeling her cheeks color. Fortunately, she had come home early, and there weren't many people on the street, but still...

There was just one thing to do: organize a vote of the co-op to ask the resource authorities to turn on fine-grained monitoring. That would enable them to identify any leaks, or to put the finger on the miscreant who was wasting resources. ■

Not all new design stories have to be as big as a building. Stories can illustrate designs that solve smaller problems as well. No matter how big or small the idea, one type of design story takes a point of pain and transforms it into a successful, happy ending. As an example, here are some short story fragments from users of a payroll program:

My co-worker usually does the payroll. When she's on vacation, we always have to scramble to get everything done right and get the staff paid on time.

The instructions in our software are fine, but they don't include little details like which set of checks we should use for payroll. We all dug through our wallets looking for a stub so we could see which number series to use.

It's not the routine things that are a problem. It's special stuff like bonuses and advances.

Maybe you used these fragments in a short story to illustrate the problems and frustrations:

Mary was filling in on payroll while the office manager, Kathy, was away. On Thursday, just as she was about to run the payroll checks, she remembered Kathy telling her about some special bonus checks due that week. She groaned. Special checks... special anything always seemed to go wrong for her. If she could just remember what Kathy said. She stared at the confusing mass of notes pinned up on the wall behind the accounting computer. None of them said anything about bonuses. She groaned again. Last time she got something wrong, it took weeks to clean up the problems.

Now you can think about how this story could end differently and write a new story that changes the pain into delight with a new feature for the payroll software.

Mary was filling in on payroll while the office manager, Kathy, was away. She didn't like this part of the job—ever since she'd made a mistake that took weeks to clean up. But Kathy told her not to worry this time and when Mary clicked on "Weekly Payroll" she saw why. All the information she needed was right there on the screen. Instead of the confusing grid of numbers that had caused all the problems last time, she saw step-by-step instructions built into the forms. Best of all, Kathy had obviously written some of the instructions, because they described the procedures in their own office, like the note that told her which way to put the checks in the printer. But the best was the reminder of the special bonuses due this week. Everything was set up, and all she had to do was click.

A short story like this not only suggests new features, but connects them to the user research and the people who will benefit from them.

Stories evolve through the design process

During the design process, your use of stories will evolve as the design goes through brainstorming (generative), concept (expressive), and specification (prescriptive) stages. As the design progresses, your stories will too, changing format and adding detail.

The number of people working with the stories expands as you move from analysis to design. In the early stages of user research, the user experience team was working most directly with the stories. Now, as you move into the design phase, more people are involved. People who were not involved in the user research (or were only involved in some parts of it) will begin to work with what you have learned and with the stories you have collected and selected.

How your company or project is organized will also make a difference. If you have a strong user experience team, your experience with using stories will be different than if you are the lone voice of user experience on a more traditional technical development team.

Brainstorming for new stories: Generative stories

In a good user experience design process, you will move into the design phase with a collection of stories to work with. But this may not always be the case. You may find yourself in the midst of the design process without having done user research and without the stories you find during that work.

This does not mean that you don't have any story ideas to draw on. But those stories will come from your own past experiences and assumptions about the product and its users. Your own history and even the language you use to think about the design challenge can be a trap, preventing you from seeing the large quantities of creative fodder around you.

While brainstorming is a technique that's been around for a long time and is practiced widely, it is not always as productive as you would like. While it is good to collect all the wild and crazy ideas a team might have, what might be more useful is to have a sort of "brainstorming helper," something that can trigger creative ideas—or at least ideas that are different and new for the team.

If you are starting to work with stories for the first time at the design stage, you can use brainstorming games to generate some new stories.

EVEN ENGINEERING PHDS CAN PLAY GAMES

Early in my career, I had to travel to a meeting of researchers and research managers for an idea generation session on a particular area of technology. These "ideation sessions" were popular because they appeared to generate a lot of ideas off the top of all the participants' heads on the chosen topic of the day. They were sessions with a lot of talking (though not a lot of listening), and the primary goal as far as I could tell was to generate patentable ideas, with a secondary goal of generating ideas that could become products.

A day or two before I was to leave for the meeting, my manager let me know that I would be leading a part of this meeting, and that our director would be in attendance. I calmly responded to him, "Sure—ok," as my panic ensued. What was I going to do with a room full of engineering PhDs? I was sure that my boss wanted to test this whole *storytelling* thing I often talked about. But at that time, I primarily had writing and performance experience, and little experience teaching and leading workshops.

What I did was use a game that I saw a friend use, which she got from Doug Lipman's bok *Storytelling Games*. I adapted a game designed for sixth graders to work for research PhDs, and prayed I wouldn't lose my job.

I had them pair up and play a game similar to Mad Libs. The objective was to choose from a list of sentence structures with blanks and fill in those blanks by choosing words from a set of word categories, all related to design and to the technology topic of the day. Once they had filled in a sentence with the appropriate words, the story supporting that sentence should leap out at them. All they had to do was write down that supporting story.

Each researcher pair was given 15 minutes to go off and write their little story and then come back to share their stories with the group.

"You mean you want us to pick words and write stories?" There was a certain level of skepticism in the room. During those 15 minutes while they were writing, I was weighing job options. Surely, I would be busted for making a room full of doctors play a childish game.

When the time was up, I checked with the pairs, and they all requested another five minutes. After that I checked again, and again they asked for more time...and again once more. At that point, I could feel the warmth of job security flowing back into my life.

When the group finally reassembled, we only had 45 minutes of scheduled meeting time left to share stories. When we were still sitting there two hours later sharing stories and identifying all the interface and technology ideas they had triggered, I knew we had something. ■

Stories can be tough to just come up with, but they can be triggered easily. Remember, we are storytelling beings. It doesn't take much to trigger a story. A simple story fragment will do.

Brainstorming helper: The storytelling game

This is a version of Doug Lipman's game, adapted for user experience brainstorming.

1. Choose one of the story sentences.

2. Choose a set of items from the People, Places, Activities, and Motivations columns to fill in the blanks in the story sentence. Modify the phrases so that they make grammatical sense for the sentence.

3. Once the sentence is completed, write a short story to provide context for that sentence.

A good story sentence will have at least one person, place, motivation, and activity. The simplest story sentence is:

A (person) in (place) needs help doing (activity) because (motivation).

You can use details that are appropriate for your company to make more complex story sentences. For example, these sentences are for constructing stories about mobile communication and computing.

- While a (person) is in (place), they need to find and meet up with a (person) because (motivation).

- A (person) who is trying to (motivation) at (place) must prepare for (activity), which they will have to do in one hour.

- A (person) at (place) just realized that they lost their keys and wallet while (activity) and needs to rearrange... everything!

The options for these categories should reflect the full range of possibilities—and even some that might seem a bit over the top. When you make your own list for a project, be sure to include some wild examples. If you are working with ideas suggested by your user research, be sure to include some of the less frequent types of users. If you stick to your current categories, you end up with the same old thing. But keep the descriptions short and easy to understand. You want broad categories, not finely drawn differences. The idea here is to free you up to think in new ways.

Table 8.1 has a list of options in each of the categories.

Here are a few of the story sentences filled with words from this list:

A small business owner in a foreign country is trying to pay household bills to stay sane.

A spy in an airport needs help feeling secure about her children when she is not at home.

While a student is at the beach, he needs to find and meet up with a supermodel because he wants to improve his social life.

A nun at a baseball stadium just realized that she lost her keys and wallet while spending her Saturday chauffeuring kids between activities, and she needs to rearrange... everything!

TABLE 8.1

PEOPLE, PLACES, ACTIVITIES, MOTIVATIONS			
People			
clergy	reporter/journalist	truck driver	farmer
fisherman	parent	national leader	professional athlete
real estate agent	nun	grandmother	supermodel
student	small business owner	sports coach	wheelchair user
teacher/professor	doctor/nurse	flight attendant	consultant
waiter/waitress	spy	researcher/scientist	lawyer
police officer	pre-literate child	pilot	building contractor
Places			
home office	a classroom	an elevator	an airplane
office building	the kitchen	a hotel room	a foreign country
driving in a car	a park	a restaurant	a shopping mall
the street corner	baseball stadium	a cab	an electronics store
a courtroom	the beach	a public transit bus	an airport
Activities			
planning a meeting	preparing a presentation	finding a lost phone	planning a vacation/trip
socializing	shopping	thinking	placing a conference call
taking notes	composing email	saving the world	job hunting
commuting	moving	studying	day trading
preventing a crime	coordinating multiple schedules	paying household bills	chauffeuring kids between activities
Motivations			
save money	spend money	stay healthy	influence people
never lose touch with friends	selectively miss meetings	generate more free time	improve social life
make mo' money	keep track of personally relevant news	become witty in conversation	get a lot of work done while sitting on the porch
spend as little time in the supermarket as possible	feel secure about children when not at home	develop/support a strong fashion sense	research personal illness
don't get lost—again	stay sane		

Your combinations can be fanciful, or you can choose ones that *seem* to make more sense. Don't be afraid to get more outlandish because you can explain anything in a story. But don't pick sentences that just tell the same story you already know. Remember, the point of this exercise is to get creative in how you think about the design challenge.

The story begins with the completed sentence and creates a narrative about how the person completed the activity. To suit the needs of different types of groups and personalities, here are two methods of doing this exercise.

- **Raw brainstorming.** Generate lots of stories for different sentences very quickly. Don't worry about the details. Just do them rapidly and without judgment. The idea is to generate many stories that might be the germ of a new idea. The method should work particularly well with groups able to loosen up and let their brains throw out ideas without the need to *fix* each one first.

- **Pick one sentence and stick with it.** Develop the best story for one sentence. This method works well with groups that like to dive deep into ideas. While they may not benefit from a wide variety of ideas, as in the first method, they will take comfort in an idea that is rich by design.

You can even use both methods. Start with the first one to generate a lot of ideas. Then select a few for the more detailed presentation in the second.

DIFFERENT WORK STYLES NEED DIFFERENT STORY STYLES

I was once paired with a young engineer in a technology brainstorming workshop. We were supposed to pick from two lists of unrelated words and use the combination of these words as sparks for generating new ideas. We were given about 30 minutes to run down the long word list and generate as many ideas as possible. Fun for me! "What better way to spend a half hour," I said.

But my partner needed to work more deliberately, grounding each piece of any idea in a technology already familiar to him. Nothing could go unanswered. Mystery was not allowed. We were not even close to fast or innovative. I kept trying to push us on—he kept wanting to ruminate. At the end of 30 minutes, we had only a few ideas completed while the other groups had 10, 15, even 20. I was frustrated.

When I thought about the experience, I realized that our different approaches gave us the worst of both worlds. If he were more like me, we would have had a lot of ideas, some of them really good. But if I were more like him, we would have had a few, well-developed ideas with deep roots in computer science, mechanical engineering, manufacturing, perhaps even product marketing. We would have fully solved some stuff. Instead, because we each had different approaches, we had a small collection of mish-mash ideas. ■

No one approach is better. While it's really good to have a lot of ideas to work with, some people just can't let go of how they naturally think. You'll have to judge whom you are working with and adjust appropriately, because much as we might wish to, we can't always make other people change.

Don't worry about wasting time. The whole idea of brainstorming is to create a lot of ideas so you have a rich mix of stories to work from. Brave New Workshop, an improvisational comedy group, comes up with 600 ideas to create a show with 25 sketches. In fact, they don't start refining any of their ideas until they have created all 600 of their one-sentence ideas. Story sentences generated quickly work in the same way, loosening you up by generating a lot of quick sketches. You'll throw most of them away, but some will spark ideas that can grow.

Here's an example of how one of the brainstorming story sentences might grow into a larger story and begin to explore the context to expose possible design concepts.

A GENERATIVE STORY

Remember Sister Sarah from the example of a points-of-pain story in Chapter 1? She couldn't find her car at a baseball game? Here's another story with a solution to a similar problem.

Story sentence: A nun at a baseball stadium just realized that she has lost her keys and wallet while spending her Saturday chauffeuring kids between activities, so she needs to rearrange everything!

The story: It had been a hectic morning for Sister Sarah. She had picked up three kids at each of their homes, taken them to the teen empowerment meeting downtown, and then ushered them off to the afternoon Phillies game. When she discovered her wallet and keys were missing, she didn't know where she could have lost them. In the parking lot? In the stadium? In the car? On the ground? Who knows?

Fortunately, she had kept her 4G mobile in an inside pocket of her habit—the pocket without the hole in it. She was able to use the bank application to lock her savings account against any future activity, knowing she would eventually have to go into the bank personally to have it unlocked.

She was worried about her car keys. If someone found them on the ground and figured out which car they belonged to, she would lose all the children's art she kept in her trunk.

From previous bad experiences, she had learned to use her mobile phone to save the GPS location of her parking space in the massive stadium parking lot. So when she went to the stadium security office, she was able to tell them exactly where the car was. Very quickly the call came back from the parking lot that her keys had been found a couple of rows away from her car. ■

This story suggests several possible concepts for new products, ready for further consideration:

- A mobile application for parking lots that records the location of a car on the parking lot grid.

- A mobile banking application that allows users to do an emergency account lock.

- A device attached to a key ring that can reply to a mobile signal with its location.

Hearing this story, an engineer or business development person may respond with these ideas:

- We could trigger the car alarm from the mobile to help find a parked car easier.

- If the mobile could unlock and start her car, she wouldn't need to carry car keys.

- An RFID tag on the phone could be made to work with ATMs so she could always get money if she lost her wallet.

Developing user research stories: Generative stories (again)

If you've been following a good user experience process, you will already have stories to work with.

- If you haven't done so already, start by creating stories from any collections of observations or story fragments you have selected. (Take a look at "Finding the Stories" in Chapter 7 for an example.)

- As you begin to work on new features, you may remember stories that will help you explore how or when people might use these features, and want to develop them further.

Remember that generative stories do not need to describe a complete design solution. The goal at this stage is to use the story to trigger new ideas as you brainstorm. Start with any of the stories and try to imagine a better solution. Your idea might remove barriers, be faster, easier, or more convenient, or suggest a completely different way of doing something.

Like any brainstorming, the goal is to use the stories to get the creative juices flowing. IDEO, the design consultancy famous for breakthrough products, talks about their "Seven Rules of Brainstorming." Three of them are particularly appropriate for brainstorming around your stories:

1. **Defer judgment.** Don't dismiss any ideas. Any idea is a good idea, no matter how crazy. Nothing can kill the spirit of a brainstorm quicker than judging ideas before they have a chance to gain legs.

2. **Encourage wild ideas.** Embrace the most out-of-the-box notions because they can be the key to solutions. The whole point of brainstorming is coming up with new and creative ideas.

3. **Build on the ideas of others.** Sometimes, people say crazy and bizarre things, like "make it on Mars," but there is some element of truth in it. When you build on the ideas of others, you might bring those crazy ideas back down to earth and make them real innovations.

Like Brave New Workshop, IDEO also suggests that you go for quantity and crank out new ideas quickly. "Aim for as many new ideas as possible. In a good session, up to 100 ideas can be generated in 60 minutes."

Incorporating your user research into the brainstorming game

The brainstorming game can also be used to generate ideas from your user research. The process is the same, except that the lists or starter sentences come from what you've collected. You can do this in two ways:

1. Create a list of people, places, activities, and motivations that come from stories you have heard or observed, or from what you know about the context, and use them to generate story sentences.

   Table 8.2 is an example of a list with a healthcare context.

TABLE 8.2

PEOPLE, PLACES, ACTIVITIES, AND MOTIVATIONS FOR HEALTHCARE STORIES			
People			
nurse	medical technician	teacher	registration clerk
medical oncologist	family practice doctor	physical therapist	professional athlete
research nurse	specialist	grandmother	care coordinator
Places			
community clinic	hospital	waiting room	home
emergency room	exam room	mountain lake	foreign country
Activities			
seeing a patient	waiting for the doctor	identifying treatment options	billing a patient
preparing for a consultation	running tests	reading the current research	planning for home care
Motivations			
worried about a symptom	stay at home	stay healthy	choose the best treatment
improve quality of life	get better	make the right diagnosis	save money

2. Create sentences based on situations you observed or points of pain that you learned about.

Here are a few examples from a healthcare project:

While a **nurse** is in the **patient's room**, she needs to find and meet up with a **physical therapist** because the **patient is having trouble sitting up**.

A **care coordinator** who is just trying to **identify treatment options** for a difficult case by looking at Web sites with results of clinical trials must **prepare for a meeting** with the care team to **present options**, which she will have to do **in one hour.**

A **home-care nurse** at a **rural hospital** just realized that she lost her keys and wallet while **visiting patients** and needs to rearrange everything!

These examples are less fanciful, but they explore the real problems of real people. Remember, the idea is to get your creative juices flowing.

Moving from brainstorming to concept: Expressive stories

So far, we've discussed using stories as a way to help generate new ideas. But stories also have a role in developing a design, by explaining the rationale behind early sketches.

One thing that happens at this stage is that you switch from describing problems to coming up with ideas that provide a better solution.

FLOW INTERACTIVE SCENARIOS INVENT A DESIGN

Here's how Phil Barrett of Flow Interactive describes the process in his blog entry (illustrated in Figure 8.1), "Telling Stories" (www. thinkflowinteractive.com/2008/12/19/telling-stories/).

Because we're not fundamentally good at imagining futures or situations different to the one we are in, we have to consciously and explicitly create stories to make sure we do things right. Interaction designers create personas (the characters in the stories), describe the context of use (situation and back story), and identify the personas' goals.

FIGURE 8.1
Visual scenario showing a task in the context of a user's main goal.

Then we create scenarios. We try to tell a compelling and realistic story of how our personas will reach a happy ending by using the product. Because we're all good at listening to stories, the team can spot the good ones, the implausible ones, and the radical amazing-breakthrough ones quite quickly. ▪

There is no single "best way" to construct a good story. Some have methodologies that distinguish between types of stories and define the difference in terms of length, structure, or format.

Ginny Redish suggests that stories that help you develop a concept should be "a very short story of a real user in a real situation."

> Sarah Smith, a 25-year-old travel agent in a small, three-person agency in a storefront in a suburb of Chicago, takes a call from her friend, Jenny.
>
> Jenny wants to go to Phoenix to see her special friend sometime in the next month. She can go any weekend, and she can take Friday and Monday off. But she can only go if she can afford it. Jenny asks Sarah to find her the least expensive flights for any Friday to Monday during the next month.

Her example blends information about users, information about users' goals and tasks, and information about users' contexts—their physical, social, and technological environments. The scenario suggests a need for finding the best fares easily. These sorts of features are now part of most travel Web sites, even though they were first discovered in research with travel agents. Ginny created this story from a real observation during user research (but changed the names for confidentiality).

In his approach, research scientist Dan Gruen of IBM describes the difference between stories and scenarios as largely having to do with specificity and motivation. In his model, scenarios are less specific and include little or no character motivation, while stories are more specific and offer more character motivation. When generating new ideas, including character motivation is useful because it grounds the events of the story in human nature and culture. When developing a design, scenarios are useful to focus attention on the tasks to be completed or the technology to be used.

Although flow charts and use cases are used in some of the same ways as stories, these models and structured formats are more focused on developing technical constructs than in explaining human motivations and context of use. If you look at it this way, you can see that stories can be useful alongside other formats that describe interaction, maintaining a focus on user experience throughout the design and development process.

We don't have a strong opinion about whether you should create specialized definitions for stories, scenarios, or some other story format. But we do have some opinions about what a story useful for design must include. It must include the following information:

- Focus on activity, describing actions and behavior, set in a specific context.

- Include a description of the motivations that trigger action.

- Describe the main characters well enough (or use one of your personas) to set them in context.

What these stories leave out is just as important: extraneous detail, technical details, anything that constrains the design too much. This is not the design. The design is the design. This is a story that describes the users and product in action. We'll talk more about choosing details for your stories later, but here's a simple example: If you make it a rainy day in your story, there should be some relevance to the fact that it's raining. Perhaps it's hard to use a mobile device with one hand while holding an umbrella in the other. Perhaps the rain changes the main character's behavior in some way. The rain would add a nice piece of environmental richness to the story, but the story should include actions that make the rain relevant.

Stories that document design: Prescriptive stories

As the design is developed, there is still a role for stories. These stories can accompany design specifications, illustrating them and filling in details from earlier scenarios. They can describe alternative user experiences for different types of users and explain complex interactions, such as those that mix several different modes or channels.

One good reason to use stories along with design specification is to keep the real-world context available for reference. As the conversation moves into technical details, it's easy to forget why a feature was added or how it might be used. Stories help keep the user experience in the picture as the team makes detailed design and technical decisions.

A STANDARD BUILT FROM STORIES

In an article in UPA's UX Magazine, Isobel Frean describes one of the more unusual use of stories in a standard for communication between different healthcare programs, HL7. These programs are primarily used by clinical healthcare professionals, such as doctors and nurses. These users felt that the people working on the technical requirements didn't understand what their work life was really like. In turn, they found it difficult to relate their daily work to the technical details of a communications standard. Their solution was to use narrative stories and use case diagrams to capture user requirements. This created a common language for the clinicians and IT professionals.

Storyboard: Request Waiting List Status Report

Purpose

This storyboard demonstrates the flow of communications associated with querying the status of a consumer's positioning on a waiting list maintained by an individual or a regionally managed waiting list.

Precondition

Peter Process, Hospital Discharge Social Worker and Good Health Hospital, has previously sent requests to several nursing homes for a bed for in-patient Mr. Adam Everyman. He has been advised by each of these places that Mr. Everyman has been placed on their waiting lists. As Mr. Everyman is keen to go to one of the nursing homes close to his family, he has his name on the waiting list for Living Legends Aged Services (LLAS) and Senior Living Retirement Villages (SLRS). Peter Process is keen to place Mr. Everyman in the next 24–48 hours and wants to establish the status of the application to determine whether he needs to approach other nursing homes.

Storyboard narrative

As he is authorized to access both the LLAS and SLRS waiting lists, Peter Process requests a status report on where in each waiting list Mr. Everyman is positioned, in order to give him some idea on the likely length of wait. He receives a response from the LLAS Waiting List system advising there are four other persons ahead of Mr. Everyman on the Waiting list.

Postcondition

Peter Process discusses the outcome of the response with Mr. Everyman, and they elect to wait for a vacancy to become available. ■

—Format for the storyboards written for the HL7 Care Provision ballot (May 2005).
© UPA, Reprinted from Frean, Isobel. Capturing User Requirements in Health and Social Care, *UPA UX Magazine*, Volume 6, Issue 4, 2007

The tech-spec story

One structure for stories that prescribe is a *technical specification story*, which is used when preparing to turn over a user experience design for a detailed specification. A tech-spec story is not a complete technical specification, but it lays the groundwork for a design, collecting information from many sources, just as personas collect information about people into a usable format. The structure for a tech-spec story includes several elements.

- **Presumptions:** Statements that illustrate the suppositions on which the story experiences are based.

- **Experiences:** Very short stories that set an image in the reader's mind in one or two sentences.

- **Goals:** Sentences that describe the ideal new experience.

- **References:** Links, books, and articles from sources that the audience would respect, as well as references to user research studies. All of these lend credence to the stories. Because many people secretly respect their own work above that of others, this is an opportunity to reference the work of audience members, when possible.

- **Takeaways:** Descriptive images that summarize the key points in a format that the audience can quickly absorb and use, perhaps even in their own presentations.

CONNECTIVITY AND INTELLIGENCE: MOBILE SHOPPING CARTS

This tech-spec story is drawn from a project to create a mobile grocery shopping application:

Presumptions

Many people need an easier way to keep track of food purchases and consumption in order to save money and manage family health concerns.

The user is part of the intelligent system. People generally know what they need and how to attend to their family's needs.

Shoppers like to save money. If a portable device clearly helps them save money, they will buy it, use it, and even pay to use value-added services on it.

Experiences

"I have a free application on my mobile called HandyShopper that lets me create a food shopping list simply by checking off what I need. Every time I shop and get something not on the list, I can add it to the list for next time."

"My HandyShopper application now accepts bar codes scanned from my mobile's camera. So I can categorize items as "similar to" or as "substitutions of" other items and do comparative shopping between my two closest grocery stores and Walmart. This saves me money."

"I downloaded HandyShopper data from the South Beach Diet site and now know when I'm shopping within Phase 2 of the diet or not."

"I just got a Bluetooth wireless earphone for my mobile."

"My mobile's Bluetooth lets me connect my mobile to printers and speakers. A special service sends digital coupons to my phone that I can use at the supermarket."

"My mobile's Bluetooth lets my HandyShopper application connect to the supermarket's smart carts. Now I'm saving time and money because I get all my coupon offers."

Goal stories

"Other families eat fast food, but the various wheat gluten, dairy, and seafood allergies, not to mention the finicky eaters in our family, mean we have to think about all the food we buy and prepare. Now, whenever I figure out a successful holiday meal or get a new list of bad and good foods from the doctor, I enter the items in my handheld. Shopping is easier because my handheld reminds me what I should buy, lists reasonable substitutions, and remembers my purchases."

"I'm accustomed to shopping around my family's dietary restrictions and tracking everything on my cell phone. But now when I shop, I connect my phone to one of the new shopping carts that track each item I put in and take out. So checkout is fast, because the scanning has already been done. All I have to do is bag it."

References

Internal report on research with shoppers:

Supermarket "smart" cart: www.msnbc.msn.com/id/5462556/

Metro Extra Future Store: www.spychips.com/metro/overview.html

RFID & Shopping: www.jefflindsay.com/rfid4.shtml

Takeaways

Shoppers like to save money and effort. If a device helps shoppers save effort, some will buy it. If a device helps them save money, more will buy it. If a device helps them save money and effort, everyone will buy it. ■

Stories can be part of the brand story

Another way that stories can be part of design is in the brand story. Like all stories, the brand story lives in the minds of your audience, blended from raw materials into a set of expectations about your product or company. If your design ideas have sprung from the stories you collect in user research, your story should connect naturally to the brand story.

> "A brand is a person's gut feeling about a product, service, or company. It's a gut feeling because we're all emotional, intuitive beings, despite our best efforts to be rational. It's a person's gut feeling because in the end, the brand is defined by individuals, not by companies, markets, or the so-called general public. Each person creates his or her own version of it. While companies can't control this process, they can influence it by communicating the qualities that make this product different than that product. When enough individuals arrive at the same gut feeling, a company can be said to have a brand. In other words, a brand is not what YOU say it is. It's what THEY say it is."
>
> —Marty Neumeier, *The Brand Gap*

If a brand is what others say about your product or company, then a company can supply the raw materials for what people say about them by telling stories—even design stories. This is a marketing strategy that seems more and more popular:

- The long-running "Get a Mac" television ads from Apple contrast a cool dude (played by Justin Long) as a Mac against a dowdy, flustered, geeky guy in a suit (John Hodgman) as a PC. Each ad creates a humorous situation in which the Mac outshines the PC.

- Scott McCloud (author of *Understanding Comics*) created a comic book that Google used to introduce its new Chrome browser. The story included sections on features, usability, and even the underlying technology.

- In 2001, BMW developed *The Hire*—a series of short promotional narrative films for the Internet. They hired a different famous movie director for each film and told them they could do anything they wanted, as long as the end product was no longer than about five minutes (though none of them ended up quite that short) and included the same driver character, played by Clive Owen.

Stories like these are a way of communicating the values and features you have put into the design. Of course, stories that are part of the external marketing may be more polished than stories you create during the design process, but they spring from the same source. Both the brand story and the design story are the logical and emotional connection between you and your audience.

More reading

"Design as Storytelling," Tom Erikson www.pliant.org/personal/
Tom_Erickson/Storytelling.html

"Notes on Design Practice: Stories and Prototypes as Catalysts for Communication" In *Scenario-Based Design: Envisioning Work and Technology in System Development* (ed. J. Carroll): www.pliant.org/
personal/Tom_Erickson/Stories.html

"Telling Stories," Phil Barrett, The Think Blog (Flow Interactive)
www.thinkflowinteractive.com/2008/12/19/telling-stories/
(December 19, 2008)

"Storytelling: The Power of Scenarios. Goldsmith Award Presentations," Ginny Redish, IEEE PCS, October 2001 www.redish.
net/content/handouts/redish_Goldsmith_Oct2001.pdf

Beyond Scenarios: the Role of Storytelling in SCSW Design,
Dan Gruen

Storytelling Games, Doug Lipman

Innovation at the Speed of Laughter: 8 Secrets to World Class Idea Generation, John Sweeney

The Brand Gap—How to Bridge the Distance Between Business Strategy and Design, Marty Neumeier

Summary

Stories have many roles in the design and ideation process, as you switch from collecting stories to using them.

Design stories can build from the stories you have collected from users and found in the data, or they can be created as part of a brainstorming exercise.

Even if you don't have user stories to work from, you can start from what you do know about the user experience to create a context for the stories.

- When you have good stories, based on good user data, they can trigger design ideas.

- You can make up stories as a way of brainstorming new ideas.

- Stories can explain your design ideas, especially if you are suggesting an innovative idea.

- Stories can describe requirements, setting a context for technical requirements.

CHAPTER 9

Evaluating with Stories

A n important part of any user experience process is to evaluate the design. We have several techniques for this, from expert review to usability testing.

Design teachers suggest tricks like looking at a drawing in a mirror to see it from a different perspective. Stories collected from users can act like a mirror, letting you look at a product from "the other side."

Although we have placed this chapter near the end of the design process in the linear organization of this book, we assume that you have been testing your work—with users and through design reviews—all along. You can use stories to improve your evaluations, whether you are doing a formal, summative usability test or a quick "hey you" test with your neighbor. Many of the ways you can use stories in evaluation are covered in Chapter 6, "Collecting Stories."

You should also be ready to collect new stories as you observe people using the product and to use those stories to improve the design.

Stories can be used in the following ways:

- To create scenarios or tasks for usability testing

- As a guide for expert reviews

- For quality testing

And you may find yourself collecting new stories during these activities, as well.

Using stories to create usability tasks

One obvious use of stories is to create scenarios for participants in a usability test. The stories establishing goals and motivations can also provide a starting point for any usability-testing task. For example, you could take Ginny Redish's story from Chapter 8, "Using Stories for Design Ideas," and turn it around for this purpose:

Her story:

Sarah Smith, a 25-year-old travel agent in a small, three-person agency in a storefront in a suburb of Chicago, takes a call from her friend, Jenny.

Jenny wants to go to Phoenix to see her special friend sometime in the next month. She can go any weekend, and she can take Friday and Monday off. But she can only go if she can afford it. Jenny asks Sarah to find the least expensive flights for any Friday to Monday during the next month.

The story as a usability test task:

You are a travel agent. Your customer, Jenny, calls to book a flight to Phoenix.

She wants to go any time in the next month, but only if she can find a ticket she can afford. She can go any weekend, and she can take Friday and Monday off.

Find the least expensive flight option for Jenny.

Turn user stories into "instant" usability tasks

Your stories can also be used as the starting point for a more open session, allowing the test participant to customize the tasks to match their own situation. This can be a more difficult session to moderate. You have to be able to think on your feet to react to the participant's ideas. But the result can be richer information from the session.

Find out what your participants want to know at the beginning of the session. Ask about their interests first—*before* you introduce the site or material you are testing. For example, if you are testing an ecommerce site, find out what they might want to purchase and why.

Some people have trouble coming up with specific ideas on the spot, so you might want to ask them on a pre-session questionnaire. This gives them time to think about their choices without the pressure of someone waiting for them to answer.

You can also ask the participants to recall the last time they were on a site like yours. Or the last time they faced a situation similar to one you want to test. Give them a chance to tell you the story.

At this point you can either let their own stories guide the sessions, or you can adapt the tasks from a prepared list, picking the ones closest to their own questions or tasks.

> "You said you wanted to know X, so let's try Y."

If you write tasks so that you can fill in the blank with information about the participants' own interests, the adaptation is easier.

> "I'd like you to purchase a sweater. You said you were looking for a red cardigan. Please try to find one, and..."

Another solution is to let them select tasks to complete from a list with some degree of variety. This way, you don't ask them to try tasks they are not interested in, or would not try on their own.

Turning tasks into stories

Apala Chavan, from Human Factors International, created a way of using stories to make usability test tasks compelling. She says that people in Asia are hesitant to say that a design is bad or to admit that they had trouble using it. Her solution was something she called "The Bollywood Technique," after the storytelling style of movies from Bollywood, the Hollywood of India. These movies are full of complex, emotionally charged plots, so Chavan created a situation in which the participants were asked to enter into a story such as this one:

> "The participant's beautiful, young, and innocent niece is about to be married. But suddenly he gets news that the prospective groom

is a member of the underground. He is a hit man! His whole life story is a sham, AND HE IS ALREADY MARRIED! The participant has the evidence and must book an airline ticket for himself and the groom's current wife to Bangalore. Time is of the essence!!!" (http://www.humanfactors.com/downloads/jun02. asp#bollywood)

The addition of a story lets participants dive in with excitement and point out things that made it difficult for them to solve the problem. You may not need to create such a broad fantasy, but a little storytelling can make your tasks more compelling than a dry set of instructions.

Collecting stories just in time for usability testing

We hate to admit it, but sometimes user experience people arrive on the scene just in time for usability testing. There are no stories and not much user research to create a meaningful set of tasks for the usability test sessions.

"JUST-IN-TIME" STORIES

Ginny Redish told us what she did when she was brought into a project late in the design stage. With no user stories to draw on, she combined story gathering with usability testing.

The developers had already created a prototype. It was based on requirements that had been gathered by asking customers—not users—what new features they wanted. No one had seen users at work. I suggested combining user site visits with usability tests of the prototype.

At each site, we spent time with users, observing their normal routine and gathering their stories about how they worked.

Then the team moved into a conference room and a few of the users came in individually to try out the prototype. The stories the team had just gathered became the scenarios for the usability test.

At the first site, the team learned that there was an entire step in the users' process that the developers had been unaware of and had not designed for. ■

Using stories for reviews

These same sorts of stories can be used for an expert evaluation or a walkthrough of the design. By establishing a minimal character (or using a persona) and walking through the task from their perspective, you are less likely to simply follow the logical flow of the application and more likely to use the product the way a real user might.

Stories and personas are a great way to add structure to the review of a design. Give each person around the table a different persona and task and ask them to do the following:

- Look at the first page or screen from the perspective of that person.

- Identify what their first action might be (including "bailing out").

- Try to complete the task.

One danger of this sort of review is that, if you don't know your users well (or don't have good personas), you may find yourself falling back into looking at the site from an insider's perspective. The group should be ready to challenge decisions that seem to simply follow the path of the design structure.

Or you may simply not have enough information to make a good decision. This is a good way to identify gaps in your knowledge; it can be the beginning of a lively discussion.

In either case, all the stories you selected while you analyzed the user research are invaluable. Use them to illustrate possible interpretations.

Collecting stories during a usability test

Like any user research, usability test sessions are an opportunity to collect stories. Sometimes, you'll find new information about the user context and learn new questions to ask next time.

THEY USE IT WHERE?

Randolph Bias teaches usability in the School of Information at the University of Texas at Austin. His students conduct usability studies for local nonprofit organizations to get experience on real projects.

One project was for a local nonprofit human services agency. The site was divided into different sections, each describing a different type of support the organization offered. The agency assumed that visitors would bookmark the home page of the section that was appropriate for them.

What my students learned was that most of their visitors did not have Internet access at home, and they were accessing the Web from the public library. This meant that relying on personal "favorites" was not going to work, and that the home page needed to help them get to the right page quickly.

As we worked through the site, my students also realized that there were other implications about using this site in a public place where there was little privacy.

The agency and the constituents they served (though they didn't know it) benefitted from my students' UCD work. ■

You can use an evaluation session for dual purposes. If you mix your specific tasks or interview questions with open questions to collect stories, you may gather enough information for two different reports: one on the specific topic of the user research or usability session, and one on the contextual information you gather.

TWO RESEARCH EVENTS IN ONE SESSION

In one usability test, we were interested in how well the users could navigate a search form with sections that could be opened and closed to reveal fields that were used only in specific circumstances. We knew that users found the original form too long, but had also learned that they didn't want to choose between a "basic" and "advanced" version of search.

The designers created a prototype for a new idea, but weren't sure if users would find the new interaction easy.

We knew that people in different situations would use the database differently, so we started the sessions by asking the participants to describe some recent occasions when they had searched this database. From that information, we chose appropriate scenarios for them so we could watch how they worked.

Some of the people observing the usability test told us that they were finding the initial discussion very useful. Not only were the participants talking about their work, but also they were showing us sites that they used and information they had found particularly useful. The observers were hearing and seeing things about how these users worked that they had never been able to observe before.

In the end, we created two reports. The first was a simple usability report on how the form design worked, which we could use to improve it. The second described everything we had learned about the context in which people might use that site, which we could use in many different ways. This gave the designers looking for immediate recommendations a short report they could work from, but also preserved the more general information in a form that the whole team could use. ■

Usability evaluation may not seem like a place for stories, but any time you work with users you have an opportunity to listen for stories.

More reading

"The Bollywood technique:" www.humanfactors.com/downloads/jun02.asp#bollywood

"The Hybrid User-Requirements Interface Evaluation (HURIE) Method," Randolph Bias, Shannon Lucas, and Tammy Latham in *User-Centered Design Case Studies*, edited by Carol Righi and Janice James

"Guidelines for letting participants create their own tasks," Whitney Quesenbery: www.wqusability.com/handouts/participant%20tasks.pdf

"Designing Web Sites for Older Adults: Expert Review of Usability for Older Adults at 50 Web Sites," Ginny Redish and Dana Chisnell: http://assets.aarp.org/www.aarp.org_/articles/research/oww/AARP-50Sites.pdf

Summary

You can continue to collect stories during usability evaluations (or start doing so, if you are jumping into the middle of a process). These stories add more rich qualitative data to your understanding of users.

You can also use stories for usability tasks in several different ways:

- Use your collection of stories to write usability tasks. The stories you collected earlier in the project can now be the starting point for a usability evaluation.

- Create stories to set a context for usability tasks, making them more relevant to the test participants.

- Start from a general story, but customize it with information you gather from each participant.

- Collect "just-in-time" stories and use them immediately in a usability test.

CHAPTER 10

Sharing Stories (Managing Up and Across)

Until now, we have focused on collecting, selecting, and shaping stories. Now, let's discuss how to use stories to communicate outside of the design team.

For many practitioners, explaining design ideas and the sources of those ideas to managers is difficult. We get enthusiastic about the specifics of the idea, drowning the audience in details before they comprehend the big picture. Or we struggle to make a connection between the idea and the real-world problem it solves. What we need is a way to engage their imagination, so they cannot simply hear the new idea, but contribute to it and thereby invest in it.

That's where stories come in. They don't replace the entire presentation; there's still a time and a place for details of technology, marketing, and budgets. The role for stories in a management presentation is to get the audience's attention, to set a context for the rest of the data, and usually to inspire action by leaving them with a clear image.

Don't worry—everyone is a storyteller

Films are full of scenes in which someone changes the minds of a group of people by telling a story. The characters always seem to have just the right words and speak beautifully. With that image in mind, you may be worried that you aren't a good enough performer to tell a story well. Don't worry. You may not be a great storyteller, but anyone can be a good one. As long as you are clear about your goals, listen to your audience, and find a story that bridges the gap between your goals and those of the audience, you have everything you need to make stories work for you.

Don't think you get just one chance to tell a story, and that it has to be perfect the first time. One of the great things about using stories to communicate design ideas is that you can refine them with input from your audience.

Help the audience build the story you tell

In the end, it's the listener's job to build the story. All you provide is the necessary information, tailored to the perspective and preconceptions of your audience. In doing so, you shape the experience so that the story that emerges in the group is a shared story, not a dozen or more wildly different versions.

It's a careful balancing act: The more you allow the people to build their own story around the structure and details you provide, the more engaged they are in their story. If you give them too much data, too many facts and details, they have nothing to do and will likely be bored. If you give them too little to work with, they may start building a story that is very different than the one you have in mind, which could cause disruption and annoyances in a presentation.

Another obstacle is that audiences vary. In user experience, the biggest difference between audiences usually lies in their role within the project or company. You may have project sponsors who are interested in the bottom line benefit, technologists who want it done the simplest way, design teams looking for new ideas, and marketers looking for insight into consumer thinking, all in the same presentation.

In any business setting, people come to a meeting (and hear your story) with different expectations and agendas. Even with a single audience, one you know well, there may be a lot of variation from day to day. No matter how good your preparation, you still have to pay attention to their body language, facial expressions, and comments while you are sharing your story to see if it is working and if the story the audience is building is the one you intended.

If you don't know your audience well, try listening

Sometimes, you will be in a situation where you know your audience well. Perhaps they are your colleagues or a client you work with on a regular basis. But you may also be thrown into a situation where you have little idea how to connect.

It may seem obvious, but the first thing you need to do in this situation is to ask your listeners what they want to hear and then *really listen* to their answers.

LISTENING WHILE YOU TELL A STORY

Once I was on a panel at a conference. There were five of us at the front of the room. It was early—8:30 in the morning. There were a hundred people in the audience. We each had five or ten minutes to talk about some aspect of business consulting.

The first person got up and spoke, and I saw all this discomfort in the audience as the person was speaking. I thought "He's not connecting with this audience; something's not right here."

But I didn't really know what the audience was looking for and how we, the panelists, weren't meeting the mark. So instead of talking during my ten minutes, I did an exercise instead. I asked everyone to write down the one thing they wanted to walk away from this workshop with. We collected answers on a whiteboard.

We were talking in general, but the audience already understood the general topic. They wanted practical tips on how to address the issue in their own work.

Now we had a more specific understanding of why people had come to this session, and we could speak directly to the goals of the audience. ■

By starting with a brief listening exercise, you not only get a better idea of the expectations the audience has brought to the room, but you also help the people in the room understand how diverse or similar they are. They may be more tolerant of material that does not seem immediately relevant to them once they know why you have chosen to include it.

A few audiences you may meet

Although each audience has its own dynamic, there are a few types that you meet often enough to generalize about them. This is not an exhaustive list, but a few of the most common personas:

- **Strategic leaders:** People who need to generate and maintain a common vision for their company, group, or products.

- **Managers:** People with a mission—often a product—who need to make the decisions that keep their entire team on track toward a common goal.

- **Technical experts:** People who implement a vision, making the myriad detailed decisions that add up to a product or service.

Your audience may include people who are experts in your field or in some part of your project. They may have their own views about the subject of your story and may listen for details that you get "wrong." We'll talk more about audiences with a special relationship to the story in Chapter 12, "Considering the Audience."

Your audience may also include other people in user experience who are not part of your immediate team. We hope that all of the people involved in user experience design work together, but that is not always the case. If you are presenting to user experience colleagues, consider what details help make a story authentic for them. Chapter 12 also looks at how a story might change to take into consideration the relationship between you and the audience.

Stories for leaders

Leaders, especially in strategic management, must connect the business and the market (see Figure 10.1). The stories you tell for leaders should do the same thing, connecting your design or research to their concerns.

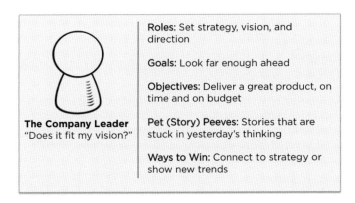

FIGURE 10.1
The company leader.

When you create a story for a leader, show how the idea you are "selling" makes a bridge between users and the business. For example, you can try one of these strategies:

- Identify a point-of-pain that users experience and then show a solution.

- Identify a gap in the market and show a way to fill it with a new product or a change in a current one.

- Identify a new approach by reconfiguring common or existing components in an unconventional way.

- Identify trends in the user experience of your customers and how that is affecting the business.

Stories can be particularly useful when you need to explain a disruptive idea, an innovation that is counterintuitive, or an idea for which there are few metrics or data points.

It's hard to separate user experience stories *for leaders* from stories *about leaders* and *leadership*.

Leadership is partially about generating and maintaining a common vision and sense of purpose. Saying, "Follow me!" is not leadership. Showing how everyone's efforts are relevant, contributory, necessary, and ultimately self-rewarding is leadership. All that can be done through telling the right story at the right time.

DOING THE RIGHT THING, NOT JUST SAYING IT

Mary Beth Rettger, a manager at MathWorks, shared this lesson about core values in action in her company.

MathWorks has very strong, publically stated core values, and our guiding principle is summed up as "Do the Right Thing." We even post this on our external Web site, with the following definition: "This means doing what is best for our staff members, customers, business partners, and communities for the long term..."

Early in my career at the company, I experienced this principle in action, and I use this story when I'm attempting to convey this message to people who work with me.

Because our software can be used in the design of defense systems, we are restricted from selling to certain countries. When we designed our Web store, one of the tricky problems was what to do when someone from outside the U.S. attempted to purchase software on the Web store—how much validation did we have to do to ensure that it was legal to sell to that buyer?

One of the team members commented that to meet the letter of the law all we had to do was some simple procedure; the implication in his statement was that would likely not prevent anyone who shouldn't be buying from actually purchasing.

The vice president responsible for the project interrupted immediately with, "No, that's not good enough; we need to do the right thing, not just meet the letter of the law. I want to be able to sleep at night knowing our software isn't getting to people who shouldn't have it." As a result, we put in additional checking, which probably also added time and expense to development. ■

User experience is not the only discipline to notice the power of storytelling. There is a growing body of work on corporate storytelling focusing on how leaders can use stories to shape and communicate strategy. Two of the leading authors in this work are Stephen Denning (*The Springboard* and *The Secret Language of Leadership*) and Annette Simmons (*Whoever Tells the Best Story Wins*).

For both Simmons and Denning, stories are a natural way for leaders to communicate. They see the leader's role as inspiring others to action, using stories to spark their imagination and engage them in working toward a goal. In this view, memos and long reports are counterproductive. Denning sees stories as a way to avoid both a hierarchical leadership style and long arguments about details of strategy and direction. Simmons recognizes the ability of a story to deliver a practical vision.

"The word 'vision' has been distorted for many of us by bad experiences of smarmy consultants, endless management retreats, and oversold and underdelivered promises. Story forces substance back into the vision process. Laminated cards with core values and quippy '$2 billion by 2010' sound-bite visions are exposed as superficial and one-dimensional when compared to vision stories. When you apply the discipline of interpreting any vision by way of a story, the process inevitably exposes any gaping holes that beg the questions: What does this mean? To whom? And who benefits if I get there? Exploitation, superficiality, and unintended outcomes are more likely to be exposed by the rigors of storytelling."

—Annette Simmons, *Whoever Tells the Best Story Wins*

Because stories are a familiar way for leaders to communicate, you can tap into this familiarity to tell stories in a way that will seem natural to them.

Stories for managers

Managers can be an easy audience because they often have clear goals (see Figure 10.2). If you can speak to their issues, crisply and clearly, they will listen.

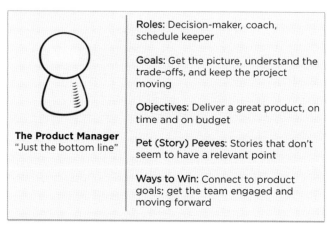

The Product Manager
"Just the bottom line"

Roles: Decision-maker, coach, schedule keeper

Goals: Get the picture, understand the trade-offs, and keep the project moving

Objectives: Deliver a great product, on time and on budget

Pet (Story) Peeves: Stories that don't seem to have a relevant point

Ways to Win: Connect to product goals; get the team engaged and moving forward

FIGURE 10.2
The product manager.

Managers don't usually have a lot of time to spare. More often than not, they like short, concise meetings, not leisurely brainstorming sessions or deep dives into user research data. Don't plan to tell long detailed stories to this audience. Instead, think about when a story can have the most impact.

Use stories to kick off a new idea, especially if you need a bit of context to explain how it will work. For this situation, the ability of stories to pack a lot of detail into a few words works for you.

If you are bringing bad news from user research, such as the discovery that the target audience doesn't really want or like a new product idea, make sure that you show how the story is typical of a group of people who are important as customers, users, or other stakeholders. If you are presenting a new idea, find a way to connect it to a well-known situation, so that it seems more plausible. You might even do both in one story: present a problem and a solution in a simple narrative. Most importantly, don't get bogged down in detailed specifications or technology.

FRAMING A NEW IDEA WITH A STORY

I once worked on a large informational Web site. During usability testing, I discovered that although visitors really valued the rich information on the site, they sometimes found themselves navigating in circles. The problem was that, although each section was written well, there was no structure to tie them together. Here's the story I told to the Web management team to introduce a suggestion for a change to the site.

You know that people really love how much good information they can find on the site. But some people, like one we saw in the last test, seem to keep going around in circles. Mary wanted to know what options she had for a specific situation. She got to this page with no problems and went from there to a deeper content page. But she just didn't recognize that the link to "more information" would take her back to the same place. She went around this circle at least three times.

Our idea is that, if we created a new banner that tied all of the information about each of the main topics together, we could improve the navigation and help Mary find the information she needs more easily.

Then I showed a deliberately rough sketch detailing how the new navigation might work. ■

In this example, a rough sketch of a new idea illustrated the story. Instead of simply plopping an idea into the middle of the meeting, the story provided a context to justify the idea. These sketches need to be concrete enough to suggest a specific direction, but open enough to accept input from the audience.

Another goal for a management story is to get a team engaged. Once people have begun thinking about an idea or how to solve a problem, it's harder to drop the topic or reject an idea out of hand. For these stories, you might focus on creating a vivid picture full of juicy images.

PARKING TECHNOLOGY

I once saw an amazing new technology come out of a company's research lab. It was an algorithm for parallel parking a car. The Australian research team demonstrated its algorithm by connecting sensors to a small Lego car and arranging obstacles for the car to park between. They sent a video to their fellow researchers in the company's U.S. headquarters; it showed the Lego car moving forward just the right amount past the forward obstacle, turning the front wheels to the right just the right amount, backing into the space at the perfect angle, then turning the front wheels back to perfectly fit in the space on the first try.

Being a city dweller, I saw gold. The researchers in headquarters saw the video, discussed it, and eventually dismissed it. I just couldn't understand why. I would have bought such a feature as an after-market device for my car or even considered buying a new car if it had this capability.

For quite a while I couldn't understand why the U.S. researchers didn't find this appealing. Then it came to me. The researchers in headquarters worked in the suburbs. In the morning when they went to work, they parked their cars in a large parking lot. And I conjectured that most of them lived in the suburbs, so when they went home they parked in their private garages, or in their driveways, or possibly in the mostly empty street outside their front doors. Parallel parking was not a daily experience for them.

It's not that they weren't incredibly intelligent in their own right; the issue was simply that parallel parking was not big on their cultural radar screen, as influenced by their personal experience. Now, there certainly could have been other reasons to reject this research, like legal liability concerns when taking over the control of an automobile. But I'm not sure that discussions of this research got that far down the pipeline. ■

In many organizations, product managers are also champions for the product and will have their own stories. These are the stories they use to motivate internal stakeholders like sales and marketing and the stories they tell to their own customers or clients. You might think about how your story will feed and change theirs.

Sometimes, you have to calm fears that changes to a product or service will cost people their jobs. Ian Roddis, Sarah Allen, Viki Stirling, and Caroline Jarrett found this out when they began work on the Open University Web site. The people at the student registration service were often the only voice a prospective student might hear before enrolling. When the Web site was developed with the promise that it would answer questions about the OU, this staff worried that it would take away their work. An analysis of email traffic showed that although there were many routine inquiries, which could easily be handled online, there were just as many that were the sort of question only a live person could answer. Armed with this user experience data, they changed the way they introduced their work to focus on reducing the "clutter" so that the support staff would have the time to provide good answers to difficult questions.

Stories for a technical audience

Technical audiences can be difficult to reach with stories, especially if the story is not firmly grounded in real details, providing concrete data for left-brain thinkers (see Figure 10.3).

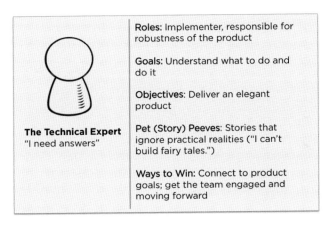

Roles: Implementer, responsible for robustness of the product

Goals: Understand what to do and do it

Objectives: Deliver an elegant product

The Technical Expert
"I need answers"

Pet (Story) Peeves: Stories that ignore practical realities ("I can't build fairy tales.")

Ways to Win: Connect to product goals; get the team engaged and moving forward

FIGURE 10.3
The technical expert.

Technical audiences can be sticklers for details. Often, this can be useful, especially when you are working on ideas that are technically challenging. You may have to deal with someone who seems to be listening only for inaccuracies in your stories:

> **Person 1:** I was thinking that we could organize the form like this (shows a mockup). It would have a lot of advantages for our users because I've changed the flow so that the fields they use the most are at the top of the page.

Person 2: (interrupting) There's a problem here. You've got a misspelling on the mockup, but the real problem is that you've drawn the fifth field too small to fit a really long entry.

This is a defensive mechanism, and may mean that your story is making them uncomfortable in some way. One way to prepare for a technical audience is to keep your stories firmly grounded in their technical reality. Craft your stories to avoid each of these pitfalls:

- **Use representative characters and situations.** Usually, stay as close to the status quo as possible. Be ready to back up your choices with hard data. The one exception is a situation when the point of the story is to show that there are types of users you don't know enough about.

- **Make the action of the story specific and tangible.** The story does not have to describe interactions technically, but think carefully about what steps or details will be important in creating a credible story for this audience.

- **Keep the story on track.** You may love the rich detail you have gathered in your user research sessions, but make sure that the story doesn't wander into pure description.

Decide which details will help make your point and focus on them. This is similar to the way wireframes or low-fidelity prototypes use visual techniques in early design deliverables.

Use technical terminology accurately. If you want to show how users talk about something, be careful to map their vernacular or idiom to the correct technical term. It's important to show that you understand everyone clearly.

In short, be sure that your story matters to the audience. Tell a story with details that relate to resources and deliverables. Use clear images to promote understanding of what needs to be done. A good story for a technical audience must present a problem they feel they can solve almost immediately, or one so intriguing they are willing to work on solving it. The choice is yours, but the first option is usually easier.

Stephen Denning makes a similar point in *Springboard Stories* when he talks about altering the level and type of detail to make a story resonate with each audience. When he tells a story about the health worker in Zambia to a general audience, he might slide over the medical details. But those details are the ones that will make a story ring true for health workers.

SMALL STEPS AND GIANT LEAPS

Simon Griffin, from Etre (www.etre.com), has written a newsletter for several years that incorporates a usability tip in the form of a short story in each issue. He uses a short anecdote at the beginning to engage the audience and set a tone or context for the rest of the story. These stories descibe a short case study or explain a technical usability principle in detail—but in a memorable way. He started one story with an anecdote about how NASA solved the problem of how to write in zero-gravity. Then he began a similar story about his own company with a line from a movie about space exploration, Apollo 13.

"Etre, we have a problem."

Last March we received a call from a company with an urgent usability problem. As part of a major Web site overhaul, they had introduced functionality to allow customers to buy gift vouchers online. However, all wasn't well. Almost immediately after launch, they began to receive a large number of calls from people who had sent the gift vouchers to themselves, rather than to their intended recipients. The vouchers were being dispatched in time for the recipients' birthdays, but were arriving at the senders' houses!

Before calling us, management had instructed the tech team to check their code for errors, yet no problems were found. They also checked their Web logs for signs of trouble, again finding nothing. This suggested that the problem was a usability issue.

It appeared that customers were inexplicably typing their own details into the form intended for their recipient's details, and their recipient's details into the form intended for their own details. The exact opposite of what they were supposed to do!

Yet the "problem page" seemed relatively straightforward. The sender and recipient forms appeared side-by-side, both containing an identical set of fields titled "First Name," "Last Name," and "Address," and both featuring a relatively unambiguous title ("Your Details" and "Recipient's Details," respectively). No obvious source of confusion was apparent. So management passed the problem over to the creative team.

The creative team, after much deliberation, put forward several options for re-design. Many involved major (i.e., "expensive") changes to the application workflow, separating the sender and recipient forms onto different pages with different layouts and different graphic identities to boot. Some even involved the addition of complex server-side validation rules that would attempt to guess whether the two sets of details were entered incorrectly based upon the customer's past behavior.

Before deciding to invest in one of the proposals, management decided to engage Etre to prototype and user-test the options. And test them we did, finding that only one of the solutions eradicated the problem in 100% of cases.

So what was this "silver bullet" solution? Did it involve major workflow changes or complex server-side validation rules? Nope. It involved the addition of just *two little words* to the problem design: "Your" and "Their."

Amending the sender form to read "Your First Name," "Your Last Name," and "Your Address," and the recipient form to read "Their First Name," "Their Last Name," and "Their Address," completely resolved the issue and the site was fixed within minutes.

"One small step, one giant leap." ■

When you have several audiences at once

Managing several audiences at once is more than just a challenge of balancing different needs. Sometimes, they have different viewpoints or worries. This can lead to a situation in which they have not been listening to each other—and may have difficulty listening to you.

Some corporate cultures find it hard to handle dissent or disagreement, so they smooth it over by not really listening to what is being said. Everyone politely takes their turn explaining their perspective on a problem, but no one points out when they are in conflict or don't connect. Have you ever attended a kickoff meeting for a project and started to wonder if everyone was talking about the same project?

CREATING A SHARED STORY

I once attended a kickoff meeting with people from the development group, marketing, and the business unit. As each described their vision of the product, it was clear that they were not just looking at it from different perspectives, they were describing entirely different experiences. The business group had a vision of some sort of artificial intelligence that would magically present just the right suggestions without much need for interaction. The marketing team wanted the whole thing to be multimedia. And the developers were imagining something in Visual Basic.

Even with piles of documents and many hours of meeting time, they had never really listened carefully enough to see the looming collision. The crash only came when someone tried to sketch a very rough version of the interface on the whiteboard.

We quickly realized that our real challenge was not only to create a good user experience, but also to help all the different people on the team share a vision for the product. ■

There is no magic wand that will let you take a project from a place where each group of stakeholders has a different vision to a happy ending. One solution is to use stories to tease out each group's starting vision. Casting their visions as stories can make it easier to talk about differences without creating a political disaster. You can use pieces of each of the stories to weave them into a single story, bringing them closer together.

Adjusting to an audience isn't just about making people feel good about themselves (though that's not a bad thing, either). It's about being able to hear what people are really saying and create the stories that let a user experience team excel.

More reading

The Story Factor and *Whoever Tells the Best Story Wins*, Annette Simmons

The Springboard: How Storytelling Ignites Action in Knowledge-Era Organizations and *The Secret Language of Leadership*, Stephen Denning

Storytelling in Organizations, John Seely Brown, Stephen Denning, Katalins Groh, Laurence Prusak, and Seth Kahan

Managing by Storying Around, David Armstrong

Wake Me Up When the Data Is Over, Lori Silverman

Around the Corporate Campfire, Evelyn Clark

Summary

When you are sharing stories with management, remember that they may be more focused on the point of the story than on the background of how it was created. This audience needs stories that help them understand easily. A good story for managing has the following criteria:

- Has a clear point.

- Opens doors to new ideas.

- Shows behavior to get beyond demographics, data, and opinion and shows how it translates into user experience.

- Is told from a perspective appropriate to the audience.

- Puts a human face on data from user research data or other analytics.

Crafting a Story

S o far in this book we've discussed *why* and *when* to tell stories in UX design. Now we are going to focus on *how*. No matter how short the story, careful construction is critical.

The idea for a story may arise spontaneously, offered to illustrate a point or answer a question. Or you may plan a story in advance as part of a report or presentation. However you discover the story and whenever you use it, your goal is always the same: You want the story to make a point. The work of crafting a story is aimed at ensuring that the story communicates what you intend and is not misunderstood.

Now it is time to turn our attention to how to craft a story. In the rest of the chapters, we will look at the following elements of a story and how you can use them to make your stories more engaging (and more effective).

The information in these chapters draws on theory and guidance for any kind of story, but is just as relevant for a user experience story. For example, you may not think of yourself as a performer, but when you tell a story to a group, that's a form of oral storytelling. Your user experience stories may not be plot-driven adventure stories, but they describe actions, giving them a structure and plot.

The elements of a story we will explore in detail are:

- **The audience:** Who is the story intended to reach?

- **The ingredients:** What does the story have to include?

- **The story structure:** How should the story be structured?

- **The medium:** How will the story be told?

What do we mean by "craft"?

"Craft" is a tricky word. It can refer to the skill it takes to make something or to an occupation requiring manual dexterity or skilled artistry. It can refer to skill in deception, but has also been used to mean the end result of skilled work, such as masterful writing. All of those meanings apply to storytelling in user experience design—except the part about deception, of course. (See Chapter 4, "The Ethics of Stories," if you have questions about authenticity and deception.)

These stories are created for a purpose. They are not primarily about *self-expression*, but this doesn't mean that they shouldn't be eloquent, fun, or engaging.

Think of a user experience story as a basket. Baskets have a purpose—they are a container to hold things. The first evaluation of a basket is whether it does its job well. But a master basket maker goes beyond function to make a basket that is not only useful, but beautiful. When a basket maker knows how to create beautiful baskets over and over again, that's craft. Similarly, learning the craft of storytelling will help you repeatedly create effective stories. As you practice telling stories, you can aim to become a master (UX design) storyteller, creating better and better stories.

Stories get better with practice

Crafting a story is an iterative process. You write a first draft, try it out, refine it based on feedback, and try it again. After Kevin taught a workshop at a storytelling conference for the first time and told an example story at the end, a wise, old storyteller named J.G "Paw Paw" Pinkerton came up to him.

"Nice story, young man," he said. "You know, you don't really know a story until you've told it a hundred times." What? A hundred times? That's ridiculous! But Kevin later realized that J.G. was right. Perhaps the number is a bit arbitrary, but stories get better with practice, whether they are intended for performance or design. The more you tell a story, the better the story becomes, and the more comfortable the teller becomes at telling it. Also, the more you tell a story, the more you can subtly (or not-so-subtly) adapt it to new audiences and situations. These opportunities allow you to see new dimensions in the story, and as J.G. said, the more you'll understand it.

You probably won't work that hard on every story you use. Some will be quick improvisations, but others will develop into workhorses of your repertoire, stories you can tell over and over again. "I have a repertoire of stories that I've built up over my years of design practice," Tom Erickson writes. "I collect them. I write them. I tell them. I piece together new stories out of bits of old ones. I make up stories about my own observations and experiences. I use these stories to generate discussion, to inform, to persuade."

To tell good stories, you have to work at it and be willing to adapt.

EVEN CLOWNS WORK AT CRAFTING THEIR STORY
One year while I was working as a lighting designer for the Big Apple Circus, the show included a famous clown, a top star of the one-ring European circus, with an act that was completely different from the red-nose, physical humor of American clowns. His first night, he bombed. The kids just stared at him with no laughs and hardly even a giggle. All of us working with the circus all waited for the tantrum, for the star to blame the audience. Instead, the next morning, while we were working on the lights, he brought his trunk into the ring and quietly rehearsed. That night, he got a few laughs, and over the next days he continued to work, changing some bits, dropping some, and adding new ones. By the end of the week, he was getting the big laughs and the applause. He didn't do it by abandoning his style of clowning, but by listening carefully to the audience and learning how to speak to them.
—"When the Show Goes On," Boxes and Arrows: www.boxesandarrows. com/view/when_the_show_must_go_on_its_time_to_collaborate_ or_die ■

Sometimes stories fail

We've stressed that anyone can create stories. We've focused on ways to successfully use stories in user experience design. But, much as we hate to admit it, sometimes stories fail. Sometimes, no matter how much you work on a story, you just can't get it right. Maybe it's you. Maybe it's the audience. Maybe it's a good story for the wrong audience. Maybe the point you are trying to make simply isn't meant to be made in a story.

THE STORY THAT FAILED
After I came out of the closet as a storyteller at Motorola, they decided that I should be responsible for crafting the use cases for my department's research technologies.

I would do version after version of these use cases, and I thought they were terrific. They went beyond "Susan doesn't know how to use her phone, so she hit the OK button and it works." There was motivation. Characters need a reason to pick up the phone—if there's a problem a user needs to solve and it doesn't make sense to pick up a phone to solve that problem, then it doesn't do any good to have a solution on the phone.

So I would write these brilliant use cases, and they'd say, "Nah, it doesn't work for us." OK, I thought. I'll try a different flow, add some more data and structure. "Nah, didn't work." Then I tried a series of different variations in a row. Still didn't work. I tried adding more of the technical aspects of the use cases, giving them a multidimensional feel. "Nah, It's a little long." Long? It's one or two paragraphs. "Yeah, it's a little long. We're not going to read that."

So what would work? I asked. "Two sentences." Should I take out the punctuation so it looks more like PowerPoint? I wondered. Would that make them feel more comfortable and familiar? I was shocked. ■

It would be easy to get angry. Kevin put a lot of work into trying to make stories work. But they didn't. He tried different ways of using stories, and he probably improved the stories as he worked on them, but they just didn't work for that audience, period.

All we can say is this: Know when to leave it behind. A good story will resurface when the time is right.

Think carefully about your goals

User experience stories should not be random anecdotes or simple jokes to make the audience laugh. Imagine that you've had a rough flight on your way to a meeting. As you start your presentation, you are still annoyed, so you try to work it into an amusing story. It seems to work. The audience laughs. The problem is that unless that story illustrates a point-of-pain relevant to your project, reinforces data from your user research, or makes some point about your user experience goals, it won't really help your presentation. Even worse, if you haven't thought carefully about the story, it could backfire, contradicting your point or distracting the audience with a lingering mental image that makes them ponder the story's relevance and pay less attention to you.

Like any design, creating a story starts with having a clear goal. User experience design stories are created for a specific audience and purpose. You might need a story that helps a researcher see and feel the user's perspectives a little more clearly. Or your goal might be to show a development team the relative advantages of different design solutions and how they balance user needs against business goals. Or perhaps your goal is to inspire a design team to think creatively about a new problem space. To be effective in each of these situations demands a story crafted to make a point to a specific audience.

Summary

The final section of the book is focused on *how* rather than *why* or *when* to use stories in user experience design.

- The work of crafting a story is aimed at ensuring that the story meets your goals, communicates what you intend, and is not misunderstood.

- Creating a story requires practice and a willingness to iterate the story until it works.

- Stories sometimes fail, and you have to let the story go and find a different way to communicate.

The next chapters look at the elements that go into creating a story. It starts with the audience, includes ingredients like perspective, characters, context, imagery, and language and covers structure, plot, and the way you tell the story.

CHAPTER 12

Considering the Audience

Astory is not just something you push out into the world; it is created in the minds of everyone in the audience. In Chapter 2, we looked at the Story Triangle (see Figure 12.1) and the dynamic relationships that connect the storyteller, the audience, and the story.

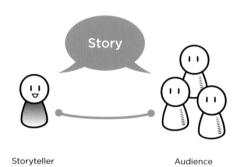

FIGURE 12.1
In the Story Triangle, there is a connection between the storyteller and the audience, as well as between the audience and the story.

Storyteller

Audience

The first step in crafting a story is to identify and understand your audience. This may seem obvious, but it's an easy point to forget when you are in the throes of story creation. This is as true in performance storytelling as it is in storytelling for user experience design. In both cases, your goal isn't just to write (or tell) a great story, but to communicate something to other people. To help a group of people understand something in a new way. To persuade. Whether this is as simple as narrating a sequence of events, or as complex as allowing them to relate to a contradictory set of attitudes, reaching your audience is the most important part of the equation.

There are two relationships to keep in mind. Both affect how the audience understands the point of your story.

- The relationship between the audience and the story

- The relationship between you and the audience

The relationship between the audience and the story

When you create a story, you must consider the *distance* between the audience and the context of the story. How far will the audience have to travel in their imaginations to understand the details of the story and the motivations of the characters? Think of the story as a bridge between the audience as they are now and the audience as you want them to be.

The shorter your story, the more important it is to gauge this distance properly. In a novel or a three-act play, you have plenty of time to gradually introduce your audience to all the quirks of the world of your story. In the brief format of most UX stories, you have to rely on the audience to fill in the gaps. If the story is based on an experience that is familiar to them, it is easier for them to do this, and you can spend less time laying the groundwork. Once you know the distance between your audience and your context, you will be able to choose the details worth including and the ones that can be tacitly implied.

Steve Denning makes this point about what he calls *springboard stories*. The example story he uses in many of his workshops is about a healthcare worker in Zambia who finds the answer to a medical question on the Web. Here is an excerpt:

> "In June 1995, a health worker in Kamana, Zambia, logged on to the Center for Disease Control's Web site and got the answer to a question about how to treat malaria.
>
> This story happened, not in June 2015, but in June 1995. This is not a rich country; it is Zambia, one of the least developed countries in the world. It is not even the capital of the country; it is six hundred kilometers away..."
>
> —Steve Denning, *The Springboard: How Storytelling Ignites Action in Knowledge Era Organizations*

The story as he told it at the World Bank went on to draw a connection between the health care worker and the work of that organization. There are many versions of the story; it is altered each time Denning tells it, as he adds and subtracts details to suit his audience. For example, if he tells the story to healthcare workers, he might include the specific information that the health worker in Zambia actually looked up. People interested in knowledge management or Web design might want details about how the health worker knew about the U.S. Center for Disease Control and Prevention or how he located the information on its site. These changes to the basic story help the audience connect to it and, more importantly, give them a context in which they can make the story their own.

Now, imagine that you are working on designing an electronic medical records system and want to create a story that would help explain the daily routine of hospital nurses as they check in on patients and keep records of their medical conditions. Table 12.1 shows just some of the relationships you might have to consider and the information they might need to connect with your story.

TABLE 12.1

AUDIENCES AND RELATIONSHIPS		
Audience	**Relationship**	**Needs**
Hospital nurses	The audience is part of the story context and has the same role as one of your central characters.	Enough detail to assure them that you understand the context they know well.
A patient (contributed to the medical record, but doesn't have access to it, or know medical terminology) or A doctor (reads the medical record and makes decisions based on it)	The audience is related to the story context, but has a different perspective than your central characters.	Details that help them see the difference between their perspective and the perspective of the nurses in the story.
A health policy analyst, who has never worked in a hospital	The audience knows the context, but is not part of it.	Specific details place the story in an acute care facility, not just a general, unspecified healthcare context.
A young, healthy adult who has not been in the hospital as an adult, and has never cared for someone who is seriously ill	The audience doesn't have any experience of the story context.	Details that show the characters as they see themselves and help the audience empathize with them.
A database designer or developer who has been assigned to work on a healthcare system for the first time	The audience only knows the context from a technical perspective.	Details that show how different people use the information in the system.

For example, you might include details such as how many patients the nurse visits each hour, or a memory of an incident where these medical records were critical. These story fragments are written from three different perspectives.

- **The nurse's perspective:** 4 p.m. Time for nursing rounds again. Mary Jo picked up her notebook, got her cart, and walked past her 10 rooms to the end of the hall. She hoped Mr. D's temperature had started to drop. She knew Dr. W would want to see how the new medication was working when he arrived for his evening rounds....

- **The patient's perspective:** 4 p.m. Mr. D listened to the rumble of the cart going past his room. That meant 15 minutes before Mary Jo, the nurse on his floor today, got done with the five rooms ahead of his. She'd take his temperature, pulse, and ask a few questions, scribbling them down into her notebook. Sometimes, he'd see her sitting at the computer station copying her notes into the computer....

- **The doctor's perspective:** 6:45 p.m. Dr. W liked to arrive after nursing rounds, so all of his patients' charts would be up to date. On an acute care floor, the daily record of vital stats helped him catch up quickly. Had Mr. D's medication started to bring his temperature down? Had the nurses added any notes on changes in the patient's condition?

User experience designers often have to work with different groups of people with different perspectives and even different technical languages. In Isobel Frean's story (in Chapter 8) about writing stories as part of the process of creating a new standard, the scenarios explained the context and activities for each function in a way that the nurses and other medical staff could understand them and review them for accuracy. The stories were connected to technical data models, so that the designers and engineers working on the standard could also understand how the computer function fit into that context.

One of the most difficult challenges I've faced in usability testing is coming up with good stories to start off tasks for nurses and doctors. I want the scenarios to be compelling, creating a realistic interaction with the site or database we are testing, but I don't have the medical training that will let me speak comfortably using their terminology.

At first, I tried creating broad, general scenarios: "A patient with breast cancer is not responding to the normal standard of care, so you want to see if there is a treatment clinical trial that might be effective for her."

These scenarios didn't work. The doctors would fire questions at me like I was a new medical student on a television show. "What has already been tried? Is there metastasis?" In other words, questions I couldn't begin to answer and that steered the discussion away from its purpose.

Since I didn't have enough clinical details to make a compelling case for a healthcare professional to respond to, I tried adding more medical details. That didn't work because inevitably I stumbled over a word, and the façade that I actually knew something about medicine came tumbling down.

The solution was to let them create their own tasks. I would start a story, using the same sort of general language. But then I would ask them to finish telling it for me. "Have you ever had a similar situation?" They could usually come up with something appropriate. I'd get them to tell me a little bit about it, and then send them off to find the answer.

Over time, I'm getting better at it. The medical professionals I work with are less likely to stare blankly, trying to imagine what I'm getting at, and more likely to come up with a good story of their own. ■

Details from user research help ground stories

In user experience design, the work is often done by people who have little to no direct experience with the context or the people in the context. User research bridges this gap. Stories are an effective way to bring the details from that research back to the project team in a meaningful way.

A good example of this is a project that Adaptive Path, a UX design group, took on after reading an open letter to Apple CEO Steve Jobs asking why the company that invented the iPod couldn't create a better portable medical device for people with diabetes. The story of this project is told in a series of blog entries at www.adaptivepath.com/blog. In one, Dan Saffer writes, "I read this plea and thought, wait, it's not just Steve [Jobs] and Jonny [chief Apple designer Jonathan Ive] who can do this stuff. Don't I work at a design firm? Don't we have the experience design tools to tackle this challenge? Why, yes. Yes, we did."

One striking aspect of this project is that they started by listening—meeting diabetics and diabetes educators—for the first three weeks. They came back with many story fragments to use in their presentation to help people understand some of what they learned:

> One participant, Alice, pointed to her big black bag and said, "Sometimes I think it would be nice to carry around a tiny stylish purse, but that just isn't possible for me."

> Between monitoring blood glucose levels and injecting insulin, most type 1 diabetics have to poke themselves with a needle 10–14 times a day.

> "I watch my diet like a hawk, and I exercise, so when my numbers are high or low I get really pissed. I feel like I am doing everything I am supposed to do, so why is this happening? It can be really frustrating."

Notice that the Adaptive Path designers didn't sit down with a list of facts and technical details about diabetes and insulin. They started by listening to people with diabetes and learning what their lives were like. These stories had a clear influence on their design process. Instead of focusing on the medical processes and data, they focused on the experience of using the device. Sharing those stories helps anyone reading about the project also have those moments of insight.

What if they think they know, but they don't?

It can be hard work gathering enough information to bridge gaps in understanding. But that's still far more preferable than situations where everyone on the project mistakenly thinks they understand the audience. These unacknowledged gaps can be the hardest to fill—both for the storyteller and for the user experience design team in general.

Rahel Baillie's story in Chapter 6 is about a company that thought it knew its users, but learned by listening that it didn't have the whole picture. While we were gathering stories for this book, we found several similar situations. All of the people we talked to mentioned how hard it is to get this information across in a constructive way. Depending on how deep the disconnect is, bringing it up can challenge basic beliefs within a company.

One tactic to bridge the gap between the story's audience and the characters in it is by building a picture that highlights not only the ways in which these situations are different from the audience's expectations, but also to show why the characters' attitudes and behaviors made sense for them.

SEEING THE BUSINESS FROM THEIR POINT OF VIEW
Our customers are the sort of folks who run a shop or a small industrial operation. It's really hard for ambitious product managers in a large company to understand the lives of their customers.

Folks on our side of the screen live and die by email, promotions, and stock options. We have people we report to and colleagues we have to collaborate with. We may worry about meeting our sales targets, but we don't usually have to agonize over the electric bill or the office rent. The hardest thing for us to understand is that someone running a small company might feel very differently.

When we go out to do site visits, we meet people who really love what they do, and often do it very well. They are printers and photographers and even auto repair companies. Their attitude toward managing payroll and their accounting is that it's a necessary evil, and the less time they have to spend on it, the better.

It's so easy for the product team to assume that they are not ambitious or that they aren't very good at what they do. What else could explain this attitude toward managing their business?

What we see is how good they are at their work and how much they love it—a printer who can do amazing things with color, or a photographer who loves taking the time to really capture a portrait, not just a picture. We try to bring back samples of their work along with the other photographs. They illustrate stories we use to close the gap so that our team can understand who our customers are and why doing the work is more important to them than management chores. ■

This story is told through the eyes of a user experience research team. It uses their role as a bridge between two worlds—the customers and their colleagues. This explicit use of the researchers' experience is a style that John Van Mannen calls a "confessional tale" in his book on writing ethnography, *Tales of the Field*. (See the section in Chapter 15 on "Written stories" for a more detailed discussion.)

Mirror stories are stories about ourselves

One variation on the problem of simply not understanding the context of the story can be found in a mirror story: stories about ourselves. Kevin coined this phrase for the stories we want to tell when we wake up in the morning, look in the mirror, and think, "I like that guy! He's who I want to work for. My stories should be about him because he's a heck of a nice guy."

There's nothing wrong with a mirror story in itself. The problem is that one main character cannot represent all people. So, if you see a pattern developing of stories that are all about the same character, or all the stories could apply to the people working on the design, it may be time for an intervention.

- If you are telling mirror stories, you may be going too far in trying to help your audience identify with the story. You want the audience to do the work of identifying with the characters in the story, not just recognize the characters as themselves.

- If the mirror stories are coming from people on your team, you need to find out why. Do they not know enough about any other customers or users? Or do they genuinely believe that they represent the model customer?

Maybe you can address this problem directly, but usually it requires a more subtle approach. One solution is to find another way to put the audience into the story. One way to do this is to make them a helpful companion to the main character. Tell the story *through their eyes*, even though the point of the story is focused on another character. In *The Anatomy of a Screenplay*, Dan Decker, a script writing coach, calls this a "window character"—the person through whom we see the real story unfold.

- Instead of telling a story about an older adult struggling to use an unfamiliar technology, tell a story about someone who is great with computers helping a parent use one.

- Tell a story about someone unexpectedly caring for a family member with a severe illness, combining the patient and caregiver perspectives into one story.

- Create a window character that can provide an explanation for what is happening in the story, from the perspective of the audience, much as a chorus in a Greek play can comment on the events.

- Set the story in a plausible future, where the advantages of the mirror character are turned around or negated by a change, such as how broadly a new technology is adopted or where a new regulation is in effect.

One value of using stories in user experience design is to get the team out of its comfort zone by helping people imagine situations they don't know much about. Using too many mirror stories defeats that purpose by limiting the number of perspectives and experiences the stories represent.

This problem is not limited to user experience. It's hard to remember that you are not the center of the universe. As John Andrew Holmes, American physician and writer, put it, "It is well to remember that the entire universe, with one trifling exception, is composed of others."

The relationship between you and the audience

The next relationship to consider is the one between you and your audience. You may find yourself:

- Part of a community of peers, such as a design or product team

- Speaking as an outsider—from a different company, discipline, or culture

- Talking "up" to managers, clients, or others with more influence or position than you

- Communicating expertise as an expert or manager

Each of these relationships brings with it different degrees of shared experience or background and different expectations for how you will communicate. Your relationship to the audience affects not only what stories you choose to tell, but also how you tell them.

And, of course, you will frequently find yourself in a group with several of these relationships, having to bridge them all at once. When that happens, you've got to shift modes, for example go from the 50,000-foot view down to the 100-foot view, and do it in short order. One audience may need a high-level perspective to understand the story, but if you stay at that level too long, the story will seem ungrounded and disconnected from real needs. Another may be focused on the details that support the high-level view. Too much low-level can bog down your story. It's one of the hardest challenges, but if you're prepared for a heterogeneous audience, you'll be better able to adjust quickly.

Both the relationship between you and the audience and the one between the audience and the story affect all communication in user experience design, especially the challenges of presenting design concepts or user research reports. In a 2005 workshop on writing usability test reports, the group identified the audience as one of the most important considerations in designing a report, saying that, "The content, presentation or writing style, and level of detail can all be affected by differences in business context, evaluation method, and the relationship of the author to the audience."

In the next chapters, as you examine the different *ingredients* in a story, plan for different presentation styles, and think about structure, keep the audience in mind. Craft a story that reflects your relationship with them.

How much are *you* like the audience?

Do you have shared references and terminology that you can rely on? These can be shortcuts, but they can also make the story impossible for outsiders to understand, so be sure you aren't excluding part of your audience. Terminology can be tricky in any world, but you also need to watch out for implicit knowledge of technical concepts and detailed facts.

"BUT AN ELAM 251 HAD PALE GREEN PAINT!"

My husband, John Chester, is an audio engineer. Worse, he's an engineer's engineer, who can tell stories based on electronic part numbers. One year, he led a panel discussion at the Audio Engineering Society on the history of live sound. He brought together some of the leading audio folks from the early days of live concerts—people who did the sound for Woodstock and the Newport festivals—to reminisce about their work and the evolution of concert audio.

I decided that this would be a discussion I might understand. I expected to hear some of the great stories about how those early festivals got their sound. And I was mostly right.

One of the photos was from the Newport Jazz Festival. John suggested that something in the photo was a U-47 and a lively discussion broke out. "No, it's an ELAM 251." "Couldn't be...those had pale green paint, and this doesn't." The final consensus was that it was a U-48.

At the time, I wasn't even sure what they were talking about. It turned out to be a debate about the exact model of the microphone in the picture. Like I said, stories based on electronic part numbers.

The point here is that everyone in the room understood. This wasn't obscure to them. They all knew these mics. It was just how they talked. ■

Is your relationship to the story the same as the audience's?

In Adaptive Path's project to create a diabetes-monitoring device, none of the project team knew much about the disease, so everyone had the same relationship to the people who would use the device. Many of the people who read their account of the project will be in the same situation. The stories on the blog describe their process of discovery and design from this shared perspective.

We can imagine that someone with diabetes would read these stories differently, based on their very different relationship. Their first questions might be, "Do they get it? Does the experience they are designing for match mine?" In this case, you want your stories to show that you do *get it*.

A similarly imbalanced relationship might exist when you are working on a system for experts such as health professionals, engineers, or people with deep experience in their business. Things that were eye-opening insights to you may be "ho-hum" to them. Your stories can acknowledge that and show how collecting the story helped you understand something the audience already knew. You might even make yourself, as the researcher, the center of the story. This approach is often used in reports from ethnographic fieldwork, as authors share not only the final conclusions, but also the story of how they reached those conclusions.

Another case in which the relationships are not the same would be one in which you have done extensive field research and are bringing your insights back to a team. At the beginning of the project, you and your story audience might have been equally distant from the context, but now you are closer to it and *bringing them in* to share your new understanding.

Do you bring different pieces of the puzzle?

Kevin's story, "Parking Technology," in Chapter 10, is an example of this relationship. He brought an understanding of the urban environment in which automated parking made a lot of sense; the other researchers brought an awareness of legal and technical issues.

User experience professionals are often brought into a project to share the perspectives that their skills give them. But other perspectives are also important. Some design challenges require an understanding of several cultural perspectives. For example, if a company wanted to make a low-cost ebook device targeted to third-world markets, it might have to consider several social and legal perspectives:

- **An educational perspective.** An ebook could be used in schools, so national ministries of education might have guidelines for what material was appropriate in their country. Education officials might want an easy way to determine that the material transferred to the ebook was appropriate for students.

- **A regulatory perspective.** The device includes communications features that could be used to send messages between people, not just used to receive purchased books. Government officials might want to know that the system didn't conflict with regulated industries.

- **A literacy perspective.** An ebook might be used by some people who were not fully literate. The interface might need to be self-teaching without advanced language skills.

- **A resources perspective.** An ebook might be used by many people for whom electric power is not always easy to come by. The ebook would need to manage power consumption efficiently.

The key is to share different perspectives with respect. Each story can acknowledge the other contexts and how they overlap. In doing this, you can explore possibilities outside of the audience's comfort zone of easy ideas. If you are pushing a group to consider a new idea, it is helpful to use examples and stories that are simple or easy to relate to their own experiences. One solution is to look for ways to recast the example. For example, you could talk about power requirements as a mobile issue, not just a local resource issue. An interface for a low-literacy population can also be about breakthrough ease-of-use.

Help them get from here to there

There are many good reasons to keep your stories short: business meetings often have a packed agenda and attention spans are short. But don't cut your stories so short that you leave out the details that will help your audience understand them. If you skip too much of the middle, they may not be able to follow you to the end.

This next story is a cautionary tale. Sometimes, you need to find the right stories for your audience or the right way to tell them. As we said in Chapter 11, you may need to be willing to try different approaches until you find one that works.

LEARNING FROM A TOUGH ROOM

Some five years after finishing graduate school and entering industry, I still had some vestiges of academia clinging to my thinking. So when I was asked to help find a way to better express a complex chart of user experience technologies to my department of researchers, my approach was based on a number of wrong assumptions. The chart was a spider chart—a graph where the axes were *Intelligence, Connection,* and *User Interface.* Scattered all over the chart were references to general and specific research areas that were colored according to which of three categories they fell in—*Capability, Technology,* and *Realization.* I'll spare you a picture of the chart here—suffice it to say that it was complex. The chart also acted as a collection of various technologies and concepts my department was interested in, and I was asked to help better express it—to help *tell it.*

We started by reducing the number of items on the chart, picking a choice few, and showing the relevant connections between them. Essentially, we were treating a few technologies as separate story characters and showing how the paths of these characters crossed. This method fell flat with the audience. I assumed that if I showed the audience a loose structure, they would fill in the meaning. They didn't.

I next created a set of short stories that specifically showed how small sets of the various technologies worked together and even evolved from one to another. For each story, I listed specific technology and cultural assumptions and references to established internal research projects. Again, my effort fell flat. I'd assumed that my audience was interested in reading. Half-page stories were simply too long, I was told.

Next, I kept the same basic structure listing assumptions and research references, but dramatically shortened each story to the bare minimum, typically using only one sentence each for the story setup/character motivation, core of the story, and then story conclusion. I also included an "experience path" for each story that listed a proposed evolution of technologies and experiences. I basically broke it all down for them. But again it fell flat. I assumed that my audience actually wanted what they asked for. I also assumed that if I gave them all the necessary component parts of a full experience, including content, structure, and a way to put it together, they would mentally construct an experience of their own. They didn't.

Distilling the stories further, I decided that for a final year report I would tell an animated visual story. For a half-hour presentation, I produced 17 short animations with the help of a graphic artist, all based on the previous story work. I finished the presentation with slides that made the case for what our department should be researching going forward, as suggested by the stories. When it was over, it was a very quiet conference room. It was not the response I was hoping for.

Out of 17 stories, one of them sparked their interest enough to say, "Hey, that looks good. Can we do that? Is that possible? Call Bob in here to take a look at this." I was lucky. One story triggered action. And that was a start. ■

When a story is rejected, you may have tried to take the audience too far in a single jump. One tactic is to start with a story that illuminates what currently exists before you tell one that reaches for something completely new.

Use stories to advocate

Steve Denning says that stories are a way to leap past logical arguments that have to be won individually, one person at a time. Pioneers in accessibility spend much of their time advocating for good user experiences for people with disabilities. Accessibility advocates have tried many different approaches, from appeals to good will to making the case for a return on development investment to new laws and litigation.

Recently, we've been seeing storytelling used as an advocacy tool. This approach is similar to the way Michael Anderson used a simple story to draw an analogy, as seen in Chapter 2.

STORIES AS A NEW APPROACH

Mike Paciello helped start the W3C's Web Accessibility Initiative (WAI) and has twice served on committees to draft accessibility regulations in the U.S. In 2009, he ran a workshop at the Cal-State Northridge Conference on Technology and People with Disabilities (CSUN). He used some of the exercises from our storytelling workshop (and this book). Here's how he described the event:

We had eight participants from many different backgrounds: one person with low vision, and one who was blind, two usability engineers, three from either the U.S. or Canadian federal government, four international, two from private industry. Two were familiar with storytelling, but none had much experience with it.

To a person, each individual was motivated to come to this workshop because of years of negative vibes from engineers, developers, and designers when it came to leveraging, prioritizing, and then implementing accessibility in Web and software applications. Two of the individuals had thrown in the proverbial towel and decided that the only tactic left was to resort to litigation.

However, storytelling gave them a new light. Properly structured stories around personas could have a strong impact. They saw how important it was to build empathetic listening skills, and liked experimenting with new ways to use perspective and imagery to make a point.

In the end, they saw storytelling as a positive approach that would help them build relationships. ■

Sometimes, a simple story can make a point by creating a situation in which the problem is inescapable. Instead of lecturing the audience that they don't "get it," the story can create a situation in which they can come to the conclusion on their own.

ACCESSIBILITY TO THE FACE

Jennifer Sutton found this story for us in a longer blog post by Rob Foster on North Temple's Web site (http://northtemple. com/2009/03/24/accessibility-to-the-face)*:*

The issues of accessibility are a daily reality for my family. For us, it's not a political issue at all. Our oldest daughter, Ramona, has cerebral palsy and uses a wheelchair to get around.

Allow me to give you a glimpse of what this aspect of our life is like. Last year, my wife and I took the kids to the Hogle Zoo here in Salt Lake. Before we left, my wife called the information desk to find out if the zoo train was an option for Ramona. Ramona loves to ride on trains.

Anna: Is the train accessible to wheelchairs?

The Girl: Yes.

Anna: So how does that work? How do I actually get the wheelchair on the train?

The Girl: Well, you take the chair to the edge and then you would lift her out and into the train.

Anna: So it's not wheelchair accessible.

The Girl: No, I guess not.

The girl on the phone had never thought of a real situation. She just had a cursory knowledge of the concept. For her, accessibility was a policy.

A few months ago, Anna called ahead to an Italian restaurant we wanted to visit to find out if we could get inside easily with the wheelchair.

Anna: Is your restaurant accessible?"

Host: Yes.

Anna: So we won't have any problem getting a wheelchair inside?

Host: Nope.

So we arrived at the restaurant. I walked up a flight of steps and let the host know we had a wheelchair. He had us meet him at the back entrance where we walked through the kitchen and ran into a very tall step.

Host: Oh, I guess there *is* that one step. Sorry about that.

Now, I'm a pretty big guy, and after 11 years of lifting Ramona and her chair into all kinds of places, one step was not going to keep me from enjoying the evening. I eat steps like that for breakfast. That said, Ramona and her current (non-electric) wheelchair weigh about 170 pounds. We've looked at electric (power) wheelchairs for her and the low-end from a weight perspective is about 150 pounds. If she had a power chair, we would not have been eating baked ziti that night. ■

The movie, *Rory O'Shea Was Here (Inside I'm Dancing)* makes the same point with a visual image. Two young men in wheelchairs are looking for an apartment. In one scene, they are following a real-estate agent down the street, listening to him describe the glories of an apartment. Suddenly they stop, and we hear the agent keep talking. The camera pulls back to show Rory O'Shea looking up a long set of stairs from his wheelchair. "See a problem?" he asks.

Bring them home safely

We've talked a lot in this chapter about pushing the audience to see a situation in a new light or getting them out of their comfort zone. Your job is to take them on a journey, not abandon them before they have finished it. As Kevin puts it in his performance-oriented storytelling workshops, you have a responsibility to "bring the audience home safely."

HOME SAFELY

Professional storyteller Laura Packer performs largely to adult audiences with original material. She knows firsthand the importance of bringing the audience home safely. UX stories are not typically this "deep," but still this is a good lesson on the role and responsibility of the storyteller. All audiences need to feel safe.

One of the great things about storytelling is the way it lets you connect with audiences on a deep level. You can talk about things in stories that you may not be able to address as easily in direct ways. Tough topics, like illness, can be touched on in a story, where the listeners can take in the tale without having to tell you anything personal or worry about you and your horrible experiences.

I do this regularly in a performance; I tell stories that talk about tough subjects with stories that touch on mental illness, abuse, homelessness, cancer, and so on. The audience listens to the story, but by the end there is a resolution, they are back in themselves and know that the experience I'm talking about is not an experience that's going to haunt them.

When I first started telling these kinds of stories, I didn't always do a good job of bringing the audience home, making sure they were in a safe place at the end. So my listeners would end up being worried about me or were just unsettled, rather than satisfied listeners. For example, I'd forget to tell them how the illness resolved (even if someone never gets better, the audience needs to know), and they would feel unsettled, some would even ask me what happened. They weren't in a safe place.

Even stories where characters are injured, die, or have other traumatic experiences can end with safety by using familiar language or tropes. Many fairy tales are quite violent, but at the end "they all lived happily ever after." Characters may die in myths, but it serves a purpose—the listener understands the symbolic value of the event.

Audience safety is part of the implied contract between teller and listeners. They need to know you won't leave them out in the woods. As a performing artist, it would be a violation of my audience's trust if I took them out to the forest and left them, unable to find their way home. ■

As a storyteller, you are in charge of managing the relationship between the audience and the story, as well as the one between you and the audience. As Laura Packer described, if you leave them feeling too vulnerable, unsettled, or just uncomfortable, they may react badly. This might be as simple as their not liking your story, or it might mean that they reject the whole idea you are trying to communicate.

This doesn't have to mean always providing a happy ending, but you do have to be sure you provide *an* ending, either within the story or during the discussion that follows. It's like taking a college course where the final exam counts for 50% of the grade. In this case, the final images that end the story are at least 50% of what the audience remembers and retells about your story. So bringing them home safely not only refers to the safety of the audience, but also refers to your effectiveness as a storyteller. As we say in "End the story well" in Chapter 4, this doesn't have to mean always providing a happy ending.

More reading

The Springboard: How Storytelling Ignites Action in Knowledge Era Organizations, Steve Denning

The story of the Adaptive Path's project to develop the Charmr is told in a series of blog entries: www.adaptivepath.com/blog/2007/08/14/charmr-a-design-concept-for-diabetes-management-devices/

"Towards the Design of Effective Formative Test Reports," Mary Theofanos and Whitney Quesenbery in the Journal of Usability Studies: www.usabilityprofessionals.org/upa_publications/jus/2005_november/formative.html

Summary

Remember that all storytelling is partly about the audience. Each person in the audience hears the story through their own perspective. When you craft your story to take that perspective and their background knowledge into account, the audience can listen to your story without distractions.

- Consider your relationship to the audience and what you both know about the context of the story.

- Choose details that will engage them and help them bridge the gap between their world and the place you want the story to take them.

- Stories can be an effective way to advocate, by helping the audience see a situation from a different perspective.

- Find a way to end the story that provides a memorable and settled resolution.

Combining the Ingredients of a Story

Now that we've considered who we are going to create a story for, let's think about what we have to work with as we put the story together.

Stories are made up of the following ingredients, each one helping shape the story:

- **Perspective:** The point of view from which the story is told

- **Characters:** The people in the story

- **Context:** The environment in which the story unfolds

- **Imagery:** The visual, emotional, or sensory texture the story evokes

- **Language:** The linguistic style in which the story is told, as well as the style of speech of the different characters

Gather your ingredients, combine according to a recipe or story structure (discussed in the next chapter), and you can craft an effective story. In this chapter, we'll focus on the ingredients.

Perspective

Every story is told from at least one point of view. In user experience stories, there is no such thing as a neutral point of view. How you present the characters, context, and events of the story is part of the point. Change the perspective, and you change the story, shaping it to either work for a specific audience or make your point more clearly.

The story of the blind men and the elephant is a classic example of perspective and how it shapes what we experience.

> A group of blind men are introduced to an elephant. The man who touched the elephant's side said, "The elephant is like a wall." The man who touched the elephant's tusk said, "No, the elephant is like a spear." The man who touched the elephant's trunk said, "No, the elephant is like a large snake." The man who touched the elephant's leg said, "No that's ridiculous. The elephant is like a tree." And the man who touched the elephant's tail said, "No you're all mistaken, the elephant is like a rope."

In this story, each of the blind men touched a different part of the elephant, and came away with a different perspective. None of their experiences were *wrong*, but none of them reflected the entire elephant, either.

When you choose the perspective for a story, you are choosing a subset of all of the experiential possibilities. The perspective (or perspectives) you choose limits what the people in the story see and experience. This determines the information you give the audience—and, more important, what you don't—and therefore changes their experience of the story.

One way to decide on a perspective is to consider the goals or attitudes you want the story to reflect. Imagine four people describing why they use an online bookstore:

> "I use it to buy books. The selection is great, and the prices are the best."

> "I use it for book reviews, reading what different people said about the books I want to buy. Then I go support my local bookstore."

> "I use it because I can send presents to my family easily. I keep their shipping information online."

> "I rarely buy anything from them, but I'm on the site a lot because it's useful for comparison shopping for things I want to buy on eBay."

Each of these perspectives could be the basis for a different story about using the site, reflecting different ideas about what this online bookstore is good for and how it fits into their lives.

So far, we don't know much about these people. When we add character, we'll add personal details like gender, culture, race, age, height, wealth, and social influence. Character affects perspective, of course, and the central character of a story can often be a shorthand way of thinking about perspective. But for now, stay focused on what story you want to tell and what perspective will help you make your point.

If you don't think perspective matters, think about *House*, the popular TV medical drama. Each show is a detective story, as the doctors try to solve perplexing medical cases. There is a central character (Dr. House) and a patient. House's medical colleagues are a set of supporting characters. Their goal is to find the bad guy (diagnose the patient's condition correctly) and save the day. There is always one other set of characters: the patient's relatives, who have to give permission for each (usually more and more dangerous) medical procedure. The stories in *House* are told from the perspective of the doctors: the disease is the enemy, and the relatives and hospital bureaucrats are barriers to be swept out of the way so they can (almost inevitably) save the day.

But what if we told these stories from the perspective of the relatives? They are worried, scared, and being asked to make life-and-death decisions instantly. They are pushed out of the way, bullied, and even lied to. For example, in one episode, House asks a colleague to call the patient's mother pretending to be from the CDC, so that she will agree to a procedure. If we told these stories from the relatives' perspective, *House* would be a very different show.

Adaptive Path did something like this when they designed their diabetes monitoring device (see Chapter 12). Instead of starting from the chemistry or from manufacturing requirements, they started from the experience of people with diabetes. That perspective changed the stories they told and the design they created.

You can use perspective in the same way in stories that explore the experiences of people who are new to technology or for whom the inner workings, language, and customs of computer use are new or unknown. You might show ways in which a product can be used that the designers and engineer never dreamed of. Used in this way, stories can help broaden the design vision.

Remember the story about a new parking technology from Chapter 10? That idea fell flat because it needed the perspective of an urban driver and the challenges of parallel parking to help it make sense. What if the researchers proposing that technology had given more weight to the parallel parking perspective instead of assuming that any and all would automatically see the value in it?

- You could tell the story from the perspective of a parking garage or garage manager, concerned about how hard it is for different cars to park well. Computer-assisted parking could mean the garage space would be better utilized or that parking and car retrieval would be much faster. (We've seen a TV ad for a car from the perspective of a tree to a curb. All the *other* cars bumped into it, but not the featured brand.)

- You could tell the story from the perspective of an urban driver, circling for many blocks, looking for a spot that would be easy to get into.

- You could make the environment or an environmental advocate the central perspective. All that time looking for a parking space and blocking traffic during slow and inaccurate parking attempts just adds to pollution and global warming!

- You could take the perspective of the city itself, showing how all the time spent trying to park adds up across the population. Imagine a visual story with an aerial view of a city block, with timers counting up all the time that's wasted.

Your own relationship to the story affects your choice of perspective

In Chapter 12, we talked about your relationship to the audience and to the story. When your story is about user experience work, you are a part of the story because you were there to collect it. You have to decide how to include your own perceptions, if at all.

Ethnographers, who may spend long periods of time in the setting of a story, always have to wrestle with this question. In *Tales of the Field: On Writing Ethnography*, John Van Mannen identifies three genres of storytelling for writing ethnography based on different relationships between the storyteller and the audience, which shape the structure of the story. His three genres are realist, confessional, and impressionist tales.

Realist tales

Realist tales are stories told in third person with the author largely absent from the finished text. This means that the narrative centers on reporting what the people in the narrative did, said, or thought. It's a documentary format, focused on concrete references. There is an implicit claim to authority—that the events described in the story really happened or might really happen.

Realist tales are useful as a way to document context of use or to create a story to describe typical events or activities. Most persona stories are written in this matter-of-fact style. They may have some detail, but primarily focus on activities and interaction rather than emotion.

This example of a realist story describes a simple context and shows the main character using an interactive system to solve a problem.

WAITING FOR THE BUS
There is nothing more frustrating than waiting for a bus in the snow and not knowing whether you are late or the bus is. Sandra didn't like snow much anyway, but she liked standing at the bus stop even less. She was pretty sure she was on time, but on her route, the bus sometimes got ahead of the published schedule. After she'd waited for a few minutes, she brushed enough snow off the sign to be able to read the stop number. She had the RideFind number in her contact list, so all she had to do was enter the number of the bus stop into a text message. A couple of seconds later, the reply came back. The bus was 10 minutes away, running late. She'd get to work this morning. ■

Confessional tales

Confessional tales are stories told in first person, which are focused on the experience of the author. As a report on research, this style most explicitly acknowledges the author's role in the work—selecting the people to work with, what to observe, and how much weight to give to various informants and observations.

These tales are a way to share experiences: what you learned, ideas about the design process, and (perhaps) how you overcame problems. Many of the stories in this book are in this style. The story "Seeing the business from their point of view" in Chapter 12 uses a confessional style to create a bridge between client and developer perspectives. By speaking directly from personal experience, these stories can help you connect directly to your audience. They can also be a disarming way to share insights, by framing them as things that surprised *you*.

Lou Rosenfeld's story, "A story can give you time," in Chapter 15, about getting a team to work together is an example of a confessional tale. Instead of trying to describe what the people within the client company were thinking, he told the story from his own perspective. This genre can be a useful way to introduce yourself to a new audience and make a connection to them.

TELLING THE STORY OF HOW I GOT THERE

Despite my passion for the subject, when I speak to groups about accessibility, I always feel like a newcomer to the field. So many others have been working in it for so much longer, and know so much more.

One year, I gave the opening talk at Knowbility's Access U conference. Everyone in the audience was there because they wanted to learn about how to make Web sites and other technology more accessible. I didn't need to convince them about the importance of accessibility, but I did want to talk about why it's important that the access be usable. Instead of diving into the "what and why" of usability, I started by telling the story of how I became an accessibility advocate.

It was a story about connecting the dots. I told them about three things that had happened to me and how they made the connection between my work and accessibility. By making the story personal, I didn't have to claim that everyone should follow the same path. By making the story personal, I could include topics that they might not think of as part of accessibility, and show why they were. And I didn't run the risk of criticizing the pioneers, because all I was doing was telling them how *I* got there. ■

This might seem like a risky strategy. After all, if you are an expert, shouldn't you be sharing that expertise, not your own problems and personal experiences? Perhaps. But you may find that telling the story through your own perspective can be a good way to acknowledge the difficulty of the topic and show the audience that they can come through the challenges to insights.

Impressionist tales
Impressionist tales mix a description of events with a strong story structure. As Van Mannen describes it, this genre holds back on interpretations "Saying, in effect, 'here is this world, make of it what you will.' ... The intention is not to tell readers what to think of an experience, but to show them the experience from beginning to end and thus draw them immediately into the story to work out its problems and puzzles as they unfold."

Impressionist tales are intended to spark ideas and actions in the readers, just as user experience stories can be the starting point for a design idea. They might start with the context of the story, perhaps including your position as an observer, but then move into a more dramatic re-telling of the events. These stories can have an ending, but might also end with an explicit or implicit question.

This impressionist story describes a missed business meeting. It draws no conclusions, but might suggest a few ideas about the people in the story. This story is told in first person, as though it is a recounting of a story as it was told to you. Third person works just as well.

MISSING THE MEETING

I work for a small consulting company. If you've ever worked in that environment, you'll know that one of the most important events is the big meeting with a potential new client. These meetings are the culmination of a lot of work, and can represent a big chunk of future income.

One January, the head of the company was scheduled for "A Big Meeting" a few hours from our office. We came in and made sure everything was ready. During the morning, it started to snow. Hard.

The traffic and weather reports started to sound dangerous, with accidents reported on the highways. "Cancel," we said. "No point risking the drive." But the boss decided to push ahead. "Have to show we are dedicated."

Presentation. *Check*. Company profile folders. *Check*. Boots. *Check*. And off he went. He left an hour early, just to be sure.

Forty-five minutes later, he called. He'd fishtailed into a snowdrift, and would we please call a tow truck and tell them he'd be late to the meeting.

We dialed the number, ready to tell them that the boss would be there, if a little late. Really. The phone rang through to the receptionist. "Sorry," she said. "He's left for the day. With all this snow, he decided the safest thing to do was to leave his car in the city and take the train home early."

Oops. We were so focused on getting to the meeting that we had forgotten that other people might go home early when it snows hard. ∎

How to add perspective

The most common way of adding perspective is by having the main character of your story do the talking. What this character says will then frame the main points in the story. This is because every character represents a different set of life experiences.

HSBC runs a series of ads based on point of view. They pair images with words describing different reactions to them. For example, a backpack might represent adventure, fear, or debt. Or a single word—"security"—might be explored through multiple images: an island compound, a teddy bear, and a password field. Each of the images suggests a story with different characters and different experiences. The message of the ads is that there are many different perspectives, and (implicitly) that you need a bank that understands them all. You can see the ads on their Web site, Your Point of View (www.yourpointofview.com).

Changes in perspective can also suggest different needs that a new design can meet. For example, one character might describe a nighttime scene as dark and ominous, while a different character might see that same scene as quiet and peaceful. If you were telling a story to explore a mobile phone for the first perspective, you might want features like a bright backlight that could be used as a flashlight and perhaps add a special-purpose emergency call button. The second perspective might suggest quick-and-easy control of ringtone volume to avoid disturbing the peaceful surroundings.

Another way to add perspective is to create an unexpected situation or context. The contrast between the expected story and the one you choose to tell creates a new perspective on the experience. Television ads use this technique because it makes the ads (and therefore hopefully the products) more memorable. A good example of this is a UK television ad for the Honda CR-V from many years ago. Narrated by Garrison Keillor, of the long-running radio show, *Prairie Home Companion*, the ad shows vehicles and people jumping out and around a car, while the driver avoids both them and the street maintenance work. The narrator talks about how adventurous one has to be because of this accepted way of life "in one of the most inhospitable places on earth." However, intercut with these images is a scene of an assembling audience watching the movie of the same driving images. The movie is being shown outdoors on the side of a building in rugged terrain, and the audience appears to be farm workers in Mexico or South America. They smile and laugh at the crazy European scene of cars and trucks barely missing each other. The ad creates a strong contrast between the perspective of people in Orpington, UK and those farm workers about what a really inhospitable place is (www.youtube.com/watch?v=b_gEqCcoh80).

As we said in Chapter 12, when you are crafting a story, you start with the audience. Their relationship to the story, and your purpose in telling them the story, are an important part of your perspective.

 THE LION'S STORY

There was a father who always told his son the same story every night. It was a story about a lion who hunted an antelope, and the antelope always outsmarted the lion. After hearing the same story every night, night after night, finally the child stopped his father and asked, "When does the lion win?" The father put the book down and said, "The lion will win when the lion tells the story."—African proverb ■

Characters

A character is a person (or other animate object) in a story. "Character" also refers to the defining traits of those people. It's the second meaning that concerns us most. Those characteristics distinguish a well-drawn persona from an actor in a use case, and help us understand the character's motivations, preferences, and goals.

One of the reasons stories are so useful in user experience design is that they add specificity and texture to the one-dimensional views of *users* that we often see. You can make your characters vivid by how you describe them. For example:

> He is proud of having been admitted and then flunking out of the best universities in the country.

In one sentence, you already have some clear ideas about this person's attitude toward life. The choice of character can help you shape the story by having the character's actions support, or contradict, expectations. You can make the audience feel comfortable by using familiar types or create tension by using unusual or disquieting attributes.

- If you have a character who is an "army staff sergeant," he might be a large, gruff man... or an understated woman.

- That "army staff sergeant" might be described as "no nonsense and to the point." Or you might describe him or her as someone who wants comprehensive information to make better decisions.

These should not be whimsical decisions, but careful choices to help craft the story. In most situations, you will want to base your characters on data or on stories you have collected. This is especially true if you are making an unexpected choice.

One exception to this rule is when you deliberately choose an *unlikely* character. We chose Sister Sarah for the story about finding a car in a large parking lot because she was an unlikely choice. She reminds us that even those we might not think of as technologically savvy have day-to-day problems that our products can solve.

Another good use of character traits is to highlight the needs of people outside the mainstream: those with less economic means, or who come from a different ethnic culture or geographic location, or who have disabilities. When these characteristics are just part of a character, instead of the central point, they can open the door to thinking about a wider vision of "the user."

The careful use of character attributes can also help address perspectives of the design team by bringing to the surface the diversity of the team itself. For example, everyone will have different feelings about baseball games: they may love them, hate them, or have never been to a baseball game at all. But that doesn't mean you can't tell a story about someone whose key characteristic is a love for the game. If you have multiple characters, you can distribute their interests so that everyone on the team has someone to root for.

How to create characters

You can use common archetypes as shortcuts to establish expectations quickly about your characters, expectations you can then either meet or refute. Of course, you need to make sure these shortcuts convey the meaning you intend with your audience. Calling someone a "soccer mom" might evoke empathy, disdain, or even confusion, depending on whom you're talking to.

The details you choose to build your character will depend on the story you are telling and the larger context of the company or project.

- **Choose details that add meaning.** Use details to make the characters real, but don't bog them down in so much detail that they (and the story) become boring. Choose details that make sense for the context of the story. Each piece of information you add should help the audience understand the character's actions a little better.

- **Show, don't just tell.** Find ways to communicate characteristics that describe actions ("show") rather than just piling on a series of adjectives ("tell"). For instance, you can describe a character as "a strong single mom who knows how to stretch a dollar." Or you could describe her as "a woman who plans out four full dinner meals every week for herself and her two kids that she stretches to seven meals." Or use a metaphor: "Here's a mom that can make a Monday chicken work all week long."

- **Foreshadow.** Set up "hooks" that you can use later in the story. For example, if a character is a cancer survivor, that fact might be used later to speak to that person's patience, experience, perseverance, and drive. You could say that a character is "both overly cautious and impatient," or you can suggest this by describing the way she drives or shops: "She drives like her 80-year-old grandmother, but sprints through stores."

- **Leave room.** Be sure to let the audience imagine some aspects of the characters on their own.

Screenwriting offers good lessons for developing characters

A lot of guidance on screenwriting focuses on developing character. Many of these techniques are best used in a longer story, where you have the time and space to explore character in more detail. There is one, however, that is useful even in short user experience stories.

Although not a widely known, the term "dictio" is used in screenwriting to refer to what a character explicitly says when it's the opposite of what they end up doing by the end of the movie. For instance, if in the first 10 minutes of a movie the main character says, "I hate dishonesty. I'll always tell you the truth," it's a safe bet that by the end of the movie that character will either lie or be heavily conflicted about the virtues of the truth or the occasional inconveniences of telling the truth. There are many good examples in American movies, especially those with particularly strong or strident main characters.

The movie has just begun. You have just met the main character, and the plot hasn't gotten started. All of sudden, a character framed in a medium shot or close-up makes some absolute definitive statement about the world or themselves. "You're coming with me and that's it." "I'll always love you no matter what." "It's the money that matters and nothing else." This is the character's dictio—or what the character claims to stand for. It's also the screenwriter saying, "*Hello, big hint here. This is where the conflict will take place.*"

Anyone who has watched a lot of usability tests will recognize this tension between what people say and what they do. People who say they don't like online forums may be the ones who end up spending the most time exploring one. Or someone who says she doesn't know how to use the Web very well may prove to be perfectly competent at browsing, just not confident about it.

In a user experience story, you might use a character's dictio to show how an early objection can be overcome by a better experience or changing conditions. For instance, there could be a character who hates the idea of having a cell phone.

> I don't need a cell phone. Besides, they're too complex with their menus and tiny buttons. I don't need the aggravation.

This would remain true in the story until he is won over by being able to talk to his 6-year-old granddaughter whenever she is free, instead of just when he happens to be sitting next to his home phone.

> Well, I get to talk to Emily when she gets home from school.

Then you can make the choice of having the character remain at that level of acceptance or push him further.

> Well, if I have my cell phone, I don't have to wear a watch. Plus, my son can send me pictures of Emily.

Personas can be your characters

If you have already created personas, you have your basic characters.

Hopefully, your personas are based on data, representing important users or customers for your products. Now, you can add some characteristics that can help you tell stories about the personas. These characteristics should not be random; base them on story fragments or other details you have collected during your user research.

If you are constructing a set of personas, one trick is to have a few characteristics that you give to each of them. The differences in the details can help you distinguish aspects of their character. Some ideas include:

- Their pets and how they relate to them (daily runs with their golden retriever, or the many toys underfoot for their pampered cat)

- Their weekend activities (sports, gardening, volunteering...)

- How they dress for rain (newspaper held over their head, sensible raincoat, raincoat with an impressionist painting)

- The kind of car they drive (or the condition of the inside of the car)

Context

Context is the environment for the story. It's the stuff that connects to and surrounds the central core of the story. Some context is explicitly stated by the storyteller and some of it is inferred by the audience. Context is also the *what, when,* and *where* of the events in the story.

It was a dark and stormy night.

It was 5 p.m., Friday, Christmas Eve.

It was Atlanta, Georgia, in July.

It was in the middle of nowhere.

The story itself might be quite simple:

I loved her, but then we broke up.

I wanted to win, but I lost instead.

She lost her keys, but found them.

He saw a woman who looked like an angel, but cursed like a sailor.

There isn't much to these simple ideas for stories. But they can be combined with contexts to become the seeds of epic tales of love, battle, mystery, or discovery. It's all a matter of context.

It was 5 p.m., rush hour, on Christmas Eve, when I first saw her. She looked like an angel, but cursed like a sailor.

She was in the middle of nowhere, but she was online.

Not a bad start.

A user experience story may not start so dramatically, but it still needs a context to build on. You can build context in just a few words, letting the audience fill in the details. All stories rely on our ability to fill in the blanks.

As with character, the details you leave out are just as important as what you put in. While there are no hard and fast guidelines about what to leave out, consider leaving out noncritical details that might be fun for the audience to fill in for themselves. For instance, when telling a story about a dog, you probably want to make sure you're clear that the animal is a dog. But you might not have to mention the breed of dog. This would allow the audience to fill in this detail themselves, possibly with the breed of their own dogs.

MI CASA ES SU CASA

I used to teach scriptwriting for multimedia in an EU program in Lisbon. In that program, half of the 20 or so students were Portuguese and the other half were from countries all over Europe. In the context section of the class, I would tell a story about my cat when I was a kid. The main part of the story described an event that took all of about three seconds in real time, but I surrounded it with explicit and implicit context, which made the whole story last about 12 minutes.

At the end of the story, I asked the students questions like, "What did my house look like? What did my living room look like? What did my bedroom look like? How was the furniture arranged in my bedroom?" They all had clear answers to these questions, though I described none of these details in the story. Furthermore, when describing my house, to the Swedes my house looked Swedish, to the Germans my house looked German, to the Spanish my house looked Spanish. I told them they were all correct. ■

When you set the context for a story, you can use those assumptions to keep the story short, focusing on the details that are important to the point of the story. Here's an example that Kevin uses in his workshops.

> As a little kid in the 1960s, I grew up listening to Motown—The
> Temptations, The Four Tops, Smokey Robinson. It's not like I
> was a big fan of rhythm & blues back then, but more that rhythm
> & blues was part of the air we all breathed. I still have a copy of
> my older sister's high school graduation picture when she had that
> popular beehive hairdo, just like Diana Ross had when we saw her
> on our black-and-white TV singing, "Stop in the name of love."

What have you learned about the context from this opening to a story?

- Kevin's approximate age

- That he's from the United States, probably from a city

- That he has an older sister

- That he is probably telling his own story and not someone else's

In this story so far, there is a strong context of time, but no specific place. The audience can fill in the place with their own experience, be it Detroit, Los Angeles, London, or Amsterdam. And when filled in with their own details, the story becomes more interesting and more relevant to them.

How to add context

There are five aspects of context we'll describe here. There are more, but these five are a good starting point. They are physical, emotional, sensory, historical, and memory.

Physical context

Here is what the physical world is like at the time of the story. It includes this information:

- Time of day (11 p.m.)

- Month or season (December, New Year's Eve)

- Physical location (New York's Times Square)

- Scale of location—large scale (the Grand Canyon), small scale (huddled under the Mr. Peanut sign on the corner of 7th Ave., craning my neck to look down Broadway), or even smaller (intimately sandwiched between my friend Mary and a very excited person from Minnesota)

Emotional context

This type of context shows how the characters are feeling emotionally. Are they happy, sad, cynical, angry, frustrated, etc.? If you, as the storyteller, are part of the story, your feelings are part of the emotional context that relates to your audience.

Sensory context

This is the context experienced through the five senses.

- What does the world *look* like?

- What is the *sound* of the world of the story?

- What can the characters *smell* or *taste*?

- What textures can be *felt*?

Kevin's story about Tokyo in Chapter 2 relies on a sensory context, the contrast between the noisy street and the quiet, peaceful shrine.

Historical context

Here, you'll find the information that places the story in a particular time or place. Historical context can be a small or quick reference to something that the audience might recognize, either specifically (like the Vietnam war) or metaphorically: "Back when the world was young," or, "Back when dialing a phone meant using an actual dial." For example:

> Back when Western Electric was the main manufacturer and supplier of American phones that were so over-engineered that they could easily be used as murder weapons, Bell Labs in New Jersey asked the question, "What if you could see the person you're talking to on the phone?"

Memory context

Memory context involves personal connections to the past. You can think of memory context as a common method of introducing flashbacks, like that old favorite, "Back when I was your age…" Often, the words used to introduce memory context are, "I remember." When a story includes those words, the audience will want to leap back in time with the storyteller. They will want to know the reason the teller is remembering these things and will travel back with them. Memory context acts like a type of glue, connecting one part of a story to another, forcing an audience to view new story material through a remembered context. The glue could be small, providing just a single image, thus making it easy for there to be multiple memory context pieces in the story.

Or the glue could be big. The movie *Saving Private Ryan* is told almost entirely in flashback. An old man is introduced walking in a cemetery presumably with his family. There's a classic flashback (facial zoom-in) to WWII where most of the movie takes place. The camera eventually brings us back to the old man and his family. The difference is that we now know who he is, what he went through, and why he's questioning his life. Anything he says at the end of the movie will be interpreted through the flashback story of the war. This is what memory context does well. It provides a lens through which the trailing part of the story or the end of the story can be seen and understood.

If you establish a memory context, you have to be sure that it resonates with the audience in the same way that it does for you. It is important to remember that for the audience each memory carries with it its own context, its own set of interpretations, and potentially even its own set of tangential stories. This is especially true for memory contexts that are strongly significant to a specific generation. People of different ages may have their own perspective on those events.

- Saying "I remember the 60s" to people born in 1985 means that their starting place for the 60s is what they've seen in the media—riots, hippies, marches, and the moon landing.

- Saying "I remember the 60s" to people born in the 50s or 60s mean they will at first refer back to their own experiences of the 60s, which are childhood experiences—TV shows, the big deal about integrating schools, classic GI Joe/Barbie, and possibly the moon landing.

These are almost two different worlds.

Context exercise

This is a version of an exercise that Kevin uses in his storytelling workshops.

1. Before the workshop, gather a collection of small objects. Look for common, insignificant objects that one might step over in the street: a small stone, a dried leaf, or a bottle cap.

2. Put people in pairs and give each of them one of the objects.

3. Each person has three minutes to use as many types of context as they can to tell a short story featuring the object.

These stories won't be perfect in just three minutes. The point is to learn to weave elements of the environment into the story.

As you get more practice, you can expand this exercise by thinking about some of the common items in the environment of your story. When you are out in the field, collect contextual details to weave into your stories later.

Here's an example that includes a number of different forms of context.

DIALING THE PHONE

When I worked for Motorola Labs PHYSICAL, there were periods of time when my job included improving the user experience for mobile phones: How might they be easier to use? What new functions might they perform? How might it be easier to call someone?

I remember, back when I was a kid HISTORICAL, I had to memorize my home telephone number, which started with Kingsley 5, or KI5. Because I would often take the bus downtown by myself to where my mother worked, I had to know how to call home in case of an emergency. So I memorized the numbers of my phone number, but that's not all I memorized.

What is also recorded deep in my being is how it felt to call home MEMORY. When you use a rotary dial, every number has its own rhythm. No matter how well you knew the number, you could only dial it so fast because the phone needed to express the number in its own time.

I'd put my finger in the holes and rotate clockwise as fast as I could, feeling the weight of the dial push back on my finger SENSORY: TEXTURE. But the dialing didn't actually happen until I pulled my finger out of the hole and let the dial recoil back. The number 2 in my phone number was quick. But the number 9 in my phone number required almost a complete turn of my skinny little finger and took forever to recoil, while I had to wait and listen to every tick—tick—tick SENSORY: SOUND. It's not so much that I dialed the number, but that the phone and I dialed together. It was collaborative.

The nature of dialing reinforced the number in my kinesthetic and auditory memory. I knew three interwoven forms of my phone number and every phone number. How can we build that interwoven reinforcing of a sensual experience of 40 years ago into modern technology? ■

Imagery

A well-defined context, a good beginning, middle, and end, interesting characters, and good timing are all important elements of a story, but as a story unfolds before an audience, all of these ingredients are really there to support the images the story leaves in the audience's mind. Listeners can forgive a lot of missing details and bad timing if there are good images.

You might think of imagery as visual pictures. Some types of multimedia storytelling can use actual images to tell part of the story. You can create images with words, too.

In performance storytelling, these images help make people laugh, cry, or think when they hear an effective story. It is the strong imagery in a story that makes them see the world differently. Even if all a story has is images, it would be almost complete. In the next chapter on story structures, there's a description of a type of story that is all images.

Perhaps you think that imagery has no place in a business story. Not so. One of the easiest ways to see the role of imagery in business stories is to look at vision stories. Annette Simmons is a business consultant who uses story as a basic element of her practice (http://groupprocessconsulting.com). In her book *Whoever Tells the Best Story Wins*, she describes a vision story as one that "raises your gaze from current difficulties to a future payoff that successfully competes with the temptation to give up, compromise, or change direction." This involves building an image of a critical moment or critical need, where the hunger for the vision is first created, then the vision supplied. Here is one example.

THEY DON'T LEAVE ONE OF THEIR OWN BEHIND
The robotics company iRobot tells a vision story around one of their products, the PackBot. (http://irobot.com/sp.cfm?pageid=171)

PackBot is a small tank-like robot designed to venture into places that would be dangerous for people, and then send back pictures or do simple mechanical tasks, all under remote control. PackBot is a complicated piece of machinery, developed over the course of many years by a large team of engineers. As with any piece of machinery, its development has included a fair share of challenges and frustrations.

One place it's being used is in war zones where there's a danger of unexploded bombs. One group of soldiers named their PackBot *Scooby-Doo*. After performing its duties admirably by detecting a number of unexploded ordinances, Scooby-Doo is now on display at iRobot headquarters. Destroyed by a bomb it was looking for, the soldiers carefully collected all its pieces and brought them back. They don't leave one of their own behind.

Scooby-Doo now sits in the company lobby, in pieces, as a reminder that this could have happened to a human being instead. So in meeting the ongoing engineering challenges and addressing the inevitable frustrations, ultimately what iRobot employees are doing is saving human lives. And Scooby-Doo reminds them of this as they enter the building everyday. ■

iRobot tells this vision story to every new employee, at internal and external company events and to a multitude of company visitors ranging from school children to the upper echelons of government. The images it leaves are powerful, even without physically seeing the robot. Images are the stuff that the audience imagines as they listen to the words and events of the story. You can help them along by providing some of the images.

How to add imagery

Imagery works with all the other ingredients—perspective, context, and character. It makes them memorable by adding word pictures that describe specific details. Consider the difference between these three openings to a story:

> It was 5 p.m. She was working on a report.

> It was late in the day. Her office walls were covered with Post-its outlining the main points they'd brainstormed that morning. The report was coming along nicely.

> She'd lost track of time, but the office was quiet. Her office walls were covered with Post-its outlining the main points they'd brainstormed that morning, and a pile of printouts was accumulating on her desk. A half-eaten sandwich lay on the side of her desk, long forgotten. The only sound was the tick-tick-tick of her fingers flying across the keyboard.

The first is strictly factual and gives few details to provide a physical context. We have a hint that she is on a deadline, because it's five o'clock and she's still working. But we don't know much else. Is she in a home office, huddled in a conference room, or at her workstation? Is she frantic or in a flow of work?

The second opening uses images to provide some hints by describing the physical context.

- She has an outline on the wall.

- She is working purposefully.

The third opening provides some hints by describing the emotional context.

- She's been working for some time, but hasn't been distracted by hunger.

- She's working steadily, but quickly.

Is this too much information? That depends on whether it's important that the audience can visualize the scene. Maybe this is a story about a collaborative tool that she will need. Or about what happens when she looks up from her report and realizes that she's supposed to meet friends across town.

The trick to adding imagery to a story lies in using just the right amount. Like character details, if you fill the story with too many images, it can overwhelm the audience. Or you can have the wrong imagery distracting the audience into focusing on something that doesn't support the point you are trying to make. Worse, you can be so specific that it leaves them no room to imagine the story themselves. But if you have too little imagery, the story is nothing more than a recitation of facts.

Language of the story

We've been talking about words used for images, but we need to say a few words about the language of the story itself. You want your stories to sound natural as you tell them (or as people read them) and to be authentic to the experience they are about. Here are a few suggestions.

- **Speak in the language of the characters.** Use the words they would use. Avoid technical language they would not know or insider jargon.

  Think about using phrasing and ways of speaking that are authentic to the characters in the story. When a story is based on real people or other user research, consider how you want the characters in the story to appear. You might choose to use their exact words, or you might clean up the language to make it more acceptable to the audience. (There is an example of this in Caroline Jarrett's story in Chapter 4.)

- **Make the story active.** Stories are active, so make the writing active, too. Make sure that the characters do, think, say, or feel things actively. Don't make them passive observers of what happens. Stories are an opportunity to let real experiences come through.

- **Focus on telling the story.** Avoid long explanations that are distracting or confusing. Focus on contextual details or imagery that support the purpose of the story. The same goes for technical details. Don't let the stories become a procedural description of how to use a product. If you find yourself stepping through actions like "clicked on a link" or "pressed a button," you may be writing great technical documentation, but not a good story.

- **Don't judge.** Let the characters, context, and events of the story speak for themselves. Don't use stories to poke fun at your characters or turn them into caricatures. Your point should come out of the ingredients and structure of the story, not be imposed as a punch line.

Putting the ingredients together

When you are constructing a story, choose the ingredients that will support the story and connect to the audience appropriately.

- Perspective and character give the story a point of view.

- Context sets it in an environment.

- Sensory and imagery details provide texture and emotion.

None of these are *extra*—they are what makes something a story and not just a chronological report. They carry information that helps the audience understand the story and make it their own, by better engaging their brains.

As you decide on the right mix, consider these questions:

- What do you have to say explicitly and what can you imply through one of the ingredients?

- What does your audience already know about the context or characters, and what do you have to be sure to tell them?

- How will the ingredients you choose fit together to make your point?

These ingredients—perspective, character, context, imagery, and language—support the events and make the story come alive in the minds of the audience, thereby creating the experience of the story.

Summary

The ingredients of a story are tools you can use to give your story meaning and texture. They are the following:

- **Perspective:** The point of view from which the story is told

- **Characters:** The people in the story

- **Context:** The environment in which the story unfolds

- **Imagery:** The visual, emotional, or sensory texture the story evokes

- **Language:** The linguistic style in which the story is told, as well as the style of speech of the different characters

Developing Structure and Plot

In this chapter, we reach the structure—the organization of events—of the story. In the previous two chapters, you have seen how you can tell a story from different perspectives or change the way you tell it to different audiences. Here, we will look at the elements of plot and structure.

- The structure is the framework of a story. It's the underlying skeletal pattern for the story.

- The plot is the arrangement of the events of the story, the sequence in which those events are revealed to the audience.

Story structure and plot are the path to bring the audience into the world created by the storyteller. When the audience can enter the story through a clear structure and plot, they can pay more attention to the story's larger themes and higher-level points, and are less likely to be distracted by logic and rational analysis. They can listen to the emotional subtext of the story, and be coaxed into its influence. They can "get it."

Story structures are patterns

Storytelling is one of the oldest art forms. We can imagine ancient hunters sitting around the communal fire at the end of the day, dressed in the skins of their kills, telling stories of their exploits. People haven't changed all that much: we still care about our families, our work, and moving forward with our lives, so some aspects of our stories haven't changed that much either. But even within a familiar structure, each story has its own pacing, images, and context. Most stories follow familiar structures. Even if there are twists and turns in the plot or surprises in how the ingredients are assembled, the basic structure is often a familiar one.

Some story structures are very simple:

- A boy meets a girl, they fall in love but are kept apart, and then finally they find each other again.

- A person is given a mission and sets out to fulfill it with the help of a band of friends. They overcome obstacles and eventually reach their goal.

Some structures are more complicated, such as stories that are in layers, each one revealing a little more of the details until a secret or underlying truth is found. Working with a familiar structure will help you build your story, and it will also help your audience understand it. You can focus on using the story to make a point.

The underlying structures of stories are found across many different cultures and languages. Although story scholars' approaches and taxonomies differ, they all look at the structure of a story as a journey that the characters take. Story scholars like Vladimir Propp and Joseph Campbell have studied the way stories have been told around the world and throughout time. Campbell and Propp's work have influenced Broadway and Hollywood. Campbell, for example, was an important influence on George Lucas as he developed *Star Wars*.

Campbell is most widely known for his book *The Hero with a Thousand Faces*. In it, he traces the hero story structure across cultures and across centuries, showing how consistent and universal it is. Many of his examples are drawn from myths. Joseph Campbell's work provides a detailed cross-cultural analysis of the hero's journey as it appears in stories from many cultures and languages. Campbell was especially fascinated by the way an individual's life story echoed the mythic hero's journey.

In the early part of the twentieth century, Propp catalogued and analyzed stories in *The Morphology of the Folktale*. Although Propp analyzed Russian folktales, his work applies to many types of stories and illustrates a relatively simple way that stories can be deconstructed. Propp identified 31 "functions" of fairy tales—classifiable actions that characters can take. He found that they occur in a consistent order, as found in Campbell's later work, but that the selection of functions varies from story to story. The combinations of these actions become grammar for story structure—a framework for how the story develops.

Propp's functions also follow a character's journey, with different events that may happen along the way. They are written in the language of fairy tales, but with a little imagination, it is easy to see how they might apply to any situation or life journey.

- The first functions set up a situation in which someone needs to be "rescued" or where there is a problem to be solved. They include warnings, ignoring those warnings, reconnaissance of the situation, trickery, deception, and outright villainy.

- In the middle of the story are a group of functions in which the hero leaves home to correct the situation and is tested. He (or she) may receive help from a magical agent and have to search for the villain, but ultimately confronts and overcomes the problem.

- Finally, the hero returns home (or is rescued). The hero may not be immediately recognized for his efforts, having to complete one more task before being rewarded.

The selection of functions determines the structure of the story. Propp believed that functions could be omitted from a story, but that they always appeared in the same order. Contemporary narrative scholars find Propp's work particularly interesting as the basis of computer models for constructing stories. You can look at one such model, called the *Proppian Fairy Tale Generator* (www.brown.edu/Courses/FR0133/ Fairytale_Generator/gen.html). We are not suggesting that you use a computer program to create your user experience stories, but these research experiments show that it is possible to create a plausible narrative with a computer program. You may find that using linear, logical structures as a framework is a helpful way to start constructing your own stories.

Both of these scholars looked at the patterns of stories in the same way that Christopher Alexander's *A Pattern Language* deconstructed architecture into a set of structures that could be rearranged and reused in endless creative ways.

Architecture is a good analogy for the function of structure in crafting a story. When you see a large building being built with its structural steel complete, you have some idea of the general shape of the finished building: how large it will be, how many floors, and so on. Even without seeing the color or external materials of the building, you can still get some sense of what the building will be like, and even how you might eventually navigate through it. (That is, with the possible exception of a building by architect Frank Gehry, with his typical use of fantastic superstructures of planes and shapes.)

It's the same for story structure—it's a framework for the finished story, before you add ingredients like character, context, or even the details of the plot. We've drawn on this tradition of analysis to suggest some story structures that you may find useful as you create your own stories.

Story structure helps the audience, the author, and the story

There are three main reasons to create a strong structure for a story.

- **It helps the audience.** When the audience recognizes the structure, they have another level of understanding of the story. They can listen to the details of *your* story more carefully, once they have a good expectation of how the story will be told; they don't have to waste time speculating on the direction of the story.

- **It helps the author.** Story structure is a navigational device, helping you figure out what's next or what's missing as you create a story.

- **It helps the story.** It can help move a story from a vague idea to something more solid, suggesting ways to organize it into a beginning, middle, and end.

Story structure provides familiarity to the storytelling process. But that doesn't mean each story has to be the same. You can play with the structure, following it closely or deliberately violating the audience's expectation with a twist. Without the platform of the structure and the expectations it creates, the twist has far less impact.

The familiarity of story structures can also provide comfort by giving the audience landmarks to use as they navigate the story. This can be particularly important if the topics of the story are unfamiliar or challenging. Familiar structural hints will help them grasp the story more easily. They may look for a wise mentor who shows up to help the hero or for flashbacks that illuminate events in the present.

User experience stories aren't on the momentous scale of an epic. And we aren't claiming they are great works of art. But UX stories are still about things that make a difference in the lives of real people. If you use a structure that is familiar to your audience, the context can add resonance and depth to a prosaic situation.

We talked in Chapter 12 about ways to let your audience see themselves in the story. In Chapter 2, Michael Anderson's persuasive story, "Using analogies to change people's minds," used analogies to allow his audience to relate their current situation to "a different story." Any story about an outsider who arrives to solve a problem that is blighting a community can be cast as Beowulf slaying the monster Grendel—that is, fixing something that is broken in a user experience. In fact, many user experience stories have the new product (and the people behind them) as implicit heroes. "Waiting for the bus" in Chapter 13, the story about Sandra and RideFind, is a story of someone rescued from distress.

Useful story structures for UX stories

From various collections of story structures, we have selected a few recognizable story structures that are useful in telling stories in user experience design. We offer them here as starting points for your stories. These structures are:

- **Prescriptive:** Structural templates that allow you to fill in the blank

- **Hero:** Using Joseph Campbell-inspired hero's journey elements

- **Familiar to foreign:** Using a different journey of sorts that begins with the comfortable and then stretches into the less familiar

- **Framed:** Stories that appear to begin and end the same way

- **Layered:** Using layered images to build a story experience

- **Contextual interludes:** Using diversions of physical or emotional details to add an extra dimension to a story

Prescriptive structures

A simple, straightforward story structure for user experience stories is prescriptive. All it requires is a fill-in-the-blanks approach, using whatever contextual details and outcomes are required for your application. Think of it as more of a logical argument structure that gets expanded into a story. *Given X, if Y, then Z.* To create a story with this structure you just need to figure out what elements in your project or environment satisfy the *XYZ* requirements of the structure. Dan North describes a prescriptive structure for what he calls Behavior-Driven Development:

1. Title

2. Given [context]

3. And [some more context]...

4. When [event]

5. Then [outcome]

6. And [another outcome]

By starting with the title, this structure immediately provides the audience with the subject matter of the story. It then requires some amount of context (where is this story, who are the main characters of the story, etc.), the major event, situation or problem, and finally the primary outcomes of the story, presumably the solutions.

This type of structure is widely applicable. While it's easy to fill in the blanks, you should pay attention to making the chain of causality plausible—to making sure that the story makes sense. While any structure is by its nature simple, it is all too possible to create an overly simplistic story. For instance, the "Widgets for prosperity" story below makes such a broad claim that it is almost nonsense. It's hard to imagine that an impulse purchase of a widget— no matter how low the price—could lead to prosperity.

WIDGETS FOR PROSPERITY

GIVEN Many people live their lives in need of more money. AND... If they could save money on their widgets, then they would have more money in their lives. WHEN When John walked downtown and saw the Acme

Widgets in the store window for half the price of the widgets from General Widget, ^{THEN} he immediately went in and bought them. ^{OUTCOME} Now John has more spending money in his life and is well on his way to prosperity. ■

All the elements of this story fit the structure. And while a bit overstated in order to make a point, the story itself is simplistic and would therefore be unconvincing. Here's an alternative:

WIDGETS (RETOLD)

^{GIVEN} John had been using his General Widget for three years. ^{AND…} Over the course of that time, he learned just how often he has to recharge it and how to navigate through the widget's menus to get to his two favorite and most used features. ^{WHEN} One day he saw an ad for an Acme Widget, which offered his same two favorite features in a way that was much easier to access. ^{THEN} John thought about all the time he would save accessing those features and decided to check it out at the store. When he did, he bought the Acme Widget, ^{OUTCOME} even more pleased that his new widget service costs half as much as his old widget service. ■

Hero stories

Many of the stories in this book have a hero—usually someone who has to overcome a problem. Joseph Campbell described this structure as a hero's journey, and identified several steps in the journey. In his structure, part of the story takes place in the everyday world and part in the world of the quest. The journey completes a cycle from one to the other and back, shown in Figure 14.1.

FIGURE 14.1
The hero story structure is a cycle. The point where the story ends can be the beginning of the next story.

1. **The call to adventure**

   Heroes start in the everyday world and receive a call to adventure. They usually resist at first, refusing to undertake the journey. (Think of the hobbits in *The Lord of the Rings* and how hard they tried to return to their comfortable life in Hobbiton.) A supernatural character (Gandalf the Grey) often comes to their aid and helps them take the first step on the journey. They may set out alone or with a band of companions (the Fellowship of the Ring). One of these companions (Sam Gamgee) acts as a window character—a reminder of life before the journey and how far the hero (Frodo) has come.

2. **The initiation and trials**

   The journey is often described as a series of trials and setbacks, which the hero must overcome (filling most of the story). Heroes meet goddesses and father figures, and are helped through their adventures by their companions. Often, each companion has a particular skill or characteristic that proves critical to the hero's success.

3. **Achieving the goal**

   The second stage ends with the achievement of the quest (destroying the Ring at Mount Doom).

4. **The return**

   Heroes must not only finish the quest, but also get out alive. They may need help to return to the world, with the object or knowledge of their quest. Ideally, they learn and grow from their mission and so return a changed person, ready to share their experience.

Hmm. Quests. Supernatural characters, goddesses. This may not sound much like user experience design, but this structure can be used for simple and prosaic "quests," as well as for epic and mythical ones. Here's a story that uses the heroic structure, elaborating on the short realist tale from Chapter 13, "Combining the Ingredients of a Story."

WAITING FOR THE BUS (RETOLD)

CALL TO ACTION There is nothing more frustrating than trying to get to work in the ice and snow, especially when using public transportation. REFUSAL Sandra pulled the covers over her head and thought about whether she could just call in sick. As she lay there thinking about just how much she didn't like the snow, she heard an announcement on the radio. She'd heard it a dozen times before, but had never really listened. SUPERNATURAL HELP OFFERED "RideFind," it said. "So you never have to guess where the bus is."

ACCEPTING THE QUEST "Right," she thought. "Time to try this one out." INITIATION AND TRIALS An hour later, she was up, dressed, and ready to leave.

TRIAL Outside, she scrambled over a pile of snow ploughed right across the entrance to her house. TRIAL Crossing the sidewalk, she slipped and fell. Sitting on the ground, she looked longingly back at her front door. She knew she could make it back there and still call in sick. TRIAL As she was picking herself up, she saw one bus chug slowly by. Her bus? Or the other one?

This seemed like the right time to try that RideFind number. TRIAL She slid into the pole with the bus stop sign, brushed the snow off the sign, and found the stop number right where the radio ad had said it would be.

ACHIEVEMENT OF THE GOAL Cell phone out. Gloves off. She typed in the number and...waited. If the bus were going to be more than 15 minutes, maybe she'd turn back. A couple of seconds later, the reply came back. THE RETURN (IMPLICIT) The bus was 10 minutes away.

MAKING USE OF THE KNOWLEDGE While she was waiting, someone else arrived, and Sandra gave her the good news. RESOLUTION They could both get to work this morning. ■

Let's look at how this story follows the hero's journey.

1. **The call to adventure**

    - An implicit call to action—have to get to work

    - A refusal—head under the covers

    - Supernatural help—the radio announcement and (by implication) the magic of the RideFind service

    - Acceptance of the quest—she leaves for work

2.   **Initiation and trials**

   - Trials and setbacks—slipping and falling, plus the temptation to give up

3.   **Achievement of the quest**

   - Trying the RideFind number

   - The information arrives

4.   **Return to the world**

   - Making use of her new knowledge—telling the other person about the bus

   - The arriving bus will take her to work

You could shift perspective and tell this story from the point of view of the network manager who keeps the RideFind service running, from the perspective of a bus driver, as the story of a band of intrepid commuters, or even as the observer coming up with this new idea from the trials of those commuters.

Familiar to foreign

These stories take the audience on a journey, starting with something familiar and comfortable, but then taking them toward the unknown. As with the hero structure, this structure starts in the "real world"—the world the audience already accepts. The goal of the story is to draw the audience into a new place, helping them make the transition by showing parallels between the familiar and the foreign and possibly illuminating something new about the familiar world.

Many TV commercials use this structure, particular for financial services and other nontangible products that may seem foreign or frightening. By setting the story in a familiar setting, the ads suggest that their service is also simple, homey, innocent, safe, smart, or practical. Like most commercials, these stories are compact and efficient, lasting just 30 seconds.

- A TV ad from Zurich Financial Services called What if? includes four short scenarios, each of which takes a common situation and asks "what if" to show an uncommon result.

- TV ads from Ameriprise Financial, starring Dennis Hopper, reverse this concept to show the familiar in the foreign. Hopper makes impassioned points standing alone in the middle of an unusual setting (a field of flowers, a deserted beach, a salt flat), followed by a sequence of familiar daily life images of people presumably acting on their dreams.

Lewis Carroll's *Alice in Wonderland* is a longer example of this structure. Alice first appears in the story as a bored girl sitting on the bank of a river in the English countryside. So far, pretty mundane. Then a white rabbit runs by. At first this is nothing amazing or unusual, except that the rabbit pulls a watch out of his waistcoat pocket and says, "Oh dear! Oh dear! I shall be late!" Since she has never seen a rabbit with a waistcoat and pocket watch, this sparks Alice's interest, and she follows him down the rabbit hole. Once inside Wonderland, she speaks with animals, a strange cat appears and disappears in front of her, and she meets a royal family of playing cards. All quite ridiculous, fantastic, and enjoyable, especially in contrast with the prosaic opening scene in the English countryside.

Starting in the familiar and moving to the less familiar or foreign is a common way to introduce new concepts to an audience. Consider this user experience story that could have been used in the early 1990s to drive product sales.

A LAWYER IN JAPAN

FAMILIAR A lawyer working for a large American electronics company took a business trip to Japan. Equipped with his pager, he knew that if someone from the office needed to get hold of him, all they had to do was dial his direct pager number, punch in a call-back number, and he'd get that message within seconds. All over the world, doctors, executives, and lawyers like himself were using pagers. He hoped to help negotiate a large deal with a Japanese company for a significant number of his company's pagers for a Japanese market of consumers like himself.

TRANSITION INTO THE UNFAMILIAR CULTURE His first night in Japan he had dinner with the customer executives. He'd never sat on the floor to eat before. Through the thick curtain of cigarette smoke, he watched the elder executives to take his cues for what to do next, such as when to drink and when to talk. The top executive suggested that he order a Kobe steak, renowned for its flavor and tenderness. He was delighted by his steak.

EVEN MORE UNFAMILIAR He didn't think of Japan as cattle country, with its big ranges, so he politely asked where the meat came from. He was told Hyogo Prefecture, where the cattle were meticulously cared for with land for grazing. It takes many people to take care of Kobe cattle, to ensure they get out into the field for grazing every day and get back to the stables for their special feed mixture and massage. He had never heard about cattle massage, but coming from cattle country in Montana, he did know some other things about cattle.

LEAP INTO THE UNKNOWN He asked if their company had ever tried marketing pagers to ranchers. With mild snickering, the response was, "No, since ranchers are not like doctors or lawyers." "Not for the ranchers themselves," the lawyer explained, "for the cattle. The cattle can be trained to respond to the beep to come back for feeding. That would mean less work for the ranchers and a pager for each head of cattle."

RESOLUTION The executives were taken aback at first by this most irregular suggestion. Then they thought about it and saw the opportunity. A sales deal was struck the next day. ■

Like most seemingly fantastic stories, this one has more than an element of truth. It is based on a story we found in the news. It begins with a very familiar scene—a lawyer on a sales trip, but with the main character placed in a different culture. The twist on the structure comes when the lawyer draws on his own experience to come up with an idea that can be applied to this new and different culture.

Familiar-to-foreign is also the structure of many stories that demonstrate new technology or design ideas.

Framed stories

In the framed structure, the story appears to begin and end in the same place. It wraps around itself, and like Dorothy back in Kansas, finds its way back home, but with a different realization or understanding from having taken the trip. So while the beginning and ending of a framed story are similar, it is their difference, however slight, that gives the story impact.

THE MECHANICS OF WRITING

FRAME When working on this book, I would sit down at my desk, turn on my computer, navigate to a particular location on the drive, open a particular document, which in turn opened a particular word processing program, scroll through to see where I was last working, look at comments and changes Whitney posted in the document, and then start thinking about what I wanted to write next.

FLASHBACK Back in the 1980s when I first started working in the computer industry as a technical writer, I would come into work, sit at my desk, turn on my DecStation computer, navigate to a particular location on the drive, open a particular application and document, scroll through to where I was last working and think about what I needed to write next. What I had hoped some 25 years ago was that at some point the writing process would be easier. Today, some of the mechanics are easier—scrolling was a lot more cumbersome on a DecStation than it is on a Mac. And I can search and navigate through scads more text and documents now than I could then.

COMPLETE THE FRAME The mechanics are easier, but they are the smallest part of the writing process. So a quarter century later, when I sit down to write, I have to remind myself, *Don't worry about the mechanics. Think first; be a mechanic later.* ■

This story is so simple that if the structure were not called out, it could be easily overlooked. It's built from an anecdote, a simple idea that you might discount all together. "That idea? Oh that's not a story!" Yeah, it is—or it can be.

Don't confuse framed stories as defined here with "a story within a story." While these two story structures are similar, the story within a story has interwoven stories, each of which can stand on its own and illuminate one another. Our framed stories are simpler and are composed of story fragments or images that only give a sense of a full story when put together.

There are three common variations on the framed structure: Me-Them-Me, Here-There-Here, and Now-Then-Now.

Me-Them-Me

This structure begins with some aspect of yourself—something you like or are good at. Then it turns to another person who does it differently (better or worse) or brings a different perspective. And it ends by returning to you.

RIDING MY BIKE

ME I love riding my bike in the summer. I regularly do hard fitness rides with a group of lovely people over a hilly and challenging terrain. Also, every summer I spend some time watching the Tour de France on TV. **THEM** I follow who's holding the yellow jersey and who the king of the mountain is for the various stages of the tour. Those guys are amazing. They go up some hills faster than I can ride on flat land. **ME** But even though I outweigh most of them by 80 pounds, I know that as long as I keep trying and never give up keeping up with the skinnier guys, I'll always be victorious. ■

This structure works particularly well for stories told in the first person, but it can just as easily be told in the third person. The main character might be someone you use as a lens for the story or someone that your audience will identify with. The next story is a Me-Them-Me frame about different ways to shop, told in the third person.

SHOPPING

ME When Melissa needed a new window shade, she had a mental picture of what she wanted. It had to roll up and down, and needed to be 50 inches wide. So she searched online, going through her usual list of Internet shopping sites to narrow down a make, model, and price. One of the sites had customer reviews, so she could see what others were saying about the models she was considering.

THEM When Melissa's mother needed a new window shade, she too had a mental picture of what she wanted. She thought about all the Manhattan stores she knew well and the malls that were most likely to have what she wanted. Then she picked up the phone and called a few of her friends and asked them for suggestions. Her friends helped her narrow down the list of stores she would visit to find just the right shade.

ME Melissa found the shade that was the best match to her mental picture and budget. And in the process, Melissa never had to leave the comfort of her own home. Which is good because living in her particular neck of Northern Vermont means that Melissa's a little removed from malls. ■

Now-Then-Now

In this structure, you start in the present, with a specific event or image. The important thing is that it be in the present—"now." Then it turns to a related detail from the past to show how it affected the character then. The story ends with a return to the present, but with an echo of the past, changing the way the character perceives the new "now."

THE CAMARO IN MY MIND

NOW At 6 feet 3 inches tall, choosing a car means choosing the one that hurts the least to sit in. Most cars are not built for tall people, and I would like to have the choice of not driving with my knees. **THEN** When I was a kid, I loved cars and had a lot of model cars. At one time, I possessed the ability to identify any car on the road within a fraction of a second with nothing but a glimpse of its front grill. My personal favorite was the 1968 Camaro, which had simple lines, a powerful engine, and an unmistakable front grill. And at 10 years old, I could fit into anything and didn't have to reach the pedals. **NOW** These days I don't drive anything like a Camaro, but the six-cylinder, all-wheel-drive practical road box I drive now is *all* Camaro in my mind. ■

The Now-Then-Now structure is a nice way of illustrating the main character's relationship with the world without focusing on the relationship. As the story jumps back and forth in time, the audience sees how the main character connects with the world. Some things will remain constant, but others will change.

Many user experience stories describe a new (or updated) relationship with technology. This structure can show how basic needs stay constant over time, but can be met in new ways. The "Mechanics of Writing" story is an example of this use of the Now-Then-Now structure.

Now: When working on this book...

Then: Back in the 1980s...

Now: The mechanics are easier...

Other examples are a doctor who still needs to treat the patient, or the delivery person who still needs to deliver packages on time. Their connection with the world is the same. But current tools can meet those needs in a better way than those they used or knew 10 or 20 years ago.

Here-There-Here

In this structure, you start with a location, where you introduce the main character. This might be "home." Then select some other place, either far away or seemingly far away. Finally, like Ulysses, you return home.

Focusing on distance can be a powerful way of talking about other cultures. This structure is easy to reverse to There-Here-There, too. Here's an example inspired by an Italian friend of Kevin's from a number of years ago.

TEXTING

THERE Back home when I wanted to meet with someone for business or pleasure, we made arrangements and met. No one used email. We simply texted each other and figured it out. Sometimes, they would get busy during the day, or I would get busy, but eventually using SMS, we'd find the gap in both of our schedules. **HERE** When I came to the U.S., it was different. People said, "We're meeting at 9 o'clock," and that was that. It was hard to get used to. What if I got busy? What if they got busy? Doesn't matter—9 o'clock. I like it in the U.S., but I also like to go back home as much as I can. **THERE** And every time I go back home, I have to change back to the old way of doing things. "You want to meet? Let's meet tomorrow. Text me." ■

Layered stories

Layered stories are told as tiny images one after the other. Very little may happen in the plot. Instead, the story is revealed through the details in the images. Each image builds on the previous one, adding layers that build up into a full picture.

This structure is a good one to spark the audience's imagination. It puts their natural story interpretation ability to work as they think about how all of the layers fit together. You can create a surprise ending by using the last image to suggest an unexpected interpretation of the sequence.

LAYERS OF SEARCH

IMAGE 1 The top of the first search results page showed 1,258 results. With 20 links per screen, the bottom of the page had links to pages one through nine and an ellipsis.

IMAGE 2 John held down the Command key and clicked on each link on the first page, opening a new tab for each one. He filled his window with tabs and learned little that he didn't already know.

IMAGE 3 A pattern emerged. Each page offered something, and each page asked for something. Energy, longevity, digestion, or appetite; all for money, compassion, or simply the time it took to read to the end.

IMAGE 4 Some pages used wild colors, some used ancient symbols, some used lots and lots of explanation of reason, method, practice, and symptoms.

IMAGE 5 John didn't know how he would design such a page if he had to, but he did know he would go beyond nine search results pages, clicking on every link. The one thing his illness gave him was time. ■

There are advantages and disadvantages to this structure. It is slow, but can be a potent method of telling a story. The story doesn't have to give away where it's going early (as in this example). If the images are engaging enough, then the audience is less likely to notice a lack of plot and be willing to focus instead on the images and their residual feelings. It is likely that the audience will remember their feelings from the story more than specific story points. Therefore, use this structure when you specifically want an emotional, as opposed to logical, response to your story.

This structure will not always work for every audience. Some people will understandably want you to "get to the point." Others will be patient and wait for the story to evolve. One way to address the needs of the get-to-the-point audience is to give them more to-the-point context either just before or after the story. You could start or follow the story example above with a statement that provides context.

> Chronic obstructive pulmonary disease (COPD) is an often slowly progressing, incurable lung disease that blocks airflow, making it increasingly difficult to breathe.

You can use the layered story structure as one element in a larger structure—for example, putting it into a section of a story where you want an emotional response, nesting it within the logic.

One of Kevin's performance stories, "Tomato Paste," uses a layered structure. It starts with a list of three things Kevin knows about tomato paste. Each element builds upon the previous element, growing in complexity. The first paragraph is fairly simple; the second is slightly longer and more involved; and the third is quite involved. The story does not give away where it's going and purposely leaves out explanatory details that would reveal its intended direction.

You can read more about this story on the book's Web site and see a video of Kevin performing "Tomato Paste" on YouTube: ﾆ www.rosenfeldmedia. com/books/storytelling/blog/tomato_paste.

Contextual interludes

Detailed descriptions of context can also be used as a structural element in a story. Like a layered story, they allow the point of the story to emerge from a collection of details, without much action or plot. Contextual interludes can help you show relationships in what may seem like scattered collections of physical or emotional details that form the context for the story. They work in two ways:

1. The contextual interludes connect the audience to the tangible, like sensory elements, or to personal experiences. They are often built on a close telling of sensory elements.

2. They are a break from the action of the plot. This can be particularly important in stories that are trying to communicate the textural details of an experience.

The following example continues the Motown story from the section on context as an ingredient in Chapter 13.

THE HI-FI

The hi-fi record player in our dinning room sat on top of a large brown record case. The cursive print on the side of the hi-fi said "Portable," which is why it had a suitcase-like handle to support the assertion, but we never carried that monster around. The speakers attached in the front on hinges so they could swing outward, but they were also easily removed if you wanted to place them even farther apart. The shiny gold fabric covering the speakers felt rough, like burlap with a little Saturday night fancy woven in. When the Supremes would sing, or Marvin Gaye, Al Green, or Ray Charles, I could run my hand along that fabric and feel them sing to me. The horns blasting out on "Hit the Road Jack" traveled from my fingertips all the way up my arm. When I heard that same song on the radio, I would sing at the top of my lungs, feeling it still in my arms. Now that's portable music. ■

This contextual interlude could be part of a larger story about media personalization or about the portability of electronics. That story might show how an MP3 player liberates music from a single location, or compare the physical texture of the old record player to the feel of a new device.

You can use contextual interlude as a story introduction to a place or time before launching into the main, action-oriented part of the story. Or it can be an ending that adds emotional elements to an otherwise straightforward narrative.

Framed stories may use two contextual interludes to contrast the starting and ending state of the characters.

- In a Here-There-Here story, an opening contextual interlude can introduce a cultural or geographic context, identifying details that are key to the experience.

- In a Now-Then-Now story, the central part of the structure might draw on a factual or fictional historical or sensory context describing the sounds that can be heard.

Using plot

Plot is the arrangement of the details of a story. It includes what happens in the story, in what order, with whom, and with what chain of causality. For many types of stories, it's the plot that carries the audience from the beginning to the end and, hopefully, inspires them to ask the question you may want them to ask, "What happens next?"

Drawing the audience in and holding them is the power of a good story plot. Professional storyteller and teacher Loren Niemi puts it this way:

> "The aim of plot and detail is to create unity, a singular thing of beauty which, when told or read, is forcefully present and inviting. When the audience hears or reads such a story, they enter its internal logic and geography willingly and find that it satisfies, sustains, and remains with them."
>
> —Loren Niemi, *The Book of Plots*

As with any other aspect of a story, the plot is crafted to capture and hold the audience. There are keys to determining the plot of a story:

- **Arrangement:** The parts of a story can be arranged and rearranged by the storyteller. By controlling the arrangement of the story elements, the storyteller can engage the audience and shape their acceptance and understanding. For example, stories don't have to be strictly chronological, even if the story is about a linear chain of events. For business audiences, it might be more effective to tell the end of a story first—to cut to the chase as it were. It's OK to show them where you are going, since the path to that point doesn't have to be predictable. But the arrangement of the events in the journey to the end of the story has to be clear and justified at every point along the way.

- **Plausibility:** On some level, a story must be believable. That doesn't mean that all stories must be factual, but they must ring true enough at every point along the way so that at no time does the audience stop listening and instead start thinking, "Is that true? Could that really happen? I don't think so, but I'm not sure." When they mentally (or perhaps worse, verbally) ask that question, you've lost their attention, and it may be hard to get them back. Plausibility is measured moment by moment, so what's implausible at the beginning of a story may not be implausible if it occurs near the end.

The goal of some user experience stories may be to change the audience's sense of what is plausible, opening up the possibility of new ideas. UX and business stories rely on plausibility. Plausibility breeds confidence and lowers feelings of risk. Take for instance the "Widgets for prosperity" story examples earlier in this chapter using Dan North's story structure. The first example would not convince major project stakeholders on the viability of Acme Widgets in the marketplace. It simply doesn't build from the starting point to the final conclusion. The second example is more effective because it builds from one "given" to another, taking small steps from the current state to a new one.

Playing with plot

There is no one right way to put together the plot of a story. Once you have the events clear in your head, the best way to figure out the best story plot is to play with it. Here is an example:

DIVING BOOTIES

Cleo, a newly certified scuba diver living in Minnesota, needed diving booties. She thought she could just walk into any dive shop and buy a pair that were her size before her winter Jamaican get-away, but none of the shops carried tropical apparel in December. So she looked on the Internet. The online dive shops did carry tropical booties, but what size should she get? Did they go by shoe size or sock size? Should she err on the side of too big or too small—after all, they were made of stretchable neoprene.

Then Cleo found the Web site for NP Dive Shop. The NP Dive Shop site offered a special service for footwear called the *No Problem* service. They asked her for her shoe size and then had her download a special PDF document. She printed the document, drew an outline of her foot on it, and then could either scan and email it back to them or send it via snail mail.

In a day she received an email back from the shop telling her exactly what size she should get, why she should get that size, and links to the booties with her size in stock. She was able to make a good purchase in plenty of time for her Caribbean winter trip. The booties fit perfectly. Then she wondered what the process would have been like had she needed to buy a wetsuit. ■

This is a simple story with a simple structure. It's a chronological chain from one event to the next—this happened, then that happened, then this other thing happened, etc. The first two sentences establish who the main character is and what problem or situation the character needs to address. The next four sentences show a first step toward solving the problem—looking to online dive shops—but then introduce another problem, of what size to buy. The rest of the story describes how the problems were addressed, with the final line added to spark the reader's imagination. *What would they have her do if she wanted a wetsuit? Lie down on a giant piece of paper?*

The plot could be rearranged to focus on the interests of a particular audience. Leaving the major events unchanged, detail and emphasis would be placed differently. The first way of telling the story is probably ideal for product management, with its balance of just enough technical details to suggest how the idea might work and the focus on differentiating the site from others.

The same story might be re-worked to address the perspective of developers:

DIVING BOOTIES (RETOLD)

A customer wants to buy diving booties online, but isn't sure what size they should order. The customer doesn't know if the sizes for any particular brand run small or large, or how much the booties would stretch. The customer clicks the link for the *No Problem* footwear-sizing service. The link downloads a specially formatted one-page PDF document to their computer. The PDF has a custom registration key graphic printed on it that defines a set RegValue.

The customer places their foot centered on the registration key graphic and draws the outline of their foot on the paper. The customer then has the choice of either scanning and emailing the document to the service center or mailing the hard copy via USPS.

The service center scans any hard copy and runs the PDF through the Scaling Algorithm, which scales the file to the exact original size according to the RegValue and registration key graphic. This compensates for variances introduced by the customer's printer and scanner. The Sizing Algorithm analyzes the customer's foot outline and maps the result to the appropriate sizes of footwear, according to each brand's sizing coefficient. The Report Generator creates a report for the customer that is emailed to them. ■

This is the same story, but told from a different perspective. Since gender is not important for this story, it is eliminated. Since the customer's point of view is of limited value for the purpose of this story, those details are limited. A developer would be interested in how the various processes and algorithms connect together to create an end-to-end service. Therefore, more of the details of those processes are included—much more than in the previous version.

The structure/plot balance

Structure and plot go hand in hand. Choosing a structure for a story will shape its plot and help you see which details fit and which don't. Knowing even a partial arrangement of plot details will help you see what structure might fit the story best. Then you can use that structure choice to further guide plot details. Here are some examples, starting with a user experience story example, and then a story that is more general.

Here is a story for a technical audience of researchers and developers about using mobile technology to coordinate large groups to be at the same place at the same time.

MOBILE CROWDS

You can write letters, send emails, or call your congressional representative all you want, but what really makes a statement is showing up. A thousand emails can be deleted in a moment, but they can't click away a thousand bodies. I manage five different affinity groups working for social change for the poor and the disenfranchised. With the Gathering System on mobiles, I can arrange for hundreds if not thousands of my groups' subscribers to be at the same place, at the same time, for the same cause, to share our passion. The subscribers enter their interests and preferences in their own mobile; the system then automatically sends them appropriately filtered time and location updates for rallies and other events. We use advanced technology to advance our society. ■

This story is structured much like a TV product ad, since the story was for a fictitious new product. Most standard TV ads use a structure that starts with a context and problem, shows how the product beautifully addresses those problems, and then has some sort of "kicker" at the end.

- The first two sentences of the story provide the context of the problem in a visual way: "... but they can't click away a thousand bodies." That image is used to impart a sense of power.

- The next section of the story describes how it works. Because the purpose of this story was to get people to see the value of new technological features, the specifics of the interface are not important. There is no mention of menus, buttons, or service contracts. The details of both the features and the design are left to the audience's imagination. The audience not only provides their own vision of the interface, but also determines whatever technology would be needed to do this. The story just speaks of the effect of the service, echoing the imagery from the earlier context.

- The last sentence is the kicker—just eight words. A *kicker* is often a slogan, such as "We bring good things to life," "Good to the last drop," or "Melts in your mouth, not in your hand." It can also be a word image that encourages the viewer to think, "Hey, they're talking about me." Or "I want my life to be like that." "We use advanced technology to advance our society" may sound a bit altruistic, but the point is to highlight, for a technical audience, the power and influence of the technology. Particularly their own technology.

Choosing a story structure and plot

As you start to craft a story, try out different structures. Look at the ingredients you want to emphasize and choose a structure that will let you explore them with the audience.

A good structure and appropriate plot points will provide you with these areas:

- **Coverage:** Does it address all of the facts without leaving out any inconvenient details?

- **Coherence and plausibility:** Does the explanation the story provides make sense?

- **Fit:** Is the story a good fit for the facts, or has it been forced into place?

- **Uniqueness:** Is it a compelling explanation, or does it seem like there are many others that would work equally well?

- **Audience Imagination:** Is the story loose enough for the audience to build their own details, or is it so detailed that there is no room for the audience to use their imagination?

One of the other benefits of working with a defined structure is that your story is more likely to be easy to retell. For you, this also means that you can learn the story well enough to adapt it to a slightly different audience as the need arises. It also means that others can retell your story. If your story is so clear that others are inspired to use it, then that is a measure of success.

Stories are more than the sum of their parts

Stories are made up of many elements. You can craft stories by carefully assembling all of the ingredients into a structure and a plot. This may feel a little mechanical at first, but as you gain experience, you will also gain a more intuitive feel for how to use these elements.

But a beautifully crafted story is something more than the sum of its parts. The many story parts described in this book are not recipes for stories or Lego pieces that fit together to create the perfect story, but paint colors and brush sizes. They can serve as guidelines to get you started, but the goal is to paint over the seams between the parts so that the audience experiences a sense of awe, not a sense of appreciation for the cleverly assembled story parts.

"Awe matters." In their book *Imagination First*, Eric Liu and Scott Noppe-Brandon describe the work of scientist David McConville (www. elumenati.com). McConville employs 3D projection technology to stir the imaginations of climate change policy makers and school children alike. McConville uses awe to affect changes in thinking and understanding. When we as storytellers allow an audience to sit back and take in all of an image, a vision, an approach, or a world through storytelling, then we too are unleashing their capacity for awe. And the audience's gratitude for that makes them ready and willing to learn and accept new ideas.

More reading

The Hero with a Thousand Faces by Joseph Campbell

Two descriptions of the stages of the hero's journey: faculty.gvsu.edu/ websterm/Hero.htm and www.mcli.dist.maricopa.edu/smc/journey/ ref/summary.html

The Morphology of the Folk Tale by Vladimir Propp

Both Wikipedia (en.wikipedia.org/wiki/Vladimir_Propp) and Answers.com (www.answers.com/topic/vladimir-propp) have good summaries of Propp's functions.

Dan North's story structures: dannorth.net/whats-in-a story

The Books of Plots by Loren Niemi

Summary

The structure is the framework of a story. It's the underlying skeletal pattern for the story, similar to other architectural or design patterns. The plot is the arrangement of the events of the story, the sequence in which those events are revealed to the audience. Look for the balance of structure and plot that helps you make a point effectively.

Useful story structures for user experience stories include:

- **Prescriptive:** Structural templates that allow you to fill in the blank

- **Hero:** Joseph Campbell inspired hero's journey elements

- **Familiar to foreign:** Begins with the comfortable and then shifts to the less familar

- **Framed:** Stories that appear to begin and end the same way

- **Layered:** A series of images that build a story experience

- **Contextual interludes:** Details that add an extra dimension to a story

Ways to Tell Stories

Throughout the book, we have talked about story*telling*, but stories can be *told* in many different ways:

- **Oral stories:** Stories told aloud with both storyteller and audience present.

- **Written stories:** Stories communicated in written form. Usually, this means that the storyteller is not present and the story has to stand on its own.

- **Visual stories:** Stories told (mostly) in pictures.

- **Multimedia, animation, or video:** Stories told using spoken words, pictures, and moving images.

There are two formats that are especially important in the world of user experience design. Both formats mix a written or visual presentation with oral presentation, blending the mediums.

- **Reports:** An obvious place for user experience design stories is in user research and usability reports or as a way to introduce a design concept, whether the report is written or presented orally.

- **Presentations:** A particularly common business format, presentations are the performance storytelling medium for user experience design.

Telling oral stories

When we think about stories, we often imagine them being told aloud in real time. The audience may be one person, a small group, or many people. The occasion may be formal or informal. But whenever or wherever they are told, spoken stories are part of the oral tradition, because they are passed down from one generation to another as a way of transmitting and perpetuating culture. They can be as natural as any conversation, or they can be a well-rehearsed performance.

In user experience design, spoken stories can be an important part of analysis or design brainstorming. Retelling events from user research can remind you of their importance, help emphasize the most relevant details, or help you share those insights with a group. Stories can be part of working through a design or explaining it. Spoken stories are also part of that all-important business skill, the great presentation.

One important difference between *telling* a story and other story mediums is that *you* tell the story, so how you shape the story is affected by who you are, your relationship to the audience, and your skill (and comfort) with live performance. You are part of how the audience experiences the story. This is true of any story, of course, but it's especially true in the case of a spoken story.

Telling a story in person lets you connect with the audience

If you are feeling a little tentative about using stories in a professional situation, it might be because you'd rather not put the emphasis on yourself as the storyteller, because you are more comfortable observing than taking center stage.

There are advantages of delivering the story yourself, however. For one thing, you can see your audience as they hear the story. This means that you can adjust the story—adding details to answer questions and making it shorter if you have misjudged the length while you are telling it. You can use their faces and body language as cues, allowing you to fill in any confusing parts, or move more quickly if their attention is failing. As Doug Lipman, a consummate story performer, coach, and author puts it, oral stories are "dynamic, interactive, and sensory," which makes them very different from simply reading a speech.

SURFING THE AUDIENCE

After years of studying film and multimedia production, I felt driven to write stories for a change, and so started working to be a short story writer. I set about the task by writing as much as I could, but my stories turned out horribly. No matter how hard I tried and no matter how well I worked with my writing partner, I wrote stories that not even *I* wanted to read.

Around that same time I found an oral storytelling community and spent many weeks just listening. When I finally got up the nerve to tell my first story, I had carefully prepared a short piece on the topic of my name to fill the eight-minute time slot. It was a very simple story. Halfway through it, I realized that I was throwing in words and inflections I hadn't practiced as I was reacting to the faces and energy of the audience.

By the end of the eight minutes, I got it. I knew why my short stories were so bad. It's because when I was writing I had no idea who the audience was—who I was writing for. But when I was in front of 40 people listening, all reacting and swaying with me, there's no mistaking the audience. I could reach out and touch them. I call this surfing the audience—that's when the storyteller is reacting to and feeding off of the energy the audience gives back such that the story comes alive for both the audience and the teller. ■

Telling a story in person adds performance elements

In a business setting, oral stories will only rarely be a stand-alone performance. They are most often integrated into a discussion or a presentation. For example, you might tell a story to illustrate a point and then make a smooth transition into a discussion of the implications of the story or a brainstorming session based on ideas that the story brings up.

Sometimes, you can create a story with the audience by suggesting the context or structure and then letting your listeners fill in the gaps, actively telling their part of the story.

 A STORY CAN GIVE YOU TIME

Lou Rosenfeld, our publisher and the author of Information Architecture for the World Wide Web, *told us about telling a story as a way to keep the attention of a meeting and how it helped him get all the way through something without being interrupted.*

I don't think of myself as a good speaker, and if you aren't very good at speaking in public, stories can help you hold the floor when you have to communicate something. The thing about stories is that they take place over time, so you can keep the audience with you while you are getting through the material. It gives them something to hang on to. Here's an example:

> I was brought in to work with the A Big Agency. Usually, my clients are trying to do information architecture across a broad enterprise. They want to unify things, but they can't because they don't have anything to unify yet. The ABA was different. They had this *huge* investment in taxonomy and this *huge* project in thesaurus development and another *huge* group working on search. Their problem was that they didn't

work together, so they were missing out on all the compound benefits of putting these things together.

What I did was say, "Let me take a stab at a high-level IA design that gets these things together a little bit." The next time I went in, I presented something. They said, "That sucks. It should be like this." And I said, "OK, let me work your input in."

The next time, they said, "That's still not good. We'll do it this way." And I started hearing more "we."

We did this for four iterations, and at the end there was very little *me* involved in the design. They were saying "*We'll* do it this way." They probably thought I was a useless idiot. And I probably am, but it got them going, and helped them start to work as a team.

The story I told was about a process. It took time. And the story took time to show the time lapses and the iterations. I found that very useful as a way to talk about this process. Telling it as a story made my audience listen to hear how it ended. ◼

Whatever the situation in which you decide to tell an oral story, you have a few extra ingredients to work with. Oral storytelling does not involve dramatic acting, nor is it simply a matter of getting the words out or reading a prepared speech.

ORAL STORYTELLING IS RICH, LINEAR, AND SYNCHRONOUS

Doug Lipman is one of the foremost storytelling coaches in the United States. He has authored multiple books on story coaching and has led hundreds of workshops in the art of storytelling to teachers, parents, librarians, and professional performers. Here he talks about the nature of storytelling and how it affects one's preparation for a performance. Part of your preparation is to think about the difference between written and oral language.

Oral language is our first language. Nearly every child comes to school with a command of it and then learns to ignore its importance as she or he acquires written language. As a result, most of us don't notice the four dimensions in which oral language differs from written language.

- First, written language is a lean medium, using only a handful of elements to convey meaning: words, capitalization, punctuation, fonts, and so on.

- Second, of these elements, words alone carry the vast preponderance of meaning.

- Third, written language is an asynchronous medium: communication is "one direction at a time."

- Fourth, written language combines linear and nonlinear qualities: words are to be read in sequence, but it's possible for the reader to skip forward or backward.

Oral language, in contrast, is a rich medium. It uses many elements to convey meaning, including words, tone of voice, facial expression, gestures, posture, eye behaviors, distance and orientation in space, and more. The elements of oral language can all carry meaning simultaneously.

Your words, your posture, and your tone of voice are like independent channels. Sometimes, those channels will reinforce each other; other times, they will diverge, creating a very rich mix. For example, think of the person whose words convey certainty, but whose pacing and tone convey hesitancy and whose eye behaviors convey a fear of being "found out."

Another difference is that oral language is strictly linear. The listener can't "rewind" a conversation to pick up a missed word or facial expression; this can make extra demands on the listener's memory. And when the speaker pauses, the listener must also pause. Such pauses—or their absence—allow the speaker to subtly influence the internal reactions of the listeners. For example, the speaker can challenge the listener to keep up with a rushing tumble of information, or pause to extend suspense or to suggest that listeners search for nonobvious implications of what was just said.

Finally, oral language is synchronous. Even in a presentation format (where only the speaker is using words), the listeners are conveying information back to the speaker via posture, facial expressions, and eye behaviors. This is not simply two-way; rather, it can create a continuous feedback cycle where the responses of listener and speaker build on each other to create a self-reinforcing sense of rapport.

To fully prepare for an oral-language presentation, you need to practice with live listeners. You need to experiment to find effective combinations of words, tone, and all the rest. And you need to practice establishing rapport—creating feedback loops with audiences similar to your intended audience, with its unique set of expectations, likes, dislikes, suspicions, and more.

In short, you can't practice two-way communication alone in a room! If you practice by reciting your words, you are actually practicing ignoring your audience. In any interactive medium, that's a sure path to failure. ■

Practice, practice, practice

There's an old joke about how to get to Carnegie Hall. The answer is "practice." Malcolm Gladwell makes the same point in his book *Outliers: Expertise* is partly a matter of time spent perfecting a skill. Gladwell estimates that 10,000 hours of practice separate people who are unusually good—i.e., outliers—from those who are just talented. Every time you craft a story or tell a story, you are banking hours of experience.

It is important to practice before you tell a story for the first time or if you are telling an oral story to an audience you can't see—if you are giving a webinar, for instance, or telling a story for the first time on the phone to an audience you don't know well. In those cases, you definitely want to rehearse. To prepare to tell a story, live with it for a while.

Barry McWilliams offers good advice on learning to tell a story: "Once you settle on a story, you will want to spend plenty of time with it. It will be a considerable period of time and a number of tellings before a new story becomes your own." His article "Effective Storytelling: A Manual for Beginners" (www.eldrbarry.net/roos/eest.htm) goes on to offer some basic advice for a new storyteller. We've adapted it slightly here.

- **Read the story several times.** Start by reading it as though you were meeting it for the first time; then proceed with concentration as you learn it.

- **Analyze its appeal.** Think about the word pictures you want your listeners to see and the mood you want to create.

- **Research its background and cultural meanings.** Prepare for questions from the audience and for flexibility in front of the audience, because you may need to adjust or explain the background of a story for various audiences.

- **Live with your story.** The characters and setting become as real to you as people and places you know. If there are important facts, be sure you can include them easily and naturally.

- **Visualize it!** Imagine sounds, tastes, scents, and colors. If you can picture the story in your head as you are telling it, it will be more real for you... and for the audience as well. Only when you see the story vividly yourself can you make your audience see it!

Develop your own performance style

There's a saying in storytelling, which is that every story is a personal story. Of course, if you tell a story about something that happened to you, it's a personal story. But also if you tell Little Red Riding Hood—it's a personal story. And if you tell a story about a research observation—it's a personal story. What this means is that when you tell a story, there is always some part of you in it. That personal stamp might be what you choose to emphasize, or the style in which you tell it. It's important to think about the authenticity of the story and your relationship to it, or what makes you interested in the story.

Unlike all the other story mediums, oral storytelling lets you shape your tale in real time, using your performance style, the pacing of the story, and the manner in which you connect and interact with the audience.

 MORE THAN SURFING THE AUDIENCE
When I was just starting to perform stories, I saw a featured performance by the wonderful storyteller Judith Black. What made her performance so amazing was not just the quality of the adult stories she told, but also how she involved the audience. In one story in particular, she portrayed a character through which the story was told. While in character, she told the story and interacted with the audience, asking them questions and inviting them to verbally fill in pieces of the story. The audience was so connected that I saw people breathing with her. There I was at that time just trying to remember the next words of my stories and there was Judith playing with the audience —way beyond just surfing the audience. "Oh, you can do that? That's allowed?" It was an eye-opening experience. ■

Any performance style requires making choices about what you want to sound like and what impression you want to make. To a tell story effectively, make those choices consciously.

Your performance style should be comfortable for you—not too different from your normal way of speaking, especially as you start out. Even professional storytellers who perform on stage must be able to incorporate their normal speaking voice in their work, as well as use their voice to serve the dramatic elements of their story. In fact, a performance voice, one that's notably different from your speaking voice, sounds insincere. Or it will once your audience talks to you after the performance. The most basic guideline is to be open, honest, clear, and sincere. If you're presenting in a conference room, you don't want to sound like you're performing in an Andrew Lloyd Webber musical. Imagine having a normal conversation with an opera singer who, when asked the time, starts belting it out in full operatic voice. Lovely—but jarring.

Another way to think about performance style is that as the storyteller, you are there to serve the story and help the audience understand it. You are there for the story. Anything about your performance that does not serve the story is superfluous. For example, you might be afraid that the audience is getting bored and start to speak faster, even when speaking faster does not serve the story. This choice, however well meaning, harms the story. Instead, you might consider changing the pace of the story or using your voice to emphasize points. If you are comfortable with the story, you can make connections between elements of the story.

As another example, some storytellers when faced with a particularly formidable audience might start speaking in a more authoritative tone with the notion that they will hold this tone throughout the story, even though it is clear that this tone is not their natural speaking voice.

As Doug Lipman described earlier, the oral storyteller has many tools to choose from and multiple channels through which to deliver their story. Relax and allow your performance style to be simple and only one of the many contributing tools you use for delivering your story.

Manage the pace of your story

After your performance style, the next element to add is pacing. Speak at a comfortable pace for both you and your audience. Don't rush through your material or be too slow. Your pace does not need to be uniform. Use pacing to draw the audience in to the particular points you want to make or to shift from a detailed level to the big picture and back. There are two forms of pacing in storytelling—presentation pacing and narrative pacing.

- **Presentation pacing** is how fast or slowly you talk, and to some extent how succinct or sharp your speech is. Think of presentation pacing as a way to influence the emotional response of the audience. For quicker, exciting, energized parts of the story, you can speed up. For slower or sadder parts of the story, you can slow down. Of course, this is only a general guideline and not a rule. You can also work with the transitions from one speed to another, using them to signal movement from one structural element in the story to the next.

- **Narrative pacing** is about how fast or slow the story goes. This is not "words-per-minute," but how much time is compressed or expanded in the details and structure of the story. For example, a story might focus on examining one small moment or jump through time from one event to another taking place much later.

A few words of caution

We like to stick to positive advice, but there are a few things you should avoid, especially as you are starting out.

- **Don't try to do voices and accents.** Unless you are *very* sure of yourself, a *very* good performer, and have a safe audience who can give you feedback on it first, you can easily turn your characters into caricatures or sound like you are making fun of the people the story is about.

- **When in doubt, keep it short.** There are no rules for how long (or short) a good user experience story can be, but no one was ever penalized for being too brief. When you are telling a story in person, you can always elaborate if you are asked to.

- **Don't be afraid of silence.** Don't fill every second with the words of your story. You can choke your story with too many words or when words flow without a break. Use silence to allow the story to breathe, emphasize important points, or provide an opportunity for the audience to build your images in their heads.

Telling a story when you can't see your audience

We've been talking about the importance of reacting to your audience and watching their reactions. With more global UX projects, much of your meeting time is spent on the phone. New media like webinars are another situation in which you may be telling a story to an audience you can't see. Here are a few tips for those situations:

- Give the people on the phone enough time to react. Don't let the performance pacing drag, but add a few seconds between sections of the story to make sure they have time to catch up.

- You might want to have at least one person in the room with you, so you have someone to make eye contact with.

- Make sure that your story doesn't rely on gestures, props, or facial expressions. If you are using a screen-sharing tool, you can show photographs, documents, or software, but pointing with the mouse just isn't the same as using your hand or being able to put something right in front of the audience.

- Explain with examples whenever possible to create a vivid description. Use metaphors and similes for their expressive possibilities. Both use comparisons of two unlike things. Metaphors use an image or a description in an unusual context: *lightening response time* or *bulletproof code*. Similes use the words *like* or *as*: *slow as a turtle* or *solid as a rock*. People on a conference call are listening to a lot of words, often spoken by people who sound alike and whose faces can't be seen. They are suffering from visual deprivation. Using verbal imagery helps them *see* what you are talking about instead of just hearing more words.

Choose the right moment to tell a story

Using stories in a business setting requires striking a balance. Stories add interest and depth to a report or presentation, but too many stories can make your work seem trivial to people who may be more used to facts and figures. This can be especially true if your stories aim primarily for an emotional response, rather than being closely tied to data.

You can tell a story to introduce a topic, illustrate a point in the middle, or sum up a series of factual points. Your goal is to find the sweet spot where a good story can help you engage the audience—that's the moment when they are ready to hear a story.

START BY HAVING FUN

Dan Szuc, who is not only a user experience designer, but also used to play a superhero for children's entertainment, talks about how you can help your audience have a good time by having one yourself.

Gerry Gaffney and I were in Wellington, walking from our hotel to the training center where we were about to run a first day of training. There's always a little bit of nervousness on the first day. I said, "You know, Gerry, let's just have a good time. Because I promise you that if we have fun, the people who come to the training will, too. The content will flow from that."

When I have presented over the years, the energy that they feel is the important thing. Yes, you have to know what you are talking about, but it's about the moments when the audience laughs, or you have a bit of fun. It's those pieces that make you say, "I loved that." ▉

Written stories

For many people in user experience design, written communication is a primary form of communication. If you work on a geographically dispersed team, you may rely on written communications to span time zones. If you are a consultant working with your clients from the outside, the written reports you leave behind may be as important as your in-person interactions.

Written stories can be a part of any design communication, such as personas, user research, usability reports, or design documentation.

The biggest challenge for including stories in written communications is that you are not there to tell the story. Many of the techniques of oral storytelling are simply not available, because the readers control the pacing and hear the words only as they imagine them. Perhaps more important, you do not know who will read your story and thus will not be able to adjust the story to fit. As you can see in Figure 15.1, this does not mean that the Story Triangle doesn't exist. But you won't get direct feedback from the audience and will only learn about the impact of the story outside of the immediate storytelling context.

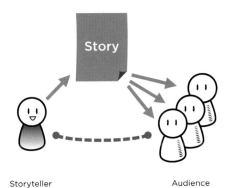

FIGURE 15.1
In a written story, communication between the storyteller and the audience is only indirect.

Written stories allow you to reflect and edit

When you create a written story, you have the advantage of being able to edit it into a single form and maybe even control the presentation. You also have an audience that can read the story at their own pace and go back over sections if they need to.

As you plan your written story, here are a few thoughts to keep in mind:

- **Keep the story as long as it needs to be, but no longer.** There is no rule for this, but in general, more people will read a shorter story than a longer one.

- **Keep the story crisp.** Set the context efficiently, choosing details that will help the audience understand the story.

- **Don't let it get weighed down with unnecessary description or side comments.** You might get away with this in oral storytelling, but it's hard to put asides into a written story.

- **Use all the tools of information design to shape the way the story looks.** White space, illustrations, and other visual elements give the story its own place on the page, and can suggest the pace of the narrative.

- **Decide on the voice for the story.** Will it be in third person, with a narrator describing the events from the outside? Or in first person, taking on the voice of the central character?

- **If you are using a story to share a detail about a user, just tell the story.** Don't make it a story about a story.

- **Think about how you frame the story in a larger document.** It might be part of the main text or set off in a box or some other device.

- **Make the point of the story explicit.** You are not present to lead a discussion or adjust the story so the audience "gets" it, so either build your conclusion into the story itself or use it as part of the framing for the story.

Before you finish a story, have someone else read it. When you read your own story, you are also hearing your own inflections on words and tone of voice. Your readers will only have the words, and will hear their own inflections as they interpret those words.

We fill in the blanks in stories

All stories rely on the listeners' ability to fill in the blanks using their own experiences and imaginations. In Chapter 2 an audience picked up small cues from Kevin's Tokyo story and used their own experience to fill in the gaps in the story and re-created it in their mind.

The IBM Research Knowledge Socialization Project (www.research. ibm.com/knowsoc/) talks about how stories "draw on common truths to convey more information than is obvious." One of the ways a story engages the audience is by providing opportunities for them to build a rich picture, with much more total "knowledge" than what is actually said (or written).

One of the tricks to writing a succinct story is to make use of your ability to pick up on social and cultural cues. Of course, this relies on knowing your audience and being sure that they will extract the same information from a story that you put into it.

In her chapter on "Storytelling and Narrative" in *The Persona Lifecycle*, Whitney followed the IBM project's example and looked at what information is suggested by even a very short fragment.

> Tanner was deep into a *Skatepunkz* game—all the way up to level 12—when he got a buddy message from his friend, Steve, with a question about his homework. He looked up with a start. Almost bedtime and his homework was still not done. Mom or Dad would be in any minute....

Here are some things we learned about Tanner in just 53 words:

- He is a kid (he still has homework and a bedtime).
- He is an avid computer games player and good at it.
- Maybe he's not such a great student.
- He has friends who also use the computer.
- Getting a message is an everyday way to communicate.
- He is probably on a cable modem or some connection where it does not matter how long he stays online.
- He is probably playing in his room, or somewhere his parents cannot see him and watch exactly what he is doing.
- We might be able to infer that his family is comfortably well off.

You can unpack any story to see what cultural or social assumptions it relies on and what details it communicates implicitly. When you craft a story, you can use those assumptions to keep the story short, focusing on the details that are important to the point of the story.

Visual stories

Stories don't have to be just words. As a friend put it, "Would it kill you to have an *illo* or two? Even if storytelling is largely auditory, some of us are pretty visual learners." He went on to point out that there are ways to create illustrations easily and cheaply.

We are not talking about drawing representative pictures or fabulous visual designs, although good graphic skills can be helpful. If you are one of the many people who think you can't draw, stop worrying. As Dan Roam, Scott McCloud, and many others have pointed out, visual thinking is not about drawing, but about thinking. The Web comic *xkcd* is another good example. It's composed almost entirely of stick figure drawings and other simple line illustrations.

If you are already a visual thinker, this kind of storytelling may come naturally to you. In his book, *The Back of the Napkin*, Dan Roam calls people who seem to want to leap up to a whiteboard and start drawing "black pen people." He contrasts them with people who are comfortable with visual stories but don't think they can draw and those who aren't really comfortable with using pictures at all.

One way to work around a lack of drawing skills is to use a tool. In an article in *UXmatters*, Mike Hughes talks about how he uses comics to end a weekly project summary and says that they help him "condense complex issues and also ... communicate them in a humorous, but illustrative way." As Mike himself admits, he is not a polished artist: he uses a free online tool called Make Beliefs Comix to get past his lack of drawing skills. You can see an example in Figure 15.2.

> "This comic was part of a weekly report that informed the team we would be conducting a specific study shadowing users. It gave me the opportunity to remind researchers that we need to stay out of the experience we are observing. Portraying the user as playing Solitaire during the study (an authentic activity but one we never get to see) was also a gentle reminder that we never truly get to observe the user unobserved."
>
> —Mike Hughes

It doesn't require a lot of drawing skills. But you do have to think carefully about what you are trying to say.

FIGURE 15.2
Using comics for team communication: www.uxmatters.com/mt/archives/2009/11/visual-methods-of-communicating-structure-relationship-and-flow.php.

Comics let you share a conversation

Comics and cartoons are gaining in popularity as a way to tell a story or share a design idea.

This idea isn't new. Comics have been used to tell stories for many years. They are often used as a way to present longer or more complex stories in a simpler, more concise format. The "classics illustrated" comic books from many different publishers retold literary classics in comic format. Even the U.S. Army publishes *PS* magazine (Figure 15.3), which uses illustrated stories and comics to communicate basic safety and mechanical tips.

FIGURE 15.3
Cover of *PS* magazine from June 1971 from the VCU libraries: dig.library.vcu.edu/cdm4/index_psm.php.

Artists who worked on the publication included popular comic book authors such as Will Eisner. The visual style of *Preventive Maintenance Monthly* has changed over the years to keep up with the current style of comic books.

You can also use speech or thought bubbles in photographs to show what people said (or thought), as shown in Figure 15.4. (If you are using pictures of real people, be sure that you have their permission to share their image.)

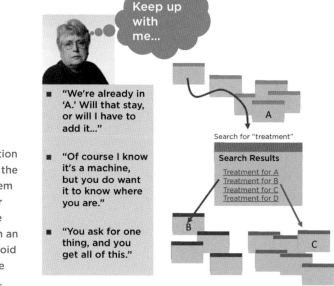

FIGURE 15.4
This image from
a usability report
combined a collection
of quotations with the
thought behind them
and the context for
the comments. The
photograph is from an
image library to avoid
using images of the
actual participants.

The attraction of these kinds of visual stories may be the pictures, but they also present a complex topic in just a few words.

Storyboards can communicate a story visually

Wireframes and prototypes are common techniques for showing the interactive flow of a product: how users will navigate from screen to screen and what they will see on each one. Storyboards can communicate a broader view of the interaction to show context and events.

You can use storyboards to think through a design problem or show how the product will answer questions that people may have as they use it. These are a little different than wireframes or even interactive prototypes. Like comics, these storyboards combine visual images with a chronological sequence and captions or words spoken (or thought). They can illustrate a complete task or allow you to show a user's thoughts and reactions to the product, as the story about Flow Interactive in Chapter 8 does.

STORYBOARDS PROVIDE EXPLICIT DETAIL
Ron Sova teaches workshops on creating storyboards. He also stresses that creating a good storyboard does not require drawing skills or large amounts of time.

Storyboards have many similarities to oral and written stories, but they have two main differences.

First, stories invite the audience to add richness, using their imagination to incorporate details. Storyboards, on the other hand, more explicitly depict whatever level of detail the author needs to accurately convey a sequence or process. Because they are explicit, everyone will see more of the same detail of the events and context in the same way. So, for example, Figure 15.5 shows not only someone using a printer, but also context about their relationship to the printer. This information can help to determine whether a printout is required in a given process.

FIGURE 15.5
Storyboard of using a printer. (Time to create: less than five minutes.)

Figures 15.5 shows Ron Sova's storyboard from field research at a call center. It not only indicates that the user accesses a printer and when in the task the printer is used, but it also shows where that printer is in relation to the user and what the user has to do to use the printer (swivel in their chair, move something out of the way, or walk down the hallway).

Second, storyboards require very little translation (if any). Therefore, they can be as easily understood among groups in different countries (speaking different languages) as they can among groups within the same building who use different terminology and have different perspectives on a project. For example, user researchers explaining a process to IT or designers explaining a process to management.

Like wireframes, storyboards provide a fast method for getting consensus on design. However, storyboards also quickly convey nonuser-interface details with context, such as timing, sequence, location, size, color, emotion, and the spatial relationship of one object to another. Figure 15.6 shows, without words, the value of iteration and refinement.

FIGURE 15.6
In this stick-figure storyboard, Ron Sova shows the importance of testing a presentation before giving it. (Time to create: less than three minutes.)

Storyboarding provides a very powerful means of visually presenting the user's story as a detailed, sequential flow of information. It's a great tool for the following:

- Visually presenting an idea

- Comprehensively showing activities, including timing and sequence

- Involving different audience groups

- Removing international and language barriers

- Facilitating audience recognition of an idea

- Enabling immediate audience feedback

- Helping to think clearly through an action

- Improving organization through establishing relationships

- Having fun—storyboards are simply fun to create and share

- Creating interest in the information by using an eye-catching communications medium

Writing the main moments of your story in visual form can help you shape the images you want to include. If you can picture the story in your head as you are telling it, it will be more real for you... and for the audience as well. ■

Visual images can add detail or show the big picture

Another role for visual storytelling is to make the imagery in a story more concrete. The audience can zoom in to the detail or pull back for the big picture. Visual stories can be unpacked just like verbal stories can.

Think back to the story about Tanner:

> Tanner was deep into a *Skatepunkz* game—all the way up to level 12—when he got a buddy message from his friend Steve with a question about his homework. He looked up with a start. Almost bedtime and his homework was still not done. Mom or Dad would be in any minute....

Look at the photograph in Figure 15.7. Does it support or contradict this story?

FIGURE 15.7
Is this Tanner?

The image gives fewer explicit details. For example, you don't know the boy's name, or his friends, or whether he has parents, and you can't see what he is doing on the computer. But you can see a boy of a similar age to the text, using a computer. You can see that he is in a city, at night, high above the street (by the lights outside the window). And you can infer a social setting:

- A private space for the boy to work unsupervised

- Computer is readily available

- A comfortable, middle-class home

- The present day

- A western culture

As with written stories, you can use visuals to add context and cultural background to the story. The photograph in Figure 15.7 reinforces the context suggested in the Tanner story. You can also use an illustration to add a twist or a surprise context. Imagine if the photograph of the Tanner story showed a boy in a very different cultural context.

Whether your story is entirely visual or adds illustrations to reinforce the words, visuals add depth to any story.

- You can use a comic style to show conversations directly, suggest time lapses in the action, and show sequences of events.

- Photographs add context, placing the story in a specific place or cultural setting.

- Simple diagrams can show sequences, infer relationships, or highlight details.

Multimedia, video, or animated stories

A few years ago, we would have said that video and multimedia were not widespread enough to consider carefully, but with the rise of YouTube (and other online formats for presenting video or multimedia), video can be an effective way to share stories.

If you are thinking about using video, however, you have to do more than just read a story into the camera. One of the challenges of using video is that film and television are so pervasive that most of the world has a clear sense of what they consider to be quality video. Just turning on a camera and pointing it is just not enough.

As with oral storytelling, video storytelling communicates on multiple levels. It includes the words of dialogue or narration, the primary and background objects in the frame, the primary elements of sound, and any secondary or ambient sound, which can include music. This is all blended together for the audience.

Some video stories use some of the same simple ideas for creating visual stories, with a sound track and animation. A new trend in Web sites that promote new products (or ideas) is the use of video instead of text to explain how they work. This style of documentation not only blends spoken words, written words, and images of the concept or interface in action, but it can also reveal more about the experience than simply *how* the product works.

- New Google products, like Google Voice, are often released with just one page describing what it is and how to use it—all of the explanations are short videos.

- The instructions for adjusting the settings for multi-touch gestures in Apple's OS X consist of a video demonstrating multi-touch gestures. Duh.

- Starfire, which we talked about in Chapter 1, created a scenario in a video to show how new technologies could change how you interact with computers.

- A company called Common Craft creates video explanations that tell short stories about how people use a product. One of their samples is *Twitter in Plain English* (**www.commoncraft.com/Twitter**).

Type the name of almost any new consumer electronics product with the word "unboxing" into a YouTube search to see more examples. Unboxing videos demonstrate the experience of first receiving a product, taking it and its accessories out of its box, and often setting it up and turning it on.

Each of these examples uses video to explain something technical and set it in a context so that you can understand *why* you might use the product. *Twitter in Plain English* is particularly effective at putting a human face on an experience that is difficult to explain before trying it.

From writing to shooting

Simply reading a script in front of a camera can be deadly boring, unless the words being spoken are incredibly interesting and you are an especially good performer. However, for most people it is natural to start composing a video by first composing the written word.

As you create the script for your video, you should keep in mind some of the different elements of the cinematic language. While video production is beyond the scope of this book, you can think about how to use these video elements as part of your story ingredients.

- **Camera:** The camera provides the visual perspective. This includes how subjects are framed, how the camera moves from place to place, and how to light subjects to visually separate them from the background. In the visual language of film, there is implied meaning and emotional effect associated with various camera angles. Think about the films you have seen for inspiration and a style that will create a good visual interpretation of your written story.

- **Time and Space:** Video is a temporal medium, meaning that things happen and develop over time, just like they do when telling an oral story. Video also uses the space of the frame. Things can come in and out of frame from the sides, and action can take place across the entire video frame, as well as forward and back within the frame, not just front and center. In a video story, you can use time and space to emphasize points and make the story more interesting, similar to how you would use your voice in an oral story.

- **Audio:** The audio can be as simple as text read by an off-camera voice, but it can also include music, sound effects, and on-camera sound. People's standards for audio are fairly high, so you have to consider what audio you want to include and how best to record it.

- **Editing and Rhythm:** All stories have a rhythm, whether they are spoken live or recorded. In a video, you have the pacing of the narrative, as well as three other rhythmic lines—visual, aural, and editorial.

Visual rhythm is the rhythm of what you see, such as the swing of the arms and legs of someone walking down the street.

Aural rhythm is the rhythm of what you hear, which includes speech, as well as other sounds, music, and silence—often the most important effect.

Editorial rhythm is the rhythm of video editing, including the frequency of cutting from one camera angle to another, the use of point-of-view camera angles, how a cut happens in relationship to on-screen action, and if cuts are continuous or discontinuous to express jumps in time or space.

In the same way that we suggest practicing an oral presentation or having someone read a written story, having someone watch an early version of your video will help you see if any rhythmic elements are distracting from the story.

You can make a video without a camera

Video does not have to involve a camera. With the many graphic tools available, you can tell effective stories without the complexities of a live "shoot."

One example is the software *Photo to Movie* (www.lqgraphics.com/software/phototomovie.php). It can take images and glide smoothly across them, fly and spin over them, or zoom in to a small region. The result is a QuickTime movie that you can then narrate, add music to, or manipulate further with other software tools. If your work involves photos taken in the field, product design illustrations, or prototype sketches, you can turn them into video and then add your script as voice-over. With only slightly more sophisticated tools, you can add overlay graphics to help tell your story.

Kevin produced a number of animations for the "Learning from a tough room" story in Chapter 12. The image for one of them is in Figure 15.8. The animation showed home electronics of the past, as an introduction to ideas for how electronics might be used in the home in the future.

FIGURE 15.8
Home electronics of the past.

To create this animation, Kevin started with a large image of the layout of a house. He placed images of different household electronics on it: hi-fi, telephone, clock radio, B&W TV, etc. The animation flew around the house, swiveling around the path, and zooming in on the individual elements as needed. A narration explaining the connection between all of the elements was added later.

Putting stories in your reports

Reports and other deliverables are part of the work of most user experience designers. Two obvious places to use stories are in user research and usability reports, as well as any deliverable that connects a design to user activities.

You may already be using a form of stories in your report, including quotes from users or brief anecdotes from your research. And you may find that thinking more consciously about using stories makes your reporting more effective. Two things we heard in our discussions about using stories in user experience reports summed this up for us:

> "I didn't think I used stories, but now I see that I do this all the time. I read out quotes or re-enact what I saw, describing what people were looking for and what happened."—Lara Keffer

> "One of the things that holds us back is the way we frame our presentations as 'research reports.' This influences their structure. Really, we should not be trying to just report on data, but to tell a story."—Daniel Szuc

We've seen many reports that include quotes from users to support important points and help bring the research to life. Figures 15.9, 15.10, and 15.11 show various layouts that you can use.

Natoque non urna donec id, feugiat vitae tincidunt commodo vehicula. Hendrerit vivamus tristique nulla venenatis.

Risus elit in felis elementum, dolor ipsum pede orci ac, libero phasellus sit platea nulla, curabitur purus nam lectus quis. At etiam suspendisse facilisi, sem non fringilla odio, quam laoreet ut repudiandae, ante donec sit dignissim. - Elizabeth

Vestibulum nisl tempus urna, turpis justo semper venenatis congue, quam suspendisse natoque senectus suspendisse, tincidunt ut sed quam cras. Quam cursus nisl dis, non fames.

Tristique nulla venenatis
Natoque non urna donec id, feugiat vitae tincidunt commodo vehicula. Hendrerit vivamus tristique nulla venenatis.

Vestibulum nisl tempus urna, turpis justo semper venenatis congue, quam suspendisse natoque senectus suspendisse, tincidunt ut sed quam cras.

Quam cursus nisl dis, non fames ut eu enim, maecenas id arcu sapien amet, felis debitis a hymenaeos malesuada.

Nec libero tempor at eget, vel magna dignissim suspendisse. Eleifend eu ultricies mattis, vestibulum in in adipiscing faucibus, platea diam ac quis, est feugiat nunc nisl hymenaeos.

Congue, quam suspendisse natoque senectus suspendisse, tincidunt ut sed quam cras.

"Risus elit in felis elementum, dolor ipsum pede orci ac, libero phasellus sit platea nulla, curabitur purus nam lectus quis. At etiam suspendisse facilisi, sem non fringilla odio, quam laoreet ut repudiandae, ante donec sit dignissim."
– Elizabeth

FIGURE 15.9
If you include stories within the body of the report, you can use a layout or visual style to distinguish them from the rest of the text.

FIGURE 15.10
Short stories or quotes can be placed in the margins.

FIGURE 15.11
If you have photographs or screen shots, you can add talk balloons around them to represent the voices of those users.

You can also be more elaborate, introducing the person the story is about and illustrating it with photographs (of user research information) or screen shots (of an online experience).

An example of this is the story from Chapter 7 about how users wandered off track while looking for cancer information. The combination of screen shots, explanations of the interaction, and quotes from the users helped tell the story of how and why users got lost. Figure 15.12 shows what it might look like on a page.

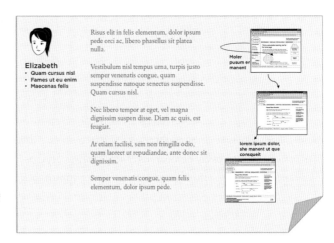

FIGURE 15.12
This mockup shows a story illustrated with screen shots and a brief summary of the user characteristics.

You could do the same thing with video clips from a usability report, either telling one user's story or combining several different people to show a pattern of interactions or problems.

These stories or story fragments can become part of the shared culture of the team. The story at the beginning of Chapter 1 about Priti, the woman who ended up selecting the *wrong* course for all the right reasons, is one that has become a shorthand for that team.

However you include stories, story fragments, or quotes, you must be sure of one thing: that the story supports the point you are trying to make. It's no good putting together a collection of juicy stories if they don't help the audience understand your point in a richer way.

If you deliver a report in person, you have another chance to use stories.

- Your company culture may be more tolerant of stories in a presentation than in the formal report.

- You can use oral storytelling to expand and illustrate points in the report.

All of the points we made before about paying attention to the audience apply here. You have to decide how many stories you can incorporate into a report and how much you can rely on them. Your colleagues may not have the same level of interest in the details of the research. You will have to decide how to engage them and win their trust for learning from stories, in addition to "harder" data.

Make presentations a story of their own

Presentations have a bad reputation as a boring sequence of bullet points, with someone droning through the information. Edward Tufte has even written an essay bemoaning *The Cognitive Style of PowerPoint* as a wasteland whose rate of information transfer approaches zero. Doug Zongker's humorous presentation at the *American Association for the Advancement of Science (AAAS)*, called *Chicken chicken chicken*, reduced an entire scientific presentation to a single word www.youtube.com/watch?v=yL_-1d9OSdk and isotropic.org/papers/chicken.pdf. Do a quick search for bad presentations, and you'll find hundreds of examples of how *not* to engage the audience.

What makes presentations so challenging is that they combine both oral and written storytelling. You are giving a live presentation to a real audience. Presentations have a storyteller (you), an audience, story material (what you say), along with written and visual elements (what's on the screen, such as PowerPoint).

Most poor presenters just start with something like a classic research report outline, and then they work through their material in a chronological order. Of course, like any other story, you have to start with the audience and what you want to communicate to them.

The trick is to think about the whole presentation as a story. You have something to say, and you need to present it in a way that will engage your audience. It's the Story Triangle again, as shown in Figure 15.13.

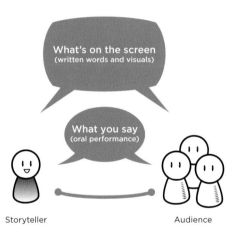

FIGURE 15.13
The Story Triangle for presentations has two story forms working simultaneously: the oral story and the visual one.

Your goal is to help the audience create the story (or hear your point) for themselves. A presentation is not only a story, but it also contains stories. When you are dealing with a story-within-a-story, you will probably find that relying on a clear, simple story structure (see Chapter 14, "Developing Structure and Plot") will help you—and your audience—stay on track.

A PRESENTATION IS A STORY IN THREE ACTS

Kelsey Ruger, an "adventure junkie who straddles the worlds of design, technology, and business," gives great presentations that mix visuals, storytelling, and performance style with compelling content. Each piece of his presentation can stand alone—for example, if you look at his slides, you will still get the main points of the presentation. But they work together, with his own performance style, to reinforce what he wants to say.

The process for creating a presentation starts with a definition of the audience, using nine questions to think about your relationship to them.

1. Who are they? What do they fear? What do they want?

2. What is the age of the audience?

3. What is the socioeconomic make-up?

4. Are you speaking their primary language?

5. How are you different than them?

6. What do you have in common with them?

7. What is their status compared to yours?

8. Have they had any bad/good news lately?

9. Do you know anyone in the audience whom it would be appropriate to address?

Next, write the "elevator pitch." This is a few sentences that sum up concisely what you want the audience to take away from the presentation. This may sound obvious, but it will keep you from simply adding slide after slide of detail, whether or not it contributes to your point.

The presentation is organized into three (or sometimes four) acts, loosely based on *Beyond Bullet Points*. Using a clear structure helps keep the presentation focused. (You can see the structure in the sticky notes in Figure 15.14.)

Act I: Set up the story: Opening anecdote, the setting, protagonist, the imbalance (inciting event), the balance, and the solution.

Act II: Expand on the problem.

Act III: Describe the solution.

Act IV (sometimes): Call to action.

The first act is especially important because it has to engage the audience in the problem *and* introduce the solution, connecting the situation to the audience's own context. Only then do you go on to provide the details of both the problem and the solution.

FIGURE 15.14
Before Kelsey Ruger creates any slides, he outlines the presentation in four acts. He starts on the wall, so he can see the shape of the presentation and keep the main points right in front of him.

This outline is the basis for a short script that you can use as notes during the actual presentation. What follows are the notes for Act I of a presentation about the changing landscape that social media has created.

Crucial Conversations in Social Media Act I

Opening Anecdote: The other day I saw a sign that said "The Easter Bunny, Santa Claus, The Tooth Fairy...Daddy. Pretty soon kids stop believing in things they don't see."

The Setting: The very act of communicating with employees and clients has been changed.

We aren't passive masses—technology has made us active participants.

We live in an attention type of economy where people do a lot more talking than listening.

New ways of communicating that don't mesh with what the corporate world considers the norm emerge daily, i.e., our ability to influence has been fractured.

A new generation that does not want to be "talked at" but rather "talked to" has emerged. Why do I say "new"? Conversation has always been a fundamental part of being human. For centuries, commerce was largely based on conversation and the interaction between people. Over the last century something has happened.

Protagonist: Despite this, business owners and communications professionals still have messages to communicate, but these messages have to work in this rapidly evolving market.

The Imbalance (Inciting Event): Companies have not evolved as quickly as markets, and the act of "commerce" has been effectively divorced from the people on whom it depends.

The human condition changes, yet never changes. The fears, hopes, and desires of a Babylonian 5,000 years ago probably closely match our own fears, hopes, and desires.

The Balance: The tools of social media don't make the conversation, they support it. By understanding the true nature of conversation, businesses can open up vibrant interactions with individuals and communities.

The Solution: Follow this three-step plan to truly understand and embrace the art of conversation.

Only when you have the entire story should you create the actual slides. With a clear story to tell, your slides can be bold and vivid, providing richness to the presentation. But they are not *the presentation*—that's the mix of all of the elements, plus you telling the story. ■

As you can see in these samples of Kelsey Ruger's slides (in Figure 15.15), the visuals are not a literal transcription of what he says in the presentation. Instead, they provide imagery along with a few words to reinforce the key point. Audiences are listening to your presentation in multiple modalities, in this case, visual and auditory. These modalities do not have to provide the same information all the time. In fact, it's usually more interesting if they don't.

FIGURE 15.15
You can see the slides for this presentation on SlideShare: www.slideshare.net/
themoleskin/crucial-conversations-in-social-media.

Choosing the medium for your story

This chapter has focused on the different ways you can share a story: telling
a story orally, writing a story, presenting visual stories like comics and
storyboards, and showing multimedia stories. We've also looked at how to
use stories in two business formats: the report and the presentation.

Each medium for telling a story has strengths and weaknesses:

- Oral storytelling allows you to create a rich experience, interacting
  directly with the audience. This medium can be woven into meetings,
  report presentations, or design brainstorming sessions. Stories and
  story structures make formal presentations more engaging.

- Written stories allow you to shape a story and share it without a
  performance. The readers can skip forward and backward to review
  the story. Stories in this medium are easy to integrate into reports,
  illustrating important points or sharing user voices and actions you
  have collected.

- Visual storytelling lets you share a conversation, show an environment,
  and provide rich cues for the audience's imagination.

- Technically mediated story forms like video and multimedia are
  informed by oral storytelling practices and visual language, using their
  own techniques and language.

More reading

Oral storytelling

- *Improving Your Storytelling*, Doug Lipman

- *The Power of Personal Storytelling*, Jack Maguire

- *The Storyteller's Start-Up Book*, Margaret Read MacDonald

- *Storytelling and the Art of Imagination*, Nancy Mellon

Storytelling performance

- National Storytelling Festival: www.storytellingcenter.net

- Local storytelling festivals and events: storynet.org

- The Moth: www.themoth.org

- MassMouth: www.massmouth.org

Visual stories

- *Understanding Comics*, Scott McCloud: scottmccloud.com

- *The Back of the Napkin*, Dan Roam: www.thebackofthenapkin.com

Digital storytelling

- The Center for Digital Storytelling: www.storycenter.org

- Hillary McClellan's Tech-Head: www.tech-head.com/dstory.htm

Presentations

- *The Cognitive Style of PowerPoint*, Edward Tufte: www.edwardtufte.com/tufte/powerpoint

- Beyond Bullet Points: www.beyondbulletpoints.com

- Pecha Kucha: www.pecha-kucha.org

Summary

There are many mediums for stories, both in person (with oral storytelling and presentations) and in a written, visual, or multimedia format.

- Oral storytelling is a performance, told in real time to an audience. It offers direct interaction with the audience in a dynamic, sensory, and immediate way. To tell oral stories well, you need to develop your own performance style and practice telling the story many times.

- Written stories enable you to reflect and edit, and let the audience experience them at their own pace. Written stories can be included in reports and other business communications.

- Visual stories let you share imagery and context without lengthy descriptions.

- Multimedia can bring together visual, oral, and written storytelling techniques.

- Presentations also blend story mediums, mixing the richness of a performance with words and visual imagery.

CHAPTER 16

Try Something New

And so we arrive here, at the last chapter. In this book, we've tried to make the case for stories as a good way to communicate. People are natural story listeners, so it's an easy way to share information. Stories can include rich information about behavior, perspectives, and attitudes. They are an economical way to communicate contextual details. When people listen to stories, their minds are engaged in the process of painting in the details. This engagement sets the stage for persuasion or a call to action.

But it can still be hard to change your own ways of communicating, especially if you are part of a team. Habits and established templates are difficult to change. It can be hard work to get to the heart of a story and tell it in just the right way for the audience. And, sometimes, stories fall flat, even when you have tried your hardest.

All we can do is urge you to take the first step and try a story or two.

At first, storytelling may be unnerving. It's a new way of talking for some business contexts. Take it at your own pace. But try it.

Remember that to tell a good story you must think about how you will engage the audience. Stories are active, so don't treat them as a target for blasting out information. Stories are a much richer way of communicating. They come to life in the imaginations of the people hearing them, in that triangular relationship between storyteller, story, and audience. Jasper Fforde conjured up this fanciful description of how stories work.

> "The reader took up the descriptive power of the book and translated it into his or her own unique interpretation of the event—channeled from [the book] through the massive Imaginotransference Storycode Engines back at Text Grand Central and into the reader's imagination...But the beauty of the whole process was that the reader in the Outland never suspected that there was any sort of process at all."
>
> —Jasper Fforde, *Thursday Next: First Among Sequels*

The relationships within the Story Triangle give stories their power to explain, to engage the imagination, to create a shared understanding, and to persuade. The discussion of sharing stories in Chapter 10 raises an important point about stories in user experience design: they are collected, created, and told with a purpose in order to make a point. If you don't know why you are telling the story, you may need to think again. If you don't know who you are telling the story to, you can't choose the details that will make the story most effective.

We are not the first people to point out the power of stories. Annette Simmons put it in the competitive language of business when she titled her book *Whoever Tells the Best Stories Wins*. Stephen Denning sums up his own discovery of storytelling in *The Springboard* by saying that the usual tools of charts, diagrams, and rational arguments are simply too limited, that dialogue is effective but impractical for large change, and that only storytelling can empower one person to persuade many by igniting the listeners' creativity.

Most—though not all—stories in user experience design start with *really listening to* other people. When you take the time to listen and observe real people, you have more opportunities. You may be surprised to find stories all around you. And when you listen deeply, the stories you find will have more resonance and will be more useful as part of the design process. They can go beyond simple anecdotes to express important aspects of behavior, goals, or culture.

There is one more reason to use stories in user experience design. It is, simply, because the power of stories allows us to see the world through a new lens. One of the hardest things to do is to understand a task, context, or experience as someone else does. But once we can see the design problem from that new perspective, we are halfway home to a solution. It might be a big, innovative new idea, or a small tweak that changes an experience from bad to good. *Really listening* is the start of *really understanding* the people who use the products, tools, and services we work on. And that's the start of creating a great user experience.

It can be scary to try something new, but we hope you will try adding stories and storytelling to your work or using them in some new ways. Tell us how you're using stories at our blog: www.rosenfeldmedia.com/books/storytelling/.

We'll end with Kevin's story about how he discovered stories and what happened when he brought storytelling and a particular storyteller into an environment that seemed like the antithesis of a place that could be moved by its power. You can learn more about the storyteller who changed Kevin's life and to whom this book is dedicated at www.brotherblue.com.

THE POWER OF STORYTELLING

There are those who tell stories and those who live stories—there is a difference.

When I first got up in front of people to tell a story, all I spoke about was my name. That's it. I don't have a long name, nor an exotic name. It's a relatively normal sounding name—Kevin Michael Brooks. My simple story was about what my name meant to me growing up, and what it meant to my mother who named me. It was no big deal. But that was also the first time I *told* a story to someone who *lived* stories. His name was Brother Blue.

At first glance, he looked like a mad man, and it's the least fortunate of this world who never managed to get past that. With blue beret, blue shirt, blue jacket, pants, shoes, and butterfly pins all over him, Brother Blue was the venerable symbol of storytelling in the Boston area and host of the evening when I told my first story. In his own special way, Blue helped me see the big deal of a simple story. As soon as my piece was over, Blue got up and told me and everyone there, these people soon to become my storytelling family, just what a big deal it was to talk simply about myself, with no pretense or fanfare. He saw deeper than I was looking. "That was GREAT. It was so sweet and simple... and GREAT! That was storytelling!" We became connected, he and I. And that connection was complex because he was complex, and storytelling is complex. Blue said that what he does is touch from the middle of the middle of himself to the middle of the middle of the people. His job was not just to reach the audience, but to reach inside the audience and connect with them there. That's what he did for me that night, and I saw him do that for each and every other person who got up to tell a story that night and every night following. Blue empowered people with his listening and elevated them with his praise. That's the moment when I was born into storytelling, or when storytelling was born into me. From then on, every Tuesday night was storytelling night.

Meanwhile, in my academic world at MIT, I was working with lots of bright technical people, trying to merge my love for writing and story with the power of the computer. It was a very different world, more heavily influenced by the deconstruction of narrative than the crafting of it. This was by no means a wrong endeavor, just a hyper-focused one. For about two years, I kept these two worlds as separate as I could: the world of construction and the world of deconstruction. I didn't want to mingle the soft rocking caress of oral storytelling with the analysis and cold computational structures of academia. Until one day I saw an opening in my department's colloquium series calendar, and I thought, "You know, why not? Why not invite Blue?"

I talked to Blue and his wife Ruth about it, and they agreed. Brother Blue would speak at MIT. Arrangements were made, the date was set, and all looked good. As the date approached, I thought more about what I had done. What *had* I done by offering to mingle my two worlds? Was I risking both? Worse yet, was I putting Blue in front of an unwinnable audience? One must understand that most of the other colloquium speakers were scientists and engineers of one type or another. They were leading theorists and practitioners, pushing the edges of their fields, helping to define the future of the world in their own special ways. Which meant that there was some similarity between them and Blue. Blue pushed the boundaries of the human heart and mind, stretching them to new capacities, telling stories for no other reason than to change the world. This is big, but still in my lab he represented a departure from the norm. The butterfly images on his face and clothing, for example—that was a departure. The balloons and ribbons tied around his arms and legs—that was a departure. A black man standing up in front of one of the world's most prestigious, predominately white, technical institutions talking about the power of story to change the world— big departure! I was afraid that people would be unable to listen, unable to absorb a message for which a mathematical equation did not exist. "Would this work?" I wondered.

It fell to me to make a poster advertising the event. Posters would be hung all over campus to help ensure a good turnout—but what to say? Come see the storyteller? No, not enough. Black man scheduled to change the world on December 11th at 4:30 p.m.? No, might give the wrong impression and perhaps a bit too 1960s. The poster ended up including a full body picture of Blue along with his full name, Dr. Hugh Morgan Hill. I thought the "Dr." part might offer people some level of comfort before the audience had their minds blown. I quoted what he and others had said about his work, like that *middle of the middle* line and how many had called him the world's greatest storyteller. But I also prayed, "Lord, let this work. I don't know what exactly to ask for, but please just let this work."

The day came, and the prearranged taxi dropped Blue and Ruth off in front of my lab. A modest crowd of 50 people assembled in the auditorium, and I was nervous. Would they get it? The audience sat there like they were waiting for the math to start. Everyone looked so serious, everyone except Blue. He was busy drawing butterfly images on the palms of his hands. I was hoping that by the end of the allotted 60 minutes those hearts and minds of technology would be softened just a little. My advisor introduced him, and Blue was on. Actually, Blue was *really* on.

Blue did his version of Romeo and Juliet, bringing on stage a pretty woman sitting in the front row to play his Juliet. By the end, she was charmed beyond belief and the audience seeing her charmed was similarly affected. He told a version of his signature story about the caterpillar that didn't know himself until he changed into a butterfly. And then Blue took questions from the audience with kindness and creativity until the time was up. The audience was stunned. Those technical hearts and minds I had worried about were pretty softened five minutes after the start. The world didn't stand a chance; everything changed that day.

When it was all over, after struggling to pull Blue from the throngs of people who came up to him, I took him and Ruth up to my lab area where we had a vegetarian dinner waiting. It was Tuesday, storytelling night, and I had to get them through dinner and on their way by 6:30. But when Blue was on, he was on! And the last thing his overflowing energy allowed him to do was eat. Surrounded by graduate students, Blue launched into his version of King Lear, as told to him by his old friend Willy, accompanied by a large cast of characters he claimed were in the original story, like Ella Fitzgerald, Nat King Cole, and John Coltrane. Nobody ate. Nobody breathed. We all just watched the master.

I learned something that day about the power of storytelling. Yes, Brother Blue was a powerful storyteller, no doubt. But the most valuable lesson that Blue taught me was that to tell a story is perhaps the most powerful thing anyone can do. Brother Blue lived story and in doing so modeled how story itself can pierce any shell, academic or otherwise, and reach the waiting heart beneath; whether one is dressed like a holy fool or not. It's the teller's job to simply launch the story on its way and then live like their story makes a difference, because it does. Governments and cynics can scoff all they want, but Brother Blue showed us that to tell a story changes lives, and when you change enough lives, you change the world. ■

Index

R

Ramey, Judy, 84, 90
realist tales, 189–190
reality, story to reflect, 50
really listening, 32
  meaning for company or team, 42
  and shared deeper thoughts, 36
reason for events, 17
Redish, Ginny, 49, 120
  on notetaking format, 88
  on usability problems, 36
  User and Task Analysis for Interface
    Design, 60, 77
references, in tech-spec story, 124
reflecting, as active listening skill, 40
regulatory perspective, 176
relationships
  between audience and story,
    164–168
  importance to design, 166
  between speaker and audience, 172
  speaker to story vs. audience to story,
    174–175
remote controller, 70
reports, 240
  putting stories in, 264–267
"rescued" situation in story, 214
research sessions, structure, 82
resources perspective, 176
restating, as active listening skill, 40
Rettger, Mary Beth, 40, 144
reviews, stories for, 134
rhythm, editing video and, 263
Riding my bike (story), 225
Roam, Dan, The Back of the
  Napkin, 254
Roddis, Ian, 148
roles of stories in user experience
  design, 20–27
  creating shared understanding,
    25–26

  engaging imagination, 22–23
  explanation, 21–22
  persuasion, 26
  sparking new ideas, 24
Rory O'Shea Was Here (movie), 180
Rosenfeld, Lou, 191, 242
Rosson, Mary Beth, 59
Ruger, Kelsey, 269

S

Saffer, Dan, 168
sales demos, for collecting stories, 71
sales stakeholders, 34
Saving Private Ryan, 203
saving screenshots, 98
scalable design process, 57
scenarios, 120
  as use cases, 59
  usefulness, 121
screenshots, saving, 98
screenwriting, ideas for character
  development, 197–198
search logs, for collecting stories, 71
selecting stories, 94
  finding stories, 97–99
  finding stories in data, 99–100
  signs of juicy story, 96–97
selling, listening as key, 42
sensory context, 202
sequence of events in story, 16
server logs, for collecting stories, 71
Shannon, Claude, 14
shared understanding, stories to create,
  25–26
sharing ideas, 64
sharing stories, abilities needed for,
  140–153
Shopping (story), 225
silence, in oral storytelling, 249
similes, 249

ACKNOWLEDGMENTS

Every book takes a village and, like authors everywhere, we have a lot of people to thank. In this case, the village includes the people who contributed stories to the book and the many people who allowed us to pick their brains about different ways to use stories.

Ginny Redish gets special thanks. Not only did she agree to write the wonderful foreword, but she was also there from beginning to end, with moral support and helping us shape the book.

A lot of people read the book at various stages. Their comments were enormously helpful: Mary Beth Rettger, Caroline Jarrett, Daniel Szuc, Karen Bachmann, Ben Weems, Ryan Evans, Laura Packer, Jo Radner, and Steve Krug.

Dirk Knemeyer and Juhan Sohin at Involution Studios in Boston took a flyer on us and hosted the first "Sex, Money, and Storytelling" workshop. We learned a lot from the great group of people as we blended some of our material for the first time.

We met Calvin Chan at User Friendly in Shanghai and convinced him to create the cartoons that introduce our stories and the storyteller people that populate the book.

And, of course, Lou Rosenfeld himself and our editors Marta Justak and David Moldawer.

From Whitney

The first time I talked about storytelling in public, I was pretty nervous. Debi Parush, Karen Bachmann, and Basil White sat up with me the night before while I ripped up and rewrote the whole presentation. The next morning, I arrived to find a room full of people and Caroline Jarrett sitting in front, notepad at the ready. Terrifying. But as the session went on, I began to see this just might work. So, thanks to everyone who got up at 8:30 a.m. and stuck with me while I felt my way through.

Thank you to John Chester, my ever-patient husband, who kept everything running and listened any time I needed to talk.

To everyone on every project I've ever worked on.

To my mother, who taught me to read and to love a good book.

And to my father, who set the bar high and drummed into me that "if you can't think, you can't write."

From Kevin

Physically writing a book is not hard; it just takes time and patience. Envisioning writing a book, that is, putting the idea in one's mind and keeping it there through all the ups and downs of the process, fighting to hold it there against all of life's competing attention attractors, is more than just hard—it's somewhat miraculous. Fortunately, miracles happen with help.

I want to thank the storytelling community for their talent and support, and all those people who sat through my workshops, helping me hone the thing that I love into concepts I can communicate.

To Laura Packer, my partner in art and life, who has laughed with me in support through all those ups and downs.

Thank you to my children, Cara, Kristoff, and Stephan, who inspire me, and to my mother who has been the teller and subject of many of my stories over the years.

And to Brother Blue, my spiritual father, who opened the door and showed me what it means to live the life of a storyteller.

ABOUT THE AUTHORS

Whitney Quesenbery

Whitney Quesenbery is a user researcher, user experience practitioner, and usability expert with a passion for clear communication. She has been in the field for too many years, helping companies from The Open University to the National Cancer Institute develop usable Web sites and applications. She enjoys learning about people around the world and using those insights to design products where people matter.

Before she was seduced by a little beige computer into software, usability, and interface design, her first career was in theatre as a lighting designer. Like every other element of the production, lighting has to help tell the story. The scenery, lighting, costumes, direction, and acting all have to work together—tell the same story. She learned a lot about the craft of storytelling from watching hours of rehearsals.

Whitney has served as president of the Usability Professionals' Association (UPA), on the boards of the Center for Plain Language and UXnet, and as a manager of the Society for Technical Communication (STC) Usability and User Experience Community.

As a member of two U.S. government advisory committees, she has worked to update the U.S. accessibility requirements in "Section 508" and to improve the usability and accessibility of voting systems for U.S. elections.

Whitney is a frequent author and presenter in industry events and is a contributor to UXMatters.com. Her first publication on storytelling was a book chapter on "Storytelling and Narrative" in *The Personas Lifecycle* by John Pruitt and Tamara Adlin. She's also proud that her chapter, "Dimensions of Usability," in Content and Complexity turns up on so many course reading lists.

You can find her online at www.WQusability.com and on Twitter @whitneyq.

Kevin Brooks

Kevin Brooks is a user experience researcher and designer for Motorola and a professional oral storyteller. At Motorola, Kevin researches new user interface technologies and expresses them using various media, as connected, user-centered experiences.

His academic career went back and forth between engineering/computer science and filmmaking. Kevin liked both, but hungered for them to be more integrated long before it was fashionable. While researching how the computer and the filmmaker could tell stories together, he found the oral storytelling community in the Boston area. There is so much natural integration between skills, modalities, tools, and techniques in storytelling that it often goes unnoticed. As he developed and performed as a storyteller and then began coaching storytellers, he learned a lot about how storytelling is a pivotal part of the creation, performance, and design process.

As a writer and performing oral storyteller, Kevin tells personal tales from his urban childhood of the '60s, his '70s adolescence, '80s adulthood, '90s parenthood, and the little things that spark our lives every day. His stories for adults and family audiences resonate with humor and poignancy, as can be heard on his CD *Kiss of Summer*. He has been a featured performer at storytelling festivals, conferences, and other venues. Kevin's coaching helps people find their stories whether they're artists, technologists, or anyone who has something to say. Kevin has given numerous storytelling workshops to engineers, designers, storytellers, and even to people with normal world views.

Kevin received his PhD in Media Arts and Sciences from the MIT Media Lab, where his area of research was computational narrative and interactive cinema. He has also studied engineering, computer science, creative writing, and film production as an undergraduate, receiving a BS in Communications from Drexel University and an MA in Documentary

Film from Stanford University. Kevin has several published papers on storytelling and interactive story design.

You can find him online at http://alumni.media.mit.edu/~brooks and read his creative nonfiction at http://wordsaboutwater.blogspot.com.

How they got together to write this book

Kevin and Whitney met at the 2006 Usability Professionals' Association conference. The theme was "Usability through Storytelling," so perhaps the writing of this book was simply a matter of fate. When publisher Lou Rosenfeld asked each of them about writing a book on storytelling, they both said the same thing: "I don't know enough to write a whole book." It didn't take long before everyone came to the obvious conclusion. Put Kevin's multimedia and performance storytelling background together with Whitney's emphasis on user research and using stories to connect to the "user" in UX, and … you can read the results for yourself.

CONTRIBUTORS

The stories in this book come from many sources. Some people contributed stories from their own history of storytelling. Others told stories from their professional experience. All made the book richer.

Adaptive Path	Lara Keffer
Michael Anderson	Doug Lipman
Phil Barrett	Laura Packer
Randolph Bias	Mike Paciello
Francoise Brun-Cottan	Steve Portigal
John Chester	Ginny Redish
Tom Erickson	Mary Beth Rettger
Rob Foster	Lou Rosenfeld
Isobel Frean	Kelsey Ruger
Simon Griffin	Ron Sova
Michael Hughes	Daniel Szuc
Caroline Jarrett	Chauncey Wilson

Calvin C. Chan created the Story Triangle illustrations.